Organisation Culture

OTHER ECONOMIST BOOKS

Guide to Analysing Companies
Guide to Business Modelling
Guide to Business Planning
Guide to Economic Indicators
Guide to the European Union
Guide to Financial Management
Guide to Financial Markets
Guide to Investment Strategy
Guide to Management Ideas and Gurus
Guide to Organisation Design
Guide to Project Management
Guide to Supply Chain Management
Numbers Guide
Style Guide

Book of Obituaries
Brands and Branding
Business Consulting
Business Miscellany
Dealing with Financial Risk
Economics
Emerging Markets
The Future of Technology
Headhunters and How to Use Them
Marketing
Mapping the Markets
Successful Strategy Execution
The City

Directors: an A–Z Guide
Economics: an A–Z Guide
Investment: an A–Z Guide
Negotiation: an A–Z Guide

Pocket World in Figures

The
Economist

Organisation Culture

Getting it right

Naomi Stanford

THE ECONOMIST IN ASSOCIATION WITH
PROFILE BOOKS LTD

Published by Profile Books Ltd
3A Exmouth House, Pine Street, London EC1R OJH
www.profilebooks.com

Typeset in EcoType by MacGuru Ltd
info@macguru.org.uk

Printed and bound in Great Britain by Clays Ltd, Elcograf S.p.A.

A CIP catalogue record for this book is available
from the British Library

ISBN 978 1 84668 340 4

Contents

Acknowledgements

My thanks go first to all the people who responded with their questions, which initiated this book. Without this start it would have been difficult to structure and write.

As I got to grips with writing it I talked to a great many people working in a number of different organisations and industry sectors. Many of the conversations and discussions were "in passing" as I got stuck, needed a perspective, or was just reporting progress. Other conversations were rather more directed – in that I wanted specific information, a point of view, or a different slant on things. Everyone has been forthcoming, interested and happy to comment, and for this I thank them. Particularly, I'd like to mention Rebecca Ratner, Jill Shankleman, Gwen Newton, Maysa Zureikat, Mike Friedl, Kamran Shaukat, Emma Sheller, Attica Jaques, Chris Rodgers, Holly Huntley, David Jackson, Martha Johnson, Wei Zheng, Frank Nicolai, Robin Bidwell, Phred Dvorak, Matt Nixon, Vineet Walia, Karen Rule, Pedro Sancha, Scott Kubly, Kenneth Hsu, Patty Flaherty, David Schutt, Bruce Brownlee, Bijan Khoozie, Simon Nash, Jo Bond, Steve Lynott, Bill Hancy, Mary Lee Plumb-Mentges, Nadine Simon, Kate Spector, Jim Shillady and Donna Hamlin for helping me think through and clarify my perspectives.

Stephen Brough has kept me laughing as he encouraged me through the writing process, exhorting GOPE (good old plain English) and relentlessly hacking out my management guff, and Penny Williams has done a sterling job in formatting, checking and clarifying the copy.

Family members have cheered the news of each completed chapter and for their warm-hearted love I thank Hannah Barugh, Rosa Barugh, Rosemary Stanford, Patty Stratton, Paula Terrey, Michael Stanford, Sonjia Stanford, John Burke and Roger Woolford.

I would also like to acknowledge the good work of the Medical Foundation for the Care of Victims of Torture (www.torturecare. org.uk), to which the royalties from this book are going.

Preface

Culture is a forbidding word. I have to use it,
knowing of none better.

> E.M. Forster, "Does culture matter?" in *Two Cheers for Democracy*

Culture is one of the two or three most
complicated words in the English language. This
is so partly because of its intricate historical
development, in several European languages,
but mainly because it has now come to be
used for important concepts in several distinct
intellectual disciplines and in several distinct
and incompatible systems of thought.

> Raymond Williams, *Keywords*

Organisation culture has always intrigued me, and over the years I have learned a certain amount about it through painful lessons and more joyful experiences. At some point in my career I started to get asked to help people "change their organisation's culture". This perplexed me, as I think of it as chaotic and multidimensional, and always changing. Thus I'm a long-time sceptic of surveys or audits that purport to measure culture, find shortfalls and fix them, which seemed to be the thing that my clients were expecting.

Later I started to wonder what the question was behind the question: "How do I change the culture?" I thought I would be able to improve my work if I had more detail on the specific aspects of culture change that my clients were interested in. I also hoped to be able to give leaders more help on the issues by providing accessible information on culture that explained the complexities of it.

Thus I sent an email to everyone in my address book, saying the following:

I'm in the early stages of writing a book on corporate culture addressed at managers and business people who are struggling to:

a) Understand the culture of their organisation

b) Get a grip on why it matters

c) Get their culture right for their business strategy

d) Avoid the common mistakes of "culture change"

e) Keep their culture from getting stuck

I'm aiming for it to be for those who need common-sense, practical, realistic and pragmatic approaches that will help them understand and work with a slippery concept that in other books is discussed in academic theory and/or in technical/"new age" jargon.

If you were going to read this book what three questions would you want it to answer?

In response to this email I got several hundred questions that I categorised and it is these categories that form the chapters of this book. As I've written the chapters I've kept the questions close by, checking that they are being covered. My hope is that the book meets the purpose that I intend it to – but readers will be the judge of that. Many people contributed to it and where quotes are unattributed it is because the company or individual requested anonymity.

Naomi Stanford
May 2010

What is organisation culture?

New to a company or seeking to introduce a new business strategy, or responding to competitive or other contextual forces, many chief executives state their intention of "changing the culture" of their organisation, often because they see the "culture" as limiting what they want to achieve.

Allen Loren, CEO of D&B (formerly Dun & Bradstreet), a company specialising in business information, until his retirement in 2005, was instrumental in creating and launching, in 2000, the company's "Blueprint for Growth" strategy. Answering the question "What was your vision for change?" in an interview in May 2005, Loren said:[1]

> The primary focus was to repair the brand, change the business model to get funds to pay for the repairs, and create a new culture. Creating a new culture was fundamental to the new strategy. The business model we adopted – we refer to it as a "financially flexible business model" – was predicated on constant re-engineering and then the reinvestment of the freed-up funds. That meant constant change for team members. We knew we needed a culture that would support continual change, but we didn't have that at all.

Loren's statement raises questions that managers in any organisation will want answered, such as: Is it possible to "create a new culture" (or change an existing one)? If it is possible what does it involve? Why was creating a new culture "fundamental to the new strategy"? What precisely gave Loren the information that D&B did not have a culture that "would support continual change"? How would he know when he had created a new culture? Would he have to create another new culture if he had another new strategy? What is culture anyway?

Popular roots of organisation culture

The concept of organisation culture dates its popular roots from the 1980s when two books were published, both in 1982, which caught the attention of business managers and consultants. (Academic interest in culture – through theories of social science and anthropology – has a longer history.) The first book was *In Search of Excellence*, by Tom Peters and Robert Waterman, and the second *Corporate Cultures*, by Terrence Deal and Allen Kennedy. *New York Times* book reviewers were sceptical of both. Christopher Lehmann-Haupt, reviewing *In Search of Excellence* in December 1982, notes:

> It is almost incidental that the authors' eight-fold way, even when elaborated, is of no prescriptive value whatsoever that I can make out. That the list is an absolute orgy of faulty parallelism is slightly more significant, because, as is always the case when apples are crammed into a series with cashew nuts and dromedaries, it is a reflection of the list-maker's hopelessly muddled thinking. The confusion becomes apparent the instant Mr. Peters and Mr. Waterman begin to illustrate their attributes concretely.

While Robert Krulwich, in July 1982, said of *Corporate Cultures*:

> Nothing in this analysis is either new or startling. These same motivational techniques apply not just to business but to most relationships ... Reduced to boldfaced headings in a manual for managers, however, they are trivialised into ugly little tricks. This book may be of some help to managers who want to be less dependent on computer printouts and systems analysis, but there are some things you can't learn from a manual. One would have no notion, jumping from heading to heading of this book, how Thomas Watson created the powerful, co-ordinated dynamo that is IBM. The elements of his genius may be here, but not the real chemistry.

Business did not go along with the reviewers. The release of these books heralded a torrent of other organisational culture books, articles and conferences aimed at the market. This resulted in a hefty income stream for consultants confident that they could work organisation miracles by identifying and addressing the cultural issues thought to be either standing in the way of, or absolutely essential for, their client's business success.

Following this awakening of business interest in organisational culture, management theorists began taking an interest in the concepts and over the years have developed a body of theory and research that seeks to explain the role of culture in organisations. Nonetheless, as James Detert, Roger Schroeder and John Mauriel said in an article in *Academy of Management Review*:[2]

> As the culture concept enters its third decade of active life in the field of organisational studies ... we seem only to move farther away from a cumulative body of theory that would benefit theorists and practitioners alike.

Accepting it is a fragmented and complex field with many competing and contested concepts and theories – it is still useful for a manager to have a perspective on organisation culture: first, because it will help answer questions like those raised earlier by Loren's statement; second, because it will help managers deal more confidently with consultants who are trying to sell them culture-change solutions; third, because it will support a realistic appraisal of what individuals can and cannot do to affect organisational culture. As one manager said:

> Those who sometimes espouse culture change often do not really have a grip on the culture of their own organisation and do not understand why the culture happens to be what it is. If you don't know what you have and do not understand why it got that way, you reduce your chances of changing it positively to a culture that supports the vision and mission.

Three perspectives on organisation culture

Joanne Martin, professor of organisational behaviour at Stanford Graduate School of Business, discusses in her work three perspectives on organisational culture making the point that each perspective is incomplete and a view of organisational culture must be drawn from a synthesis of the three perspectives.[3] Briefly, the three perspectives are as follows:

▶ **The integration perspective** suggests that an organisation has a single culture that is clearly identifiable and potentially measurable, and that employees are committed to supporting it (or at least go along with it).

▶ **The differentiation perspective** sees organisations as complex, many-faceted sets of subcultures, within one overarching culture, interacting to manage their diverse and often competing interests and objectives.

▶ **The fragmentation perspective** "emphasises ambiguities of interpretation, irony, paradox and irreconcilable contradictions that cross-cut, undermine, and confuse any organisation-wide or subcultural claims of consensus or clarity".

The integration perspective

The way business people talk about organisation culture generally reflects specifically the integration perspective. This is evident when they "label" either the culture they have or the culture they want to have. Thus Apple is described as having "created a culture of secrecy" (*New York Times*) and Walmart "an austere culture built by old man Walton" (*The Economist*). In another example, commenting on the appointment of Markus Dohle as chief executive of Random House (a division of Bertelsmann, a global media company), an observer wondered whether Dohle, "known for his entrepreneurial zeal", would be able to lead Random House "without harming its creative culture".[4] It may puzzle some people as to why entrepreneurial spirit should be at odds with creativity, but it is explained by the view of one Random House author:[5]

On the face of it, it looks like the guy is a complete production bean counter. It doesn't look hopeful that he'll share the romantic idea of literature and publishing.

The problem with labels is that they are shallow, working only in terms of stereotypes along the lines of "all Frenchmen eat frogs", and confusing: the painting of a pipe by Magritte labelled "*Ceci n'est pas une pipe*" (this is not a pipe) illustrates this.[6] The confusion lies in labelling something that looks like a pipe as "not a pipe". It is not of course a pipe but a two-dimensional representation of a pipe. Similarly, a label of culture is not the culture but a severely abbreviated verbal description. Confusion and sometimes conflict arise because too little is done to create a shared meaning around what the label stands for. As an example, "a culture of collaboration" will mean different things to different people unless there are explicit and shared explanations and expectations around the label.

Lehman Brothers is a good example of the limitations of addressing the culture at the level of a label. When he took over as chief executive in 1994, Richard Fuld determined to establish "a culture built on teamwork", as in his view:[7]

(This) leads to the best business decisions for the firm as a whole, and paying employees in stock helped reinforce that culture. I wanted them all to think and act and behave like owners.

The premise implied is that the employees will understand and respond to the label in the same way. Some fundamental flaws in this approach are:

▶ assuming that his (Fuld's) notion of "teamwork" is the same as each employee's;

▶ presuming employees have a common view of what thinking, acting and behaving as an owner is (and want to be an owner);

▶ acting as if people are motivated by the same rewards, in this case stock;

▶ believing that "teamwork" leads to the best business decisions.

Fuld's main action to develop a "culture of teamwork" was to link compensation to the overall performance of the firm through equity awards (Fuld himself being awarded colossal sums – somewhere between $350m and $485m between 2000 and 2008). This type of one-track action to culture change may show some results in the short term but is highly unlikely to be effective in the longer term. Indeed, when Lehman Brothers filed for bankruptcy during the financial sector collapse of 2008 it became clear that the "culture of teamwork" was one based on greed, lack of oversight and accountability, and blame – not the characteristics commonly associated either with teamwork or with well-run, owner-managed businesses.[8]

Lehman Brothers could have taken an approach that recognised that:

▷ teamwork is a system of operation that has mutually interrelated parts including tasks, personalities, timescales, goals, values and incentives;

▷ each of these interrelated parts has an impact on the others;

▷ none can be manipulated independently from the others if the goal is to establish and reinforce a well-articulated and shared view of teamwork;

▷ leaders must support the principles and role-model the behaviours of the teamwork they expect in others.

This would have been a more subtle, nuanced, multifaceted, systems approach to establish "a culture of teamwork" and might have led to a different outcome for Lehman Brothers. Of course it may not have, and that is one of the fascinations of examining organisational culture, because despite theories, perspectives, definitions, labels and inventories that claim to measure it, culture is largely an unknown quantity. Donald Rumsfeld, former US defence secretary, could have been talking about organisational culture, instead of Iraq, when he commented:[9]

> As we know, there are known knowns. There are things we know we know. We also know there are known unknowns. That is to say we know there are some things we do not know. But there are also unknown unknowns, the ones we don't know we don't know.

Grappling with the issues put down to the culture of his organisation, one executive commented:

> *There's the question of what it (culture) is. I suppose every company has a corporate culture of a sort, and certainly every executive I've met claims to be promoting one ("we have a culture of accountability", etc). But such widespread usage makes the word "culture" feel flabby to me. It would be wonderful if it could be described more crisply or provocatively so I could know what it is and then do something about it.*

The differentiation perspective

That manager's frustration in trying to understand organisation culture is not helped by the academic approach to organisation culture. The competing theories and contested research result from the many different definitions of culture that theorists use. Below are five typical definitions of culture that reflect the more nuanced perspective of differentiation:

▶ The collective programming of the mind which distinguishes the members of one category of people from another.[10]

▶ The pattern of values, norms, beliefs, attitudes and assumptions that may not have been articulated but shape the ways in which people behave and things get done. Values refer to what is believed to be important about how people and the organisations behave. Norms are the unwritten rules of behaviour.[11]

▶ A pattern of shared basic assumptions that the group learned as it solved its problems of external adaptation and internal integration, that has worked well enough to be considered valid and, therefore, to be taught to new members as the correct way to perceive, think, and feel in relation to those problems.[12]

▶ An active living phenomenon through which people jointly create and recreate the worlds in which they live.[13]

▶ A system of shared values, defining what is important, and norms, defining appropriate attitudes and behaviours, that guide members' attitudes and behaviours.[14]

Beyond these five definitions is the popular one of uncertain origin defining culture as "the way we do things round here".

For five reasons these definitions, although they allow for a differentiation perspective, are as unhelpful as labels in getting to a crisp and provocative understanding of organisation culture:

▶ There is little agreement at a practical level of what culture "is". In the same way that "beauty is in the eye of the beholder", so it could be said that "culture is in the mind of the experiencer". (Additionally there is a philosophical difference between researchers who take the view that organisations "have" a culture and researchers who take the view that culture is what the organisation "is".)

▶ Where there is agreement about the constituents of culture they are stated as "patterns" of values, norms, beliefs, attitudes, behaviours and suchlike that can be shared. This may be useful as a generalisation but is less so when it comes to taking actions at a local or individual level. If the various ingredients of a pie (the culture) are a proxy for value, norms, beliefs, and so on, when the pie is assembled, cooked, cut and shared out each person will experience it differently and have their own response to it. Similarly with culture – the "ingredients" of culture are meaningless before combination, and when combined are experienced differently by each individual.

▶ There is confusion as to whether culture is static – and therefore easily teachable to, say, newcomers to an organisation – or dynamic and inherently less predictable and teachable.

▶ It is not clear whether culture is influenced by people or whether culture influences people. Is it "done to" people or "done by" people? Or, more likely, is it a continuous interplay of people and circumstance?

▶ The definitions are inwardly focused. They do not allow for the external framework in which the organisation is situated, which, simply put, is evident at three levels:
– the organisational regulatory and tax compliance requirements;
– external relationships with governments and communities;
– the legal frameworks and mutual expectations surrounding the rights and responsibilities of workers and employers, for example whether employees are barred from joining a union.

Thus the disparity in definitions demonstrates the difficulty in giving leaders the kind of "right" answers they are looking for when they ask questions about their organisation's culture. Taking the threads inherent in the various definitions, it is evident that culture is about pervasive, implicit, subtle, complex and dynamic ways of community being that might be generalisable across an organisation but are experienced individually and subjectively. However, this notion is too vague and slippery to be useful to someone who wants to create or change or protect an organisation's culture.

An analogy for organisational culture

One way of getting to an understanding of organisation culture is to consider it as analogous to something else – climate and weather is a good analogy. Following the Köppen climate classification system the world is divided into six major climate zones. For example, one of these is "tropical humid". This is analogous to the integration level of an organisation – an organisation might be described as having "a culture of collaboration".

Each climate zone has a number of subclimate zones: those for "tropical humid" include "tropical savanna", and "subtropical steppe". These are analogous to the differentiation perspective where business units and departments have variations of the culture within the overarching culture.

Within each subzone are the daily weather patterns. These are analogous to the fragmentation perspective, discussed in the following section, and help explain how the day-to-day culture of the organisation plays out. The point to note is that climate and weather are inseparable from each other (reflecting Martin's view that organisational culture is a synthesis of three perspectives).

The US National Aeronautics and Space Administration (NASA) explains the difference between weather and climate as follows:[15]

> Weather is what conditions of the atmosphere are over a short period of time, and climate is how the atmosphere "behaves" over relatively long periods of time.

Weather is basically the way the atmosphere is behaving, mainly with respect to its effects upon life and human activities. The difference between weather and climate is that weather consists of the short-term (minutes to months) changes in the atmosphere. Most people think of weather in terms of temperature, humidity, precipitation, cloudiness, brightness, visibility, wind, and atmospheric pressure. In most places, weather can change from minute-to-minute, hour-to-hour, day-to-day, and season-to-season.

Climate, however, is the average of weather over time and space. An easy way to remember the difference is that climate is what you expect, like a very hot summer, and weather is what you get, like a hot day with pop-up thunderstorms.

When we talk about climate change, we talk about changes in long-term averages of daily weather.

Table 1.1 applies the weather/climate analogy to an organisation's culture and suggests why it is a helpful one.

Table 1.1 **Weather/climate analogy**

Analogy	Applying the analogy	Why this helps
Climate (average of weather over time, space, and climate zone). The most commonly used climate zone classification describes six zones each with subzones. Factors determining assigning a region to a specific zone include biome distribution, latitude, humidity, elevation, distance from the sea and direction of the prevailing winds.[a]	Organisational climate (the label of the culture). Patterns over time of cultural similarity across business units and geography are often reflected in visual representations, shared IT systems, a single mission or vision statement, etc. This element reflects the integration perspective.	It paints the picture of macro-level consistency across an organisation. So, for example, a visitor going to an HSBC bank in any country will recognise common HSBC characteristics both visually and through apparently seamless IT systems. (The bank's strapline is "the world's local bank".)

Analogy	Applying the analogy	Why this helps
Subclimate varies, within recognisable boundaries by terrain, geographic location, etc, within the climate zone.	Culture evident in terms of values, norms, beliefs, attitudes, assumptions, facilities, etc, at a business unit or department level, often dependent on the unit's leadership and the stamp they put on their part of the organisation which leads business units to have a different "feel" one from the other. This element reflects the differentiation perspective.	It makes it clear that culture is more than the sum of its parts. It cannot be reduced to discrete elements for manipulation (in the same way that rain cannot be separated from other weather elements). Klaus Kleinfeld, former chief executive of Siemens, tried to manipulate only one element when he embarked on changing the firm's culture to one "of delivery". He set aggressive internal earnings targets. In doing so he incurred the wrath of employees, became the subject of a bribery probe, unbalanced the organisation and was dismissed.

Analogy	Applying the analogy	Why this helps
Weather (short-term, minutes to months) determined by interactions of temperature, humidity, precipitation, cloudiness, brightness, visibility, wind, and atmospheric pressure.	Organisational culture (short-term, minutes to months) varies as the immediate context changes – people join and leave, crises hit, demands change, people's emotions switch – resulting in the culture feeling chaotic and unpredictable within certain bounds.[b] Also related to the external context in which the organisation is situated (including regulatory, relationship, and worker/employer expectations), which leads multinationals to have a different "feel" in different countries of operation. This element reflects the fragmentation perspective.	It suggests that culture could and should reflect local conditions. Starbucks' ability to maintain a presence in China is due, in part, to its willingness to try different types of ownership structure, and with these some differences in the "Starbucks experience" depending on geographic location.[c]

Analogy	Applying the analogy	Why this helps
Climate change does occur but over time (NASA measures over 30 years). It happens as a result of natural activity such as a volcanic eruption, or human activity such as through the build-up of greenhouse gases.	Organisational climate change does occur but over time. It happens as a natural result of environmental and context changes such as technology advances and social changes or as a result of a specific set of planned activities/interventions such as long-term efforts to achieve a specific business strategy in a particular way.	It reinforces the fact that although the culture (here meaning short-term, minutes to months) changes or might be changeable, to see or introduce sustained change in the organisational climate (here meaning across a whole organisation in the long term) takes time and – where more than the "normal" rate of change is desired – effort on multiple fronts. In answer to the question "Does a radical change agent lie behind the cultural conservatism?", Alan Lafley, chief executive of Procter & Gamble, paused at the "radical" label because, at least until the Gillette deal, the transformation had been the cumulative effect of a series of small, interlocking changes. No single dramatic event during the previous five years defined the period, just as no evocative vision statement served as its road map. "I guess I'm a serial change agent," Lafley says.[d]

a For more about weather and climate see the Köppen climate classification system, which is the most widely used for classifying the world's climates.
b For a readable book see Gleick, J., *Chaos: Making a New Science*, Penguin, 2000.
c http://seattlepi.nwsource.com/business/228728_sbuxchina16.html
d "Leading change: An interview with the CEO of P&G", *McKinsey Quarterly*, August 2nd 2005.

In summary, the weather/climate analogy is helpful when thinking about organisational culture because it represents culture in two time measures – short-term/immediate and longer-term. It paints the picture of local differences or patterns that are locally variable (the fragmentation perspective) but can be defined (the differentiation perspective) within an overall set of patterns that can be labelled (the integration perspective).

Sticking with the analogy, it works to illustrate how people make sense of the world around them by responding to patterns that they experience over time. (Sensemaking is discussed in more detail in Chapter 6.) People make judgments, even in the absence of weather forecasts, on what clothing to wear and what accessories to take (hat, umbrella) by looking at the sky, feeling the air temperature, listening to wind noise, seeing the light level, noticing what other people are wearing, and so on. They are making these decisions based on their experience of weather patterns. This works well when they stay in the same geographic area, because the weather patterns vary within certain parameters. When moving to a different geographic area either within the same climate zone or in another climate zone, a person has to respond to different weather patterns and, initially, finds it much harder to make good choices on what to wear or bring in case of weather variation, and often seeks or is given advice. *Frommer's Complete Guide to San Francisco* (2007), for example, asks:

> Have you packed a warm jacket or coat? When the fog's in and the wind picks up, San Francisco will feel like winter regardless of the time of year.

Similarly, people make sense of an organisational culture by picking up the patterns of the organisation – things like what type of person gets promoted, how offices are allocated, what gets noticed or who talks to whom. Where these patterns can be discerned across the whole organisation (equivalent to a climate zone) they are usually reinforced in policies, performance management systems, common visual symbols or decor, among other things. At the "weather" level, within a local department or team, the patterns are local (as in weather), depending on the nature of the work, the personalities of the managers, and so on, but are still potentially predictable because they are within the parameters (climate) of the organisation.

The experience of a long-serving executive moving from the marketing department to the strategic planning department of her organisation illustrates this. She said: "Marketing was very gregarious and outgoing. Here it is unbelievably intense." She found this change difficult to adapt to, commenting:

> It was a gruelling experience at first. I nearly gave up several times. What saved me was knowing at the broader level how the organisation worked and knowing where to go to get things done.

This executive's experience of the climate of the organisation aided her in her initiation to local cultural conditions.

People who move from one organisation to another (as from one climate zone to another) have to get to grips with not only the climate but also the local culture ("weather") patterns. This can be extremely hard. Another executive, recruited from outside to the same organisation as in the previous example, when asked six months into the role if he felt attuned, noted:

> Not completely. I want to bring some fresh things in. But I've had to adapt. I've had to learn to fit into the culture and accept some of its strangeness if I'm going to be accepted. For me there's a bit too much consensus and discussion: meetings for two hours are not what I'm used to. But I need to be careful. I need to understand why people do what they do. I'm confident enough now at the whole organisation level, but the local departmental differences are still worrisome to me.

Recognising organisational climate and organisational culture as distinct but interlinked and inseparable allows for both natural evolution and planned changes to the culture over the long term. It reinforces the notion that culture is not a set of independent variables but a series of complex, dynamic, interactive and pervasive "ecosystems". (An ecosystem is a dynamic complex of plant, animal and micro-organism communities and their non-living environment interacting to form a whole functional system.) It implies that local interventions in the short term may have little impact on the overall patterns in the longer term (but they may, in the same way that a local volcanic eruption can have an immediate and dramatic effect on global climate which is then sustained over time).

The fragmentation perspective

The climate/weather analogy is also helpful in reflecting on organisation culture from a fragmentation perspective. Although weather forecasting continues to improve it is not right all the time: there are unpredicted thunderstorms; a tornado veers in an unpredicted direction; a mudslide, a forest fire or an earthquake occurs; the weather forecaster may say there will be heavy showers and there is brilliant sunshine or vice versa. All these events are analogous to the "ambiguities of interpretation, irony, paradox, and irreconcilable contradictions"[16] that people who listen to weather forecasts are aware of, and learn to work around or adapt to.

Similarly in organisations there are the inherent contradictions, shocks and "out of the blue" jolts that shake the company. Take the Shell example, when it was revealed in January 2004 that the company had overstated its oil reserves. *Business Week* reported:[17]

> *The antagonism between Watts and van de Vijyer must have been hard to ignore. "I am becoming sick and tired of lying about the extent of our reserves issues and the downward revisions that need to be done," van de Vijyer wrote to Watts in November 2003, after a critical performance review. Yet ... [the law firm investigating the matter surmised that] van de Vijyer's team chose to "play for time", hoping that Shell could discover its way out of the reserves shortfall, rather than take these concerns to the board.*

For this senior manager the news came not as a climatic trend that he had missed (that may or may not have been evident to analysts) but as an unexpected shock. As he commented:

> *I feel betrayed by the leaders of the company I work for, but the*

fact is I am a leader in it myself. I don't know what my respon-
sibility is in this mess that we're in, and I don't know how to
keep my staff motivated and supported as we work things out
in a way that demonstrates we are still committed to our busi-
ness principles.

Recap points

▶ An organisation's culture is not a "thing" where a label suffices
to "tell it how it is", nor is it a set of discrete elements that can be
easily manipulated either separately or together.

▶ Organisational culture is like the climate and its weather – climate
reflecting the more predictable pattern, applicable to the larger
entity, and its weather being chaotic and unpredictable in a more
limited arena.

▶ An organisation's culture, like the climate and weather, is
simultaneously shaping and is shaped by the context. Over time
it can and does change – whether by design or by default.

▶ In the same way that people are conscious of the climate and the
weather, they are conscious of organisation culture – and make
choices in relation to it.

▶ People experience, adapt to, interact with and have an impact on
an organisation's culture in subjective and singular ways.

▶ Academic research on organisation culture is a contested field
with many competing theories (so, at this stage, has limited
practical application in the day-to-day life of managers).
Nevertheless, it indicates to managers the complexities of
trying to get to grips with organisation culture and the risks of
oversimplifying what it is.

▶ Thinking about organisational culture as analogous to climate,
sub-climate and weather helps explain why changing the culture
is complex.

One manager, who immediately saw the power of the climate/
weather analogy, commented:

I would say that organisational culture is the outcome of a set of dynamics and, at the same time, an influencer of those dynamics – in the same way that the nature of the weather at any particular time will be affected by the weather patterns that have gone before and the ways in which these have affected wind patterns, temperatures, land contours, and so on. For me, this is a powerful insight into the culture of my company – in the jargon, "the way we have done things around here" is a shaper of the way we do things around here, and of the way we will be able to do things around here. I've come to realise that "changing the culture" is not something I will undertake lightly and that learning how to work with, influence and sculpt it is likely to be more effective.

One company's culture: McDonald's

McDonald's celebrated its 50th anniversary in 2005. It was the topic of a US National Public Radio broadcast, "Talk of the Nation", on April 14th 2005. Here is the host, Neal Conan, opening the discussion:

> McDonald's is a multinational giant whose famous Golden Arches can be found in more than 119 countries. But what would future anthropologists infer if, long after our civilisation crumbled, they unearthed thousands of Ronald McDonald toys or an ancient franchise? What would that say about who we were? Whether you love it, hate it, dine there often or never, McDonald's revolutionised the fast-food industry, and it changed not just the way we eat, but our language, our architecture, advertising, our culture.

Conan is talking here about the American culture. But taking it a step further, his comment also illustrates the interrelationship between an organisation and its market, and how McDonald's customers' buying patterns and feedback have an impact on the company's culture and behaviour. As a caller to the radio programme said:

> When I was a kid, there were three of us children, and we never went out to eat much, but when we did, going out to eat meant going out to McDonald's ... My favourite was their fish with the orange drink ... And actually now I'm a vegetarian and I see they've kind of adapted. They've got salads and yogurt and stuff like that, so I can still eat there.

In turn McDonald's has an impact on the national cultures it operates in. A manager who joined the company in Pakistan notes:

> *The whole food industry changed in Pakistan as a result of McDonald's opening there. They introduced technologies such as trash compactors, supply chain management, and quality and hygiene standards. They employed women in the restaurants. As a result of these types of business practices the culture of the country started changing too.*

Interestingly, the word "culture" hardly features on the McDonald's website in relation to the company. The "Plan to Win" phrase, on the other hand, gets hundreds of mentions. This is a strategy "focused on restaurant operations and our four cornerstones of quality, service, cleanliness and value" (QSC&V – a benchmark used by the corporation to assess the standards of its restaurants). For McDonald's it appears that Plan to Win is equivalent to a label of its culture. CEO Jim Skinner says:

> *"Better, not just bigger" became our mantra, and the customer-centric Plan to Win became our playbook ... Every decision that we make, whether it affects thousands of restaurants or just one, has customer relevance as its primary driver ... we take our cue from customers.*

Across McDonald's the integrator is the Plan to Win strategy. Training managers and "crew members" in what it means to Plan to Win, drumming home the requirement to "live" the four cornerstones (QSC&V) and reinforcing/role-modelling the values of the organisation demonstrate that there is no need to use the word "culture" to have a culture.

Illustrating the differentiation perspective is the ability of franchisees to make the Plan to Win work in their environments while sticking to the QSC&V. As James Watson, editor of *Golden Arches East: McDonald's in East Asia*, talking on the radio programme mentioned earlier, notes:

> *One of the hallmarks of the brand is that they try to standardise everything, but increasingly in many markets, including East Asia, they're introducing new kinds of items that are not covered in other parts of the world. I teach a course at Harvard called Food and Culture, and I ask my students to bring me tray liners from McDonald's all over the world, and I have a huge collection of these, and it's amazing the variety of foods that are available.*

However, there's one central feature about McDonald's that never varies. The sandwiches may differ, you don't find beef in India, and you find fish burgers being preferred in places like Hong Kong, but the one thing that never varies are the fries. [Because they comply with local laws] everyone can eat the fries, and it cuts right across religions.

The standardisation is what many detractors of McDonald's rail against to the extent that the "McDonaldisation" of things has become a commonly used pejorative. As Watson says:

[Look how] we are using a capital M, small C in front of a lot of things and it is now a pejorative: "McJob", "McPaper" – USA Today was derided as "McPaper" when it first came out. And a lot of people who live in those big houses built in suburbia [which] are referred to as "McMansions" ... I've been collecting these prefixes, and it has penetrated the language to the point where it is now perceived as a kind of pejorative everywhere. It's interesting that it's also spreading in other languages as well, and sometimes the "Mc" in Roman script or in English is attached to Chinese script or Korean script, and it has the same kind of implications. So you find it everywhere.

The demonising of McDonald's highlights the fragmentation perspective (the unpredictable events) that McDonald's manages – and does so for the most part without reputational/brand damage. In recent years the company has been the target of physical attacks. In 2002, for example:[18]

One was torched in Riyadh, Saudi Arabia, on November 20th. Another blew up in Moscow on October 19th, while less than a month before, a small bomb ripped through a franchise in a suburb of Beirut. According to Reuters, militants arrested in July for the bomb attack on the US consulate in Karachi had also been planning to bomb McDonald's. In December 2001, a McDonald's was bombed in Xian, in central China, and in September 2001 a pipe bomb exploded on a McDonald's in Istanbul.

There are also media/pressure group assaults on worker conditions, the nutritional value of the food (most strikingly in the film *Super Size Me*), pricing policies and various other campaigns.

An example of the latter that was widely reported in Europe and the United States was the 1999 case of Jose Bove, a French farmer, who "became something of a national hero ... for leading an attack on a

McDonald's restaurant". In July 2001 the *New York Times* reported:

> *From the beginning it was clear that Mr Bove's attack on the American fast-food giant had tapped into a deep well of public discontent and a feeling of powerlessness on subjects ranging from genetically modified food to ... the United States' decision to levy high tariffs on Roquefort cheese ... in retaliation for the EU's decision to ban American hormone-treated beef.*

These cases illustrate the tensions between business interests, national interests and competing interests, and also the unpredictable nature of events – the fragmentation perspective.

Further examples of this perspective playing out in McDonald's occurred in 2004 when the company's sixth CEO, James Cantalupo, died of a heart attack while at a company convention in April. Charlie Bell, who replaced him, learned 16 days later that he had colon cancer, leading him to stand down in November that year, whereupon Jim Skinner took over as CEO. In spite of unexpectedly having to take the reins, Skinner successfully continued with the Plan to Win strategy and was named 2009's Chief Executive of the Year by *Chief Executive* magazine. According to the press release:[19]

> *"Skinner successfully transformed an iconic brand by shifting strategies to being better versus bigger and introducing a range of quality enhancements from introducing new, healthier menu options to the innovative redesign of restaurants," said J.P. Donlon, editor-in-chief of Chief Executive magazine. "He has been respectful of McDonald's legacy while engineering an inspirational strategic leadership that reinvented the industry."*

One of the reasons Skinner could pick up the reins and carry on successfully is that McDonald's had a clear organisational culture, one that was able to successfully deal with the unexpected. Although McDonald's does not use the word "culture" in describing the organisation or its operation (those who take culture to mean sophistication, discernment or refinement may be pleased to hear this), it clearly has culture based on "fast, clean and cheap" – what food historian Bruce Kraig calls "the American credo of food", which is manifested in the Plan to Win strategy, the Quality, Service, Cleanliness and Value principles, and the resources geared up to deliver all this.

Learning from McDonald's

Three lessons come out of the McDonald's approach to its culture:

▶ **Be clear what the company stands for from the three cultural perspectives.** McDonald's is an example of a company that is clear about:

- what its strategy is (Plan to Win): integrated perspective; what it stands for (Quality, Service, Cleanliness and Value): differentiated perspective;
- the way it practises its corporate values as events unfold: fragmented perspective.

▶ **Be culturally relevant in each market.** This means adapting the company's culture to the local culture as appropriate. Skinner makes the point that taste, trends and needs are so diverse in every country that McDonald's cannot use the same business model for every location. That means adapting to local customs and traditions. Examples include closing McDonald's five times a day for prayer in Saudi Arabia or serving shrimp entrees in Japan. McDonald's most successful market in Europe has been France, thanks to its adaptation efforts in that country. "If the French love us, who can hate us?" Skinner jokes. "We're doing something right."

▶ **Be alert and respond to changes in the external culture.** Any response to external changes needs to be made with finesse and in the knowledge that it will have an impact on the internal culture (see Chapter 7). In April 2009, under the heading "Big Mac, hold the CO_2", the *Sunday Times* reported:

> *The hamburger giant still arouses strong feelings among activists but it has been working hard to adapt, particularly in the environmental field. Introducing fairtrade coffee and organic milk, for example, has won some plaudits, but perhaps the most striking example can be seen in the south side of Chicago where, next door to the Swap-O-Rama flea market, it opened a prototype "green" restaurant last year.*

Summary

▶ There is no value in taking a reductionist approach to organisation culture. It is not a phenomenon that can be reduced to a meaningful short label or a single agreed-upon definition.

▶ Organisational culture is an organisationally specific "experience" felt both subjectively and individually by insiders and outsiders.

▶ People living in one of the six climate zones become familiar with the characteristic weather patterns and respond to the day-to-day variations in weather. In a similar way they experience an organisation's culture.

▶ Across an organisation there is an overarching "look and feel" that is expressed differently but relatively predictably within business units.

▶ On a day-to-day basis employees respond to whatever comes up within appropriate and culturally acceptable norms.

Exercise 1: Getting to grips with an organisation's culture in Appendix 3 helps you discover how the three organisational cultural perspectives of integration, differentiation and fragmentation manifest (or not) in a specific enterprise.

Can culture be measured?

When the new CEO of General Motors (GM), Fritz Henderson, appointed in March 2009 following Chapter 11 bankruptcy filing, was asked at an early meeting to discuss GM's culture, he gave what some members of the task force[1] described as a long, meandering answer, which concluded with "I've been here 25 years. This is the only culture I know", after which he quickly added that he was determined to change it.[2]

Others who are similarly unable to describe their organisation's culture yet are convinced that they need to change or manage it often turn to quantitative organisational culture surveys to help them decide what to do in the belief that "what gets measured gets managed", a well-worn management phrase usually attributed to management guru Peter Drucker. (In this chapter the words "measurement" and "assessment" are used interchangeably.)

Typical is this manager's challenge:

> My boss has read Collins and Porras's book Built to Last, and tells me that it celebrates a clear, sustained culture that is stronger than any one individual, as a factor in continued success. She's asked me to find out the levers that need to be pulled consistently to enable such a culture to be built. She wants to know what the biggest influence on the culture of our organisation is: top management, our business environment, our location or something else. I'd like to know how you measure, identify or assess what the culture is in an organisation so I can give her the answer.

The manager looked to quantitative surveys as his first port of call in his desire to find the "levers", measures, or "checklist of elements" that would help him – all understandable given the desire to manage if not totally control the culture and the widespread strong belief that what cannot be measured cannot be managed.

There are many quantitative surveys available to buy "off the shelf" (see Appendix 2 for some available ones). Choosing one is almost a matter of personal preference as they all share similar characteristics. What follows is a list of these similarities, but for each one a different off-the-shelf survey is given as an example to illustrate the characteristic:

▶ Having a specific language in which they describe culture: for example, the Human Synergistics Organisational Cultural Inventory (OCI) assesses culture in terms of style. Constructive, passive/defensive and aggressive/defensive are the three main dimensions, each having four subdimensions. (See Figure 2.2 on page 34 for a worked example.)

▶ Asking individuals to score or tick their answers to a series of questions that relate to each of the dimensions that the survey covers. The Culture Sync Survey, for example, is based on the language of "Tribes", suggesting that there are five cultural stages – "life stinks" (Stage 1), "my life stinks" (Stage 2), "I'm great" (Stage 3), "we're great" (Stage 4) or "life is great" (Stage 5) – and that organisations should aspire to be at Stage 5. In this survey individuals indicate which statement is closest to their experience of the organisation. The following question illustrates the approach:

a) Which best describes people's relationship to the organisation's mission, vision, and/or values:
  i   Hostile antagonism
  ii Sarcastic jokes and/or no real effect on behaviour
  iii Inspires individuals to do a better job
  iv Inspires collaborative behaviour that overcomes personal differences
  v   Mission, vision and/or values tells people in the organisation who they are

▶ Being internally focused, that is, asking all or selected samples of employees to complete them, not external suppliers, customers or other stakeholders (though these groups may be asked to complete a different survey). The Denison Culture Survey has four culture traits – mission, involvement, adaptability and consistency – each with three subculture traits. Each of these has five questions, and employees are asked to score on a scale of 1–5, rating their agreement with a statement, for example: "It is easy to co-ordinate projects across different parts of the organisation."

▶ Asking for a single response to a complex question. The Corporate Culture Survey, for example, asks respondents to circle one number for each statement on an agreement scale of 1–5 for statements including:

Creativity
a) I am encouraged to invent new ways to do things.
b) X company rewards ingenuity.
c) Employees are rewarded for improving work processes.

Ethics and Values
a) The people at X company always behave in an ethical manner.
b) The people at X company will not tolerate unethical behaviour.

Managers may initially think that these types of quantitative survey will be helpful, but on closer examination, or even use, it is evident that they may not take them very far. Edgar Schein, a professor at MIT Sloan School of Management, discusses several reasons "why culture surveys do not and cannot measure culture":[3]

▶ There is no way of knowing what cultural dimensions are important in any one organisation. Even so, the surveys make an assumption that the dimensions they pick up are the same for all organisations that take that survey. In the examples above, each survey labels cultural dimensions differently. Some focus on behaviour and include people's relationship to the organisation's mission, vision, and/or values; others focus on the "mood" of the organisation, or the activities of leaders, or what people complain about most and the structure of people's relationships. Without doing a lot more digging for information it is not clear on what basis these dimensions have been chosen, whether they are relevant to the organisation being surveyed and, if so, the relative contribution of each to the culture of the organisation.

▶ There is little recognition, at least in off-the-shelf surveys, that culture covers all aspects of a group's external tasks and internal integration processes and the ways these interact, integrate and endlessly recombine. This is likely to be because these dynamic factors cannot be adequately addressed in a survey.

▶ There is no way of knowing what a respondent is reading into the questions. In the last example above, is "ingenuity" being experienced in the same way by everyone? Are individuals consistent in their thinking about what constitutes an "ethical manner"?

▶ There is no way of knowing if the respondent is answering honestly or in good faith.

▶ There is too much complexity in culture to assume that individual responses can be aggregated into a perspective on the whole organisation's culture. In this regard, Warren Bennis made the point that "you can't just pop a culture in a microwave and out pops a McCulture".

▶ There is an implication that if the survey results reveal issues or problems then something will happen to address these. However, there may not be a will to do anything; for example, if there are "clusters of people who feel they have little impact on how the organisation is run", so what? If the organisation is performing well, although lack of impact may be of importance to the responders, it may not be a material finding to their managers. (This in itself says something about the culture of the organisation.)

Other reasons surveys "do not and cannot measure culture" are as follows:

▶ They take a reductionist view of culture that attempts to isolate independent cultural variables (norms, attitudes, values, behaviours, management practices, etc) and "treat" them. The problem with this is that even if surveys had meaningful variables, they are not independent. Every variable is dependent in some way on every other. Chapter 1 argued that this approach is like taking an element of the weather (such as hours of sunshine in a given period) and assuming that manipulating this as an independent variable (were it possible) would change the weather in a desirable direction.

▶ They imply that "fixing" a culture that is "broken" or working out what is great about a culture and needs protection can be quick and painless. Neither is the case (see Chapter 7).

▶ They assume, by using the same dimensions in the survey, that organisation culture is homogeneous and shared among all employees. Again this is not typically the case. In organisations of any size there are subcultures, countercultures and variations in culture (as in the day-to-day weather analogy described in Chapter 1).

▶ They take the view that organisation culture is "transmitted" through the behaviour and actions of employees within an organisation. This does not allow for the complexity of the interplay between internal and external "transmission" routes and the chaotic and dynamic nature of culture.[4]

▶ They purport to be more than a snapshot in a particular time period, overriding the dynamic and constantly changing nature of culture.

The popular Dilbert cartoon series created by Scott Adams has generated the "Dilbert Metric", which neatly and absurdly makes the point about trying to measure an organisation's culture using surveys:[5]

> *The Dilbert metric involves showing ten Dilbert cartoons selected at random to members of an organisation. Each member rates the cartoons on a scale of zero to ten. Zero means the cartoon is wholly applicable to the organisation while ten means the cartoon is not at all relevant. Each individual's score is totalled up and an average score of all the totals is taken. The resulting figure is an indication of the health of the organisation's morale and culture: the closer the figure to zero, the closer the organisation to the Dilbertesque, chaotic view of corporate life; the closer to one hundred, the better.*

If culture must be measured

Given that the desire to identify, assess or measure an organisation's culture seems unshakeable and that quantitative surveys
are a shaky method of conducting those activities, what can help
managers make sense of all the measurement possibilities that are
available, and of these what would help them in their quest to
know what culture their organisation "is" or "has"?[6] The following
sections give practical help on this topic.

In a nutshell, there are three ways of trying to measure the culture
of an organisation:

▶ quantitatively (as in surveys);

▶ qualitatively (as in interviews or focus groups);

▶ a combination of the two (known as mixed method).

Quantitative methods

Quantitative methods isolate certain dimensions and then measure
them. In the weather analogy used in Chapter 1 the measurement
of certain dimensions associated with weather gives the weather
forecast for the day. Figure 2.1 overleaf shows the forecast for Tripoli,
Libya, on May 20th 2010. Note that what is being measured is temperature, wind, humidity, pressure, sunrise, sunset, highs and lows
for the day, and an indication of cloud cover. This gives some clues
on what to expect that day but it does not give any kind of vivid
impression of someone's experience of that weather.

Qualitative methods

Qualitative methods aim to build a richness and depth to the
assessment through the use of narrative, storytelling, personal
example and imagery. Here is the opening paragraph of a novel
set in Tripoli:[7]

> I am recalling now that last summer before I was sent away. It
> was 1979, and the sun was everywhere. Tripoli lay brilliant and
> still beneath it. Every person, animal and ant went in desperate
> search for shade, those occasional grey patches of mercy carved
> into the white of everything. But true mercy only arrived at night,

A weather forecast

Weather in Tripoli, Libya

Current Conditions in Tripoli

 77°F / 25°C

Wind:	NE at 14 mph / 23 kh
Humidity:	50%
Pressure:	30 inches / 1016 mb
Sunrise:	6:06 AM
Sunset:	8:02 PM

Conditions updated at Thu, 20 May 2010 12:50 pm EET

Today's forecast

Clear
Hi: 81°F / 27°C
Lo: 63°F / 17°C

Tomorrow's forecast

Sunny
Hi: 81°F / 27°C
Lo: 61°F / 16°C

Source: Worldtimeserver.com

*a breeze chilled by the vacant desert, moistened by the humming
sea, a reluctant guest silently passing through the empty streets,
vague about how far it was allowed to roam in this world of the
absolute star. And it was rising now, this star, as faithful as ever,
chasing away the blessed breeze. It was almost morning.*

In this the writer is giving a vivid impression of how he experiences the weather conditions of Tripoli, and doing so in a way
that cannot be achieved by survey, where the items are set and
there is a check box to tick a response. Notice how the writer mentions "the grey patches of mercy", which reflect in the quantitative
weather forecast as a sun graphic with a cloud across it. Notice
too how the qualitative paragraph mentions the "breeze chilled
by the vacant desert" that arrives at night. This is shown in the
weather forecast in Figure 2.1 as "Wind: NE at 14mph/23kh", which
is a daytime wind speed.

As far as trying to measure organisation culture goes, both

quantitative and qualitative methods have strengths, and both have limitations. Table 2.1 summarises these.

Table 2.1 Quantitative and qualitative methods

	Quantitative method (eg, surveys)	Qualitative method (eg, self reports, 1:1 interviews, focus groups, observation)
Strengths	Objective (though this can be disputed)	Subjective (gives depth and richness)
	Hard facts, data, numbers allowing for trend spotting, tracking over time, comparison between business units, etc	Multiple realities: focus is complex and broad
		Aims to discover, describe to get to understanding, shared interpretation
	Reduction, control, precision	
	Measurable	Interpretive
	Can be conducted quickly	Context-dependent
		Describes meaning, discovery
		Provides information on "which beans are worth counting"
Limitations	One reality (limited by survey items)	Searches for patterns and theories developed for understanding (takes time to do this)
	Focus is concise and narrow. The aim is to generalise, leading to prediction, explanation and (mis) understanding	Soft data: basic elements of analysis are words/ideas that are more difficult to see patterns across or compare
	Mechanistic: the parts equal the whole	Develops a story often with a timeline
	Context-free (surveys can be bought off the shelf)	
	Establishes relationships, causation (where, in the case of culture, none might exist)	
	"Counts the beans"	
	Snapshot in time	

Mixed methods

Rather than using just one of these methods, a better way to try to measure or assess culture is to use a combination of both. The Tripoli weather example illustrates why. Briefly, a survey instrument cannot list all the items that might be material to someone's experience, nor does the survey allow for the impression that makes the numbers come alive. But a qualitative assessment does not provide any yardstick. Is the "desperate search for shade" the result of temperatures in the 100s or in the 80s? Do the humidity and wind factors make it feel hotter? Nor does it allow for easy comparison. Another person describing the weather in Tripoli might experience the heat differently and use completely different vocabulary in describing it.

This mixed method works as:[8]

> [An] approach to inquiry in which the researcher links, in some way (eg, merges, integrates, connects), both quantitative and qualitative data to provide a unified understanding of a research problem.

This sounds like an academic quote and it is. But it is useful because it confirms that a mixed-method approach starts to provide "a unified understanding", and it implies two questions that are often missed in the drive to measure an organisation's culture:

▶ What is the "research problem"? That is, what is the reason for commissioning an evaluation or metric tool to measure the organisation's culture? What is the issue or opportunity that the piece of work is supposed to address?

▶ Who is "the researcher" in measuring organisation culture? That is, who is the person responsible for designing the measurement approach, analysing and disseminating the results and ensuring that any actions arising are agreed and taken?

Good answers to those two questions will help determine more exactly what to do to get to some level of assessment of the organisation's culture, bearing in mind the following:

▶ Information resulting from the measurement project will not be clear on what the organisation's culture is, neither will it give much that is certain in the way of pointers towards "levers" to pull to keep it as it is or make it different. This is not to say that culture cannot be changed (see Chapter 7).

▶ A mixed-method approach is the best one to take of the three measurement possibilities. Do not rely on surveys alone (or much).

What measuring the culture aims to address

Unless there is a clearly expressed, well-understood and good reason for attempting to measure the organisation's culture, it is pointless to even consider undertaking this complex process, and the reason must always relate to the business strategy – its issues or opportunities – and have an external perspective. Here are four examples where organisational leaders decided to measure their culture. Each addresses a specific business issue or an opportunity; each has an external focus; and each was a mixed-method approach to culture measurement.

Merger or alliance opportunity

When two airlines were considering an alliance in the mid-1990s to cut costs and fares and offer more efficient travel routes to customers, they undertook a cultural assessment process to gain insights into whether their cultures were compatible.[9] Figure 2.2 overleaf shows the results of the survey.

A member of the alliance team said at the time:

> We sent the survey to around 100 managers in each company and asked them to complete it. The results didn't surprise us that much – in that we kind of knew that there were cultural differences. But it was helpful to see them quantified and then be able to discuss the implications through interviews and focus groups with a wider group of people – the survey outcomes were one of the several factors which led us not to pursue the alliance.

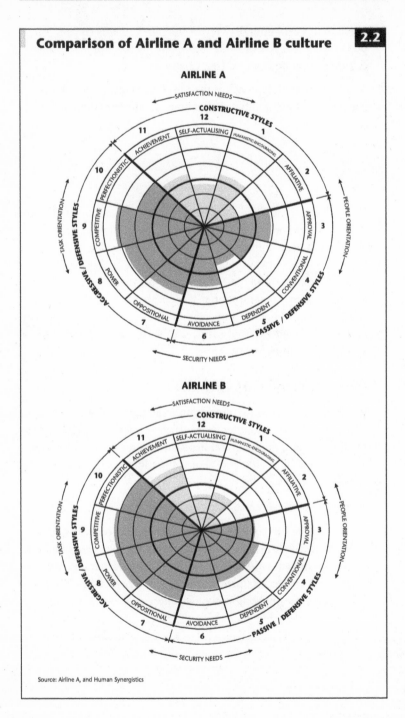

Comparison of Airline A and Airline B culture 2.2

Issues related to a new business strategy

An engineering maintenance company determined that it would be able to grow the business by changing its strategy from task focus to customer focus, as it was wasting a lot of money being reactive on maintenance rather than proactive, and customer satisfaction scores were falling. Engineers were repairing in response to call-outs rather than looking for patterns of equipment failure that could be managed on a before-breakdown basis. The maintenance general manager made the point:

> Our business strategy was cost-driven not performance-driven, and we needed to change. Particularly sensitive was our cadre of engineers – we had to help them see the value of getting the proactive/preventive/reactive balance right. We had to get to the position where, for example, we measured uptime and not downtime, which we knew would make the users of our equipment much happier and also save us money. We also knew that the way people are managed doesn't work in favour of proactivity, but we wanted a dipstick to "prove" that. We combined a culture survey with workshops, customer visits and training designed to help swing the business from task to customer. It's a slow process but we're getting there.

Opportunities related to growing the business

A successful American online retailer had developed a strong customer-oriented perspective that it felt was a key differentiator and could not be imitated by other online retailers. Determined to keep the culture dynamic and responsive, it instituted annual employee surveys backed up with monthly "pulse checks", monthly departmental focus groups, and a raft of related incentives and events to keep the culture "going in the right direction". The human resources director says:

> We've been very successful in keeping our customer satisfaction high – most of our business comes from repeat customers and their referrals, and we have one of the best retention rates of employees in the call-centre industry. We think that if we can keep the culture on track we'll be able to double the business in a couple of years.

Issues related to competitor challenge

A major consultancy and systems integrator had a culture that "was stuck in the dark ages". The vice-president of culture change (her actual job title) commented:

> We had to change the business – it was horribly old fashioned and we were losing market share. I decided to develop a short survey with the help of an external consultant. The seven categories were not complete or sized similarly or anything. But they were a place to start and they seemed to "stick". I wasn't about orchestrating some huge cultural change but about getting some change happening in the culture to loosen it up and give them confidence. So, I didn't really care, nor did I think it mattered, that we got the seven categories (or even the survey) right, so to speak. The survey wasn't the only, or even the major, approach I took. It was, in fact, a small part of a much wider multi-pronged process that included competitions like the Giraffe Competition – for sticking your neck out, collaborative events, storytelling, and other stuff that helped people break out of their rigidity and their need to avoid all risk.

Responsibility for the measurement and its outcomes

Who "owns" the culture is discussed in Chapter 5. Here the discussion is about who is responsible for making the tactical decisions about measurement choices, such as if a survey, which one; if not a survey, then what qualitative approaches. Who is responsible matters, because that itself is almost certainly a cultural indicator. If the CEO initiates the culture-measurement project and hands responsibility to someone from the strategy department, it sends a different signal from having the HR or corporate social responsibility (CSR) director handle it with someone from their department. Before assigning responsibility to someone ask the following questions:

▶ **Does the person have the necessary understanding and insight?** Culture is a complex and chaotic phenomenon. Treating it as a management tool for performance improvement is a mistake. The person responsible for the culture measurement process must be able to identify and deal with those who claim quick fixes, consultants who sound convincing, numbers presented as objective facts or generalisations about what the culture is. He or she must be able to present a legitimate case on the value and limitations of any culture-measurement process.

▶ **Can the person make informed choices about the measurement approach to take?** This means being able to answer questions like: What is the business reason for undertaking this project? What is the expectation around results? Is the issue local to a department or across the whole organisation? If a survey is used, what dimensions should it cover? Should the process used be a packaged solution or tailored to the organisation? If packaged, which to choose from all those on offer? Who should participate in the process? How will results/outcomes be communicated?

▶ **Is the person sufficiently interested and curious?** Culture investigations demand a curiosity that brings with it the ability to look out for factors that prove or disprove that the measurement approach is working. Because organisation culture is "counter, original, spare, strange, fickle, swift, and slow",[10] the findings need to be framed as interesting indicators, but not definitive statements; though this may be at odds with what the management sponsor of the measurement project is looking for (again a possible cultural indicator).

▶ **Does the person know what the sponsor is looking for or expecting, and their likely reactions?** In the maintenance project mentioned on page 35 (where the company was changing from task focus to customer focus), the sponsor of the measurement project was not pleased to have commissioned an expensive and time-consuming cultural audit and then learn that the business unit employees reported "a culture of micro-management, command and control, with little evidence of trust, collaboration or participation. People are keeping their heads down trying to manage what other people think of them". She demanded to know, by name, who had completed the survey and participated in the focus groups so she could "have a word" with them. It pays to know from the start which vested interests are involved. Given the nature of organisational culture there are always vested interests. Before using an assessment, consider the potential impacts, psychological, social and political, on those who will be affected by it.

▶ **Is it clear who "owns" the results of the measurement exercise?** It might be the sponsor, or the person with the day-to-day tactical responsibility for the culture assessment or someone else. Schein commented on this, saying:[11]

> For me the most difficult dilemma is that when we work with organisations the ... goals get very fuzzy. In my work with organisational culture, I frequently find that there are strong subcultures at work in the organisation, and that these subcultures have different goals. Is my job, then, from a systemic point of view, to align them, to integrate them, or to let them fight it out for dominance?

Deciding on the measurement approach

Each of the four organisational examples mentioned earlier (airlines, engineering maintenance, online retailer, consultancy and systems integrator) took a different tack in their approach to assessing their culture. Deciding the methods by which to make the assessment is culturally dependent – for example, focus groups will not work well in an organisation where employees are frightened to speak up. A survey with technical or difficult language will not work well if people do not understand the words being used in it, or if they don't know the "answer" to the question. Paradoxically, to decide on an assessment approach the manager or consultant has to be familiar with the organisation's culture. The following steps help in reaching a decision on the measurement approach to take.

Step 1: Get a feel for the organisation's culture

Consultants to organisations have to get to grips with their clients' organisational culture quickly. One consultant uses a range of techniques to help her do this. She has developed her skills in these over a number of years, and depending on the situation will use some or all of them. She tends to think of what she does in three categories but advises that each person has to develop their own "horizon-scanning style". By this she means the way to look out for threats, opportunities, and likely future organisational developments.

Internal networking

▶ Horse-trading information (giving information in return for information).

▶ Listening in to gossip, for example in the staff restaurant.

▶ Getting unstructured information from people and meetings, for example chatting to the receptionist.

▶ Scheduling time to talk about anything, for example informally over coffee.

▶ Talking to the key players, that is, those with power or influence.

▶ Reading internal documents where available, for example induction or orientation material.

▶ Observing what is going on and what the visual symbols of the culture are, for example assigned or non-assigned parking spaces.

External networking

▶ Asking questions of, and listening to, the organisation's suppliers and service providers.

▶ Gleaning unstructured information from people and meetings.

▶ Finding time to talk about anything, for example informally over coffee.

▶ Finding out who the key players are.

▶ Joining social networks and email lists where the organisation has members.

▶ Attending related industry groups' conferences.

▶ Going to places without a clear agenda but just to see what is out there.

Desk research

▶ Checking out the literature the organisation produces, such as annual reports, marketing/recruitment collateral.

▶ Finding out who the players are from, for example, press reports, blog sites.

▶ Reading academic or consultancy reports/articles on the organisation.

Step 2: Pinpoint the business issue/opportunity that the assessment aims to address

John Chambers, CEO of Cisco Systems, a networking and technology company, has been taking the company through a massive, radical, often bumpy reorganisation. He is doing this to move the company away from being a supplier of gear "guiding data through the internet". He sees a business opportunity in pushing the company into the server market, further into consumer territory, and into the smart grid. The goal is to spread its leadership and decision-making far wider than any big company has attempted before. This move, Chambers says, reflects a new philosophy about how business can best work in a networked world. "We want a culture where it is unacceptable not to share what you know," says Mike Mitchell, Cisco's director of technology communications.

Step 3: Determine the level of the assessment

Will the assessment be at the whole organisation level (climate zone/integration), and/or at the business-unit/departmental level (sub-climate zone/differentiation), and/or at the team/group level (weather/fragmentation)?

An electronics company has over 25 R&D labs worldwide. It is competing in a tough market, and the European R&D director felt that the company was missing innovative product opportunities because each laboratory worked in isolation from the others:

We wanted to know what the cultural barriers were to sharing information. Traditionally, individual labs are protective of "their" work and compete with others but organisationally this is a mistake. We decided to do a cultural assessment across all the labs but not the whole company as we felt the R&D body was distinct in its own right and, quite frankly, we were only interested in identifying possibilities and traits for research co-operation.

In this example, the level of assessment was at the business-unit level, because collectively the R&D labs were considered a distinct business unit.

Step 4: Decide the overall approach within the budget/resources available

Agree the scope, sample size and timescale, and whether there will be a quantitative element and/or a qualitative element. There may be existing information that precludes the need for additional data gathering. For example, an employee opinion survey may have all the survey questions needed, or a regular staff briefing (as in Pret A Manger, a UK-based takeaway sandwich chain, each morning before opening) might be a forum for discussing the culture.

Designing an in-house survey requires skills that may not exist in the organisation and have to be learnt or bought in. The qualitative element can be conducted through, for example, one-to-one interviews, focus groups, workshops, observation, online feedback forums, larger conferences. The choice of interviewer/facilitator is a factor to consider.

Recap points

▶ Gauging an organisation's culture involves not only qualitative and quantitative approaches but also factoring in the interests of competing cultures, subcultures, individuals and groups.

▶ There is no comprehensive checklist of elements to look for when trying to size up an organisation's culture. There are some fairly consistent cultural characteristics (see Chapter 8) but these do not adequately express an organisation's culture.

▶ Culture cannot be measured by looking at variables in isolation or even collectively. It is not possible to get to an "actionable" understanding of culture through this route because the interactions between variables are not predictable and variables cannot be accurately isolated.

▶ Measuring the culture may or may not help in the drive to change or manage the culture.

▶ Treating organisation culture as a management tool that can be quickly deployed to improve business performance will not guarantee a successful outcome.

▶ Gaining some efficacy in measuring an organisation's culture requires having experience in that specific culture.

▶ There are as many external factors influencing organisational culture as there are internal ones. Most off-the-shelf survey tools that purport to measure organisational culture focus on internal factors.

One company's way of measuring culture: Zappos

Rob Patterson, writing on the fastforward blog, says:[12]

> Zappos sells shoes – lots of them – over the internet. The company generated sales of more than $1 billion in gross merchandise sales in 2008, up from just $70m in 2003. Part of the reason for Zappos's meteoric success is that it got the economics and operations right ... so the value proposition is a winner. But it's the emotional connection that seals the deal. This company is fanatical about great service – not just satisfying customers, but amazing them.

Established in 1999 and making consistent year-on-year financial gains, Zappos has become a household name in the United States. However, in July 2009 it was announced that Amazon was acquiring Zappos in a $10m share stock swap. Confidently, Tony Hsieh, Zappos's CEO, stated:[13]

> We plan to continue to run Zappos the way we have always run Zappos – continuing to do what we believe is best for our brand, our culture and our business ... Our goal is to build the Zappos brand to be about the very best customer service and the very best customer experience. To do this, our number one priority is company culture. Our belief is that if you get the culture right, most of the other stuff, like delivering great customer service and building an enduring brand, will happen naturally on its own.

For ten years Hsieh has shown his commitment to that belief, consistently emphasising the importance of the company culture in building the brand and delivering outstanding customer service. He believes that a company's culture and a company's brand are really just two sides of the same coin. The brand may lag the culture at first, but eventually it will catch up. True to his catchphrase "Your culture is your brand", he systematically and consistently assesses the Zappos culture in a number of ways:

> It starts with the hiring process and two different sets of interviews. The hiring manager and his/her team will do the standard set of interviews looking for relevant experience, technical ability, fit within the team, etc. But then the HR department does a separate set of interviews, looking purely for culture fit. Candidates have to pass both sets of interviews in order to be hired.

> After hiring, the next step to building the culture is the 4-week training which covers company history, the importance of customer service, the long term vision of the company, the philosophy about company culture – and then you're actually on the phone for 2 weeks, taking calls from customers. Again, this goes back to our belief that customer service shouldn't just be a department, it should be the entire company. No matter what grade of job, department or title every new employee takes this training.

Zappos is looking for culture fit in its employees. Being clear about the culture that it has, and the aspects it wants to keep, it assesses individuals against this. Zappos has formally defined its culture in terms of ten core values:

▶ Deliver WOW Through Service

▶ Embrace and Drive Change

▶ Create Fun and A Little Weirdness

▶ Be Adventurous, Creative, and Open-Minded

▶ Pursue Growth and Learning

▶ Build Open and Honest Relationships With Communication

▶ Build a Positive Team and Family Spirit

▶ Do More With Less

▶ Be Passionate and Determined

▶ Be Humble

Interviewers ask specific questions about each of the ten values. Table 2.2 lists the questions for the value "Deliver WOW Through Service", which respondents are asked to score quantitatively on a scale of 1–5 and answer related qualitative open-ended questions.

Table 2.2 **Deliver WOW Through Service**

The applicant understands what a great customer service is, what Zappos customer service is. "What does great customer service mean to you?" "In your last job, how did you know if your customer was satisfied?"	NA	1	2	3	4	5
The applicant views his/her job as more than 9–5, more than his/her job description, and is eager to go above and beyond. "Give an example of a time you went above and beyond, why did you do it? Any regrets?"	NA	1	2	3	4	5
The applicant knows how to WOW. "What's the best work-related compliment you've ever received?" "What's something that you did at work that maybe no one else knew about but you are very proud of?"	NA	1	2	3	4	5
The applicant can be innovative and unconventional. "Tell me about a time you came up with an innovative solution to a problem." "Tell me who you think is the most unconventional person you have worked with. Do you think they were successful? Did they do a good job?"	NA	1	2	3	4	5
Did the applicant WOW you?	NA	1	2	3	4	5
Overall rating (average of above ratings)						

This does not measure the culture *per se*, but rather people's fit with it, which is something Zappos considers of huge importance. Hsieh explains:

> At the end of the first week of training, we make an offer to the entire class. We offer everyone $2,000 to quit (in addition to paying them for the time they've already worked), and it's a standing offer until the end of the fourth week of training. We want to make sure that employees are here for more than just a paycheck. We want employees that believe in our long-term vision and want to be a part of our culture. As it turns out, on average, less than 1% of people end up taking the offer.

Zappos is explicit and consistent in its approach to culture and measures it in a number of ways, both formal and informal. Rebecca Ratner, HR director, explains:

> We have a twice-yearly 35-item employee opinion survey that goes to all staff with about a 95% return rate. The survey was one that we developed ourselves internally. Questions relate to how employees feel about their role, about Zappos, about their fit to the company and to the work that they do, as well as the goals and direction of Zappos. The same 35 questions are asked in each survey.

> We also do a monthly five-question pulse survey (the term "pulse" comes from the medical use of the word and gives a quick indication of the "health" of the organisation) with about a 60% return rate, again going to all employees. These questions ask about the level of happiness with the job, whether they are able to develop the role, whether the company has a higher purpose than simply retailing. The same five questions are asked each month so we can track trends.

> Additionally we participate in five external surveys: Best Place to Work (nationally, in Kentucky and in Nevada), Most Democratic Company (new in 2009), and Psychologically Healthy Workplace. This participation gives us a good external take on how we compare and how we are doing because the surveys share the results with us in detail about our employee responses.

Zappos is unusual in running its employee opinion survey twice yearly. Limitations it might have as a result of being designed in-house are offset by the further information the company gets about its culture from participating in external surveys.

Ratner describes what else Zappos does to develop its culture:

We have HR generalists each responsible for between two and six departments. Each month they hold a focus group in each of their departments with between five and eight employees, randomly selected. Essentially it's an "exit interview" for people who are not exiting. It's a free form approach – not directly related to the questions in the surveys but aimed at finding out if there are issues to deal with or things to celebrate. Over time the generalists are building up a good story of their departments and then partner with recruiters to help select people who are a good fit for that part of Zappos.

Managers play a big part in developing the culture using the information from these surveys and through teambuilding. Every manager at Zappos is encouraged to spend 10–20% of their worktime doing teambuilding and socialising with their employees. We believe that building these bonds that come from casual, fun, non-work-related interaction together is critical to building strong culture, so teams can often be found out bowling, doing charity work, having restaurant lunches, throwing team happy hours, and dozens of other activities together. Managers ensure these happen and intuitively measure culture during these events.

We also invite employees to contribute to the annual culture book, that we give out at the vendor conference, and which is also available on our website. It is something that Tony (Hsieh) has done for the last five years. It has about an 85% participation rate.

Additionally employees are encouraged to blog (http://blogs.zappos.com/) and to use Twitter. Hsieh explains:

We decided to introduce Twitter to Zappos as a way of growing our company culture. We've found that it's been great for building more intimate bonds with both employees and customers, essentially an opportunity to learn about each other in a way they otherwise couldn't have. Another way we get to share what the Zappos culture is like is through our employee Twitter page, which we make publicly accessible to the world.

Zappos has had a meteoric rise since its establishment in 1999. Hsieh is convinced this is because it takes culture seriously. The company uses a number of complementary ways of measuring and assessing the culture (that are woven into the fabric of the organisation as part of "business as usual"). It is also committed to investing in, sustaining and developing its culture:

We believe that it's really important to come up with core values that you can commit to. And by commit, we mean that you're willing to hire and fire based on them. If you're willing to do that, then you're well on your way to building a company culture that is in line with the brand you want to build. You can let all your employees be your brand ambassadors, not just the marketing or PR department. And they can be brand ambassadors both inside and outside the office. Some might argue that a model that considers customer service and culture as investments (rather than expenses) can't be sustainable. But by the end of 2008, we'd achieved a couple of the most important goals we set for ourselves during the early days of Zappos.

The assessment and measurement that Zappos does is directly correlated to the CEO's belief that "your culture is your brand" – confirming the point made earlier in this chapter that culture must be measured in relation to a business issue or opportunity. For Zappos, the issue is the creation, identification and exploitation of opportunities for business growth. It is working so far and not just in the financials – customer stories endorse the approach Zappos takes:[14]

I wanted to thank you so much. Like I told the representative the last time I called to change my last order because of the size, the way I was treated over the phone and how well I was accommodated and how fast the shipment came in, I was so impressed and grateful. Your staff treated me with the best customer service I have ever had with any company that I have ever used. I couldn't have been more pleased. My mother called me and told me that your company sent me flowers to congratulate me on my wedding and I was so surprised and grateful that your company would do something like that for your customers. I really do thank you sincerely. I will and always will recommend your website. Thank you again. Xiomara

Sarah Gaede, an Episcopal priest in Florence, Alabama, is also a great fan of Zappos. Laughing, she says:[15]

I am a fervent evangelist for Zappos. If I were half as enthusiastic about how Jesus can change your life, we'd be adding on to the church to contain all our new members.

Learning from Zappos

Three lessons come out of the Zappos approach to its culture:

▷ **Be clear and explicit in defining the culture in terms that work for the organisation.** Zappos has defined its culture in terms of ten core values. This is not necessarily the route for all organisations, and certainly another organisation could not lift Zappos's values and expect similar results. However, in knowing what the values are, making the expectations surrounding them an explicit part of daily organisational life and supporting them through policies, practices, processes and structures, Zappos is able to assess its culture in a way that works for it.

▷ **Align measures/assessment along all three perspectives (integration, differentiation and fragmentation) of organisation culture.** It is important to remember that the three perspectives cannot be disaggregated and there are no single

---

Customer service value proposition   `2.3`

Customer service value proposition in action...
Zappos is committed to WOWing every customer.

- *Customers come...*
  - § *Over 10 million total purchasing customers*
  - § *Over 4 million have purchased in the last 12 months*

- *Customers come back...*
  - § *On any given day, about 75% of purchases from returning customers*
  - § *Repeat customers order >2.5x in the next 12 months*

- *Customers come back, order more and order more often...*
  - § *Repeat customers have higher average order size*
  - § *$123.86 – first time customers in Q407*
  - § *$156.27 – returning customer in Q407*

Zappos

Source: Presentation at the Tony Robbins Ultimate Business Mastery Summit, Las Vegas, April 2009

---

levers to pull. Table 2.3 illustrates how Zappos has aligned its cultural assessment with the three perspectives.

▶ **Make clear the links between business issues and the culture.** For Zappos "the culture is the brand". In order to WOW the customer in a way that is not easily imitated by competitors Zappos has linked what they define as the culture to their business growth opportunity. Figure 2.3, taken from Tony Hsieh's presentation "Delivering Happiness", illustrates this connection.

Table 2.3 **Alignment of cultural assessment with three perspectives**

Culture perspective	Analogy (see Chapter 1)	Zappos	Measurement/ assessment
Integration	Climate zone	Customer service culture ("Delivering Happiness")	External survey participation Customer testimonials Repeat business Customer referrals
Differentiation	Subclimate zones	Ten core values (the values are held by all employees but reflect somewhat differently depending on business unit and job role)	Mixed-method measurement including: employee surveys, pulse checks, employee culture fit, focus groups
Fragmentation	Weather patterns day-to-day	Blogs, Twitter, teambuilding, Zappos Culture Book, activities and events (work and non-work)	Nothing formal but being tracked by CEO and others (who are also participants) Intuitive gauging

Summary

▶ Organisation culture cannot be measured through off-the-shelf surveys alone.

▷ It can be assessed to the level of "good enough" through a mixed method of quantitative and qualitative approaches.

▷ It is better if the assessment or measurement instruments are tailored by someone who knows the organisation and is curious about it.

▷ The dimensions and questions should relate to the specific company and the presenting business issue or opportunity pertinent at the time. However, no process can measure the "experience" of the culture.

▷ At best, the measures are indicators that help determine a course of action, they are not usually usefully or reliably comparable across organisations

Exercise 2: Developing a tailored measurement process in Appendix 3 gives an approach to developing a process for assessing a particular organisation's culture.

Does culture matter?

The immediate answer to the question "Does culture matter?" is "Yes, of course". Intuitively people know that culture matters but they have difficulty in explaining why it does. All organisations have assets. Most managers have no difficulty recognising that these comprise both financial assets and tangible assets: plant, equipment, inventory. They are less clear about the intangible assets: technologies, information, management skills, brand image, consumer loyalty, patents, distribution channels, and so on. But they are increasingly aware of the value these hold and most would assert that the competitive position and potential of their enterprise rests on how well the three "baskets" of corporate assets – financial, tangible and intangible – are managed and deployed.

Sticking with the third, Robert Kaplan and David Norton, who developed the balanced scorecard, identified "three categories of intangible assets essential for implementing any strategy" – human capital, information capital and organisation capital – the last including the company's culture, which they note is "perhaps the most complex and difficult dimension to understand and describe".[1] In their view, not only is an organisation's culture essential for implementing any strategy, it is also distinctive and inimitable, with the ability to create strategic advantage, to differentiate an organisation and to add (or diminish) value.[2] For these reasons, if no others, culture matters.

But knowing that the culture is one of several of an organisation's intangible assets is not enough. What is needed is a clear understanding of it. Specifically, what its characteristics are, how these collectively and individually matter to a particular organisation, how they can be augmented to create more value, whether they are inadvertently being depleted – which diminishes value, with potentially tragic consequences for the organisation[3] – and how the culture relates to the other types of assets.

Grameen Bank, which offers microcredit to the poor, for the most part women, is based on the assumption that borrowers will repay their loans. The style and operation of the bank, reversing the principles of most conventional banks, started from the belief that credit is a human right. Those who possess the least are first in line to get a loan. The operation of the bank (described as the "methodology"), according to its website, is not based on "assessing the material possession of a person, it is based on assessing the potential of a person". Grameen believes that "all human beings, including the poorest, are endowed with endless potential".

David Bornstein, a writer on social innovation and author of *The Price of a Dream: The Story of the Grameen Bank*, in talking about a visit to Bangladesh as part of his research for the book, makes the point:[4]

> It's very clear that in this rural economy the bank is working and then I looked at the institution which employs today 20,000 people, who work in 70,000 villages, and it was clear it had a culture that was really ... like the IBM man of the 50s if you think about it, the sort of puffed chest, blue suited pride ... of course they're not in blue suits, they're in saris, but there was a real culture of excellence that ran through the Grameen Bank.

This pride come from the employees and customers sharing the beliefs and values that underpin the bank's operation and that are evident in the way it does things – for example, its cultural fit to its borrowers, the rules that surround the services provided, its attitude to learning, its ethical stance, its management interests and its leadership modelling.

No other bank is able to replicate the precise mix of cultural characteristics that make Grameen what it is, although several offer similar microcredit services. For Grameen Bank, "the way we do things round here" (one of the definitions of culture mentioned in

Chapter 1) gives it the cultural distinctiveness that contributes to its success.

The climate zone, subclimate zone and weather culture analogy presented in Chapter 1 is helpful at this point because it underscores the fact that culture is a mix of characteristics that collectively form the culture but that individually do not express the culture. (In the same way that the various ingredients of a pie do not individually give the experience of eating the pie made from them.) Table 3.1 illustrates this in relation to Grameen Bank.

Table 3.1 Grameen Bank: "The way we do things round here"

	Described as:	Characteristics of:
Climate zone (integration perspective)	"A real culture of excellence"[a]	An operational methodology with the components of: 16 Decisions 10 Indicators Credit Delivery System Breaking the Cycle of Poverty Method of Action
Subclimate zone (differentiation perspective)	"A unique management culture"[b]	"Field level authority where the actual work of planning and implementation takes place. The groups and centres have their own identity. At the same time, they work with the Grameen bureaucracy in a very integrated way."

	Described as:	Characteristics of:
Weather (fragmentation perspective)	"A rewrite of the entire village culture"	"Grameen requires members to form groups and relies on the social pressure of the group to promote accountability and fiscal discipline. Members agree to a set of '16 Decisions' related to discipline and self-empowerment, which along with the Grameen credo – 'Discipline, unity, courage, and hard work in all walks of our lives' – are repeated at the beginning and end of each group meeting. Bank staff are trained to engage with members. 'Instead of trying to solve other people's problems, first find out whether they have an idea how to solve their own problems', is how one staff person describes the mindset. All banking staff visit members in their villages on a weekly basis, in order to foster familiarity and trust between staff and villagers and to promote the principles of hard work and discipline. Each employee undergoes a six-month training internship at a branch location to learn the way Grameen works."[c]

a www.allbusiness.com/lecture/11758637–1.html
b Sarker, A.E., "The Secrets of Success: The Grameen Bank's Experience in Bangladesh", *Labour and Management in Development Journal*, Vol. 2, No. 1, 2001.
c Stephen LaFrance, "Scaling Capacity 4: Culture – Cultivating and Perpetuating the Culture", October 17th 2006 (www.socialedge.org/blogs/scaling-capacities).

Looking at Table 3.1, it is evident that the Grameen Bank culture is consistent and carried through all three organisational perspectives (integration, differentiation and fragmentation). Also evident from Table 3.1 is that the bank has some specific cultural characteristics: among others, it has an explicit credo, an operational methodology to deliver the credo, an articulated attitude to people (borrowers and employees), a reputation for supporting the poor and a relationship with the borrowers. It is the mix of these that makes Grameen Bank's culture different from other microcredit institutions and inimitable by them.

In much the same way that a climate zone (discussed in Chapter 1) is characterised by a common set of constituents – including biome distribution, latitude, humidity, elevation, distance from the sea and direction of the prevailing winds – and it is the mix of these that distinguishes one zone from another, so it is, to a large extent, with organisational culture. Although cultural characteristics vary, there are ten that are common to most organisations. These are present in different combinations and "strengths" and are, of course, interdependent, just as the constituents of a climate zone are. Additionally, as with climate, cultural characteristics are influenced and affected by various mediating factors, such as the business model, which are discussed in Chapter 4. The value of the culture lies in the way its characteristics manifest, combine and interact with each other and in relation to the mediating factors. There are consequences – foreseen and unforeseen – if they are treated as independent levers to be pulled.

These ten characteristics, discussed in the following section, form the typical characteristics of organisational culture:

- A story or stories
- A purpose and a set of values
- A strategy
- An attitude to people
- A global mindset
- A relationship network
- A digital presence
- A reputation
- A customer proposition
- A horizon scanning ability

The characteristics that contribute to organisation culture

1 A story or stories

Stories abound in organisations and serve as powerful descriptors and shapers of the culture. Who has not heard of stories about two people starting up a venture in a garage (Hewlett-Packard) or trying for years to establish a business (Kentucky Fried Chicken)? Stories come from various sources: founder stories (Ray Kroc of McDonald's), customer stories (Zappos – see Chapter 2), success and crises stories (NASA and Challenger), product stories (3M and post-it notes), legacy stories, and so on. The stories told about an organisation act to reinforce (or deny) a company's vision, values and ways of doing business. They send strong messages to the listeners and readers of the stories, both internal and external.

Steve Jobs, founder of Apple, tells his story in the 2005 Stanford University Commencement Address (a speech given at the students' graduation ceremony), starting with his dropping out of college:[5]

> It wasn't all romantic. I didn't have a dorm room, so I slept on the floor in friends' rooms, I returned coke bottles for the 5¢ deposits to buy food with, and I would walk the seven miles across town every Sunday night to get one good meal a week at the Hare Krishna temple ... Because I had dropped out and didn't have to take the normal classes, I decided to take a calligraphy class ... I learned about serif and sans serif typefaces, about varying the amount of space between different letter combinations, about what makes great typography great ... None of this had even a hope of any practical application in my life. But ten years later, when we were designing the first Macintosh computer, it all came back to me. And we designed it all into the Mac. It was the first computer with beautiful typography.

At age 20 Jobs started up Apple with a friend and "in ten years Apple had grown from just the two of us in a garage into a $2 billion company with over 4,000 employees". At that point Jobs was fired by the board of directors:

I didn't see it then, but it turned out that getting fired from Apple was the best thing that could have ever happened to me. The heaviness of being successful was replaced by the lightness of being a beginner again, less sure about everything. It freed me to enter one of the most creative periods of my life. During the next five years, I started a company named NeXT, another company named Pixar, and fell in love with an amazing woman who would become my wife. Pixar went on to create the world's first computer animated feature film, Toy Story, and is now the most successful animation studio in the world. In a remarkable turn of events, Apple bought NeXT, I returned to Apple, and the technology we developed at NeXT is at the heart of Apple's current renaissance. And Laurene and I have a wonderful family together.

Jobs ends his address talking about death:

Your time is limited, so don't waste it living someone else's life. Don't be trapped by dogma – which is living with the results of other people's thinking. Don't let the noise of others' opinions drown out your own inner voice. And most important, have the courage to follow your heart and intuition.

Finally, he urges listeners to "stay hungry, stay foolish".

In Jobs's stories, told and retold inside and outside the company, are the characteristics that continue to help shape Apple's culture (and its business success): thoughtful design, making innovative connections, taking risks, being unconventional and having the courage to follow a different path.

2 A purpose and a set of values

In the same way that a country's constitution and legal framework lay down guiding principles for the state and the behaviour of its citizens, leaders talk about their organisation's vision, mission, purpose and values (see Appendix 1) in annual reports, company presentations, and so on, because these statements are, for the most part, intended to be instrumental in providing the guidance that shapes the conduct of the company.

Coffee company illy is known for "one blend one brand". A family-owned business with headquarters in Trieste, Italy, it operates in 140 countries. Ernesto Illy, son of the founder, Francesco Illy, had run the company until his death in 2008 at the age of 82. "He has left us this legacy: 'our conduct is guided by a compass of ethics'," says his niece. This is one of the two values mentioned on the company website, the other being the pursuit of excellence.

The stated mission of the company is to be "the world reference for coffee culture and excellence". Ernesto Illy and his son Andrea (now CEO) both trained as scientists and worked with the chemical properties and processes to get to what they considered the perfect cup of coffee. Andrea Illy says:[6]

> *In the production plant beans endure 114 quality tests, with samples eyeballed and scratched – and every bean is put through a laser-driven sorting machine that rejects one bean before and after any defective ones just for good measure. Rooting out that one bad bean is essential because it can spoil an entire tin. That's why illy pays 30% above market rates to top farmers. We are completely obsessed about quality – close to crazy.*

How much the purpose and values of an organisation matter depends on how well they are "lived" and experienced by the organisation's employees, its other stakeholders, customers and suppliers. In illy's case it is evident from a variety of stories that the purpose and values are lived. For example, one tells of a barista in one of the illy coffee shops in Copenhagen who refused to sell the customer a cup of coffee because "our espresso machine is not working quite the way it should, which means that the illy coffee does not taste quite right".[7] Consistent adherence to its aims and values is one of the hallmarks of a successful organisation.

Failing organisations, by contrast, are notable in part for the confusion and cynicism around the mission, vision or values. When this occurs, as Jim Collins observes in his book *How the Mighty Fall*:[8]

> *People cannot easily articulate what the organisation stands for; core values have eroded to the point of irrelevance ... Instead of passionately believing in the organisation's core values and*

purpose, people become distrustful, regarding visions and values as little more than PR and rhetoric.

3 A strategy

An organisation's strategy summarises the desired future for the organisation. It expresses where those running the organisation want it to be and where they believe it can be. It indicates the areas of significant change that will be involved and the hoped-for outcome of such changes. It takes into account the competitive environment in which the organisation operates and is attuned to the aims and values of the organisation, though it may stretch the organisation's aims and bring a new dimension to its values. Put simply, the strategy outlines the future "what, where and how" of the business and as such it shapes and reflects aspects of the culture.

Trader Joe's – owned by Aldi, a privately held German company – has built a chain of grocery stores in the United States. Established in 1967 with the opening of one store, the company ran 270 stores in 22 states with revenues exceeding $5 billion by 2007. Its business strategy is to develop from its current base to offer more and more Americans the convenience of a neighbourhood grocery store – Trader Joe's differentiator being to sell low-price, high-quality, mostly own-brand products. Its stores are small (approximately 15,000 sq. feet) and the product mix changes, creating "a sense of adventure that appeals to customers". The stores' tagline is: "We tried it! We liked it! If you don't, bring it back for a full refund, no questions asked." Stores are all themed around an "island paradise". "Crew" members wear Hawaiian shirts, the store manager is called the captain, the decor is "shipwreck style" (see www.traderjoes.com) and there is a red plastic lobster in each store.

To remain true to the neighbourhood grocery store concept, growth is carefully managed:[9]

> Because the challenge associated with migrating its unique culture requires a meticulous selection and training process. Store location is determined by three key factors: density of population, educational level of the consumer, and distribution efficiencies.

Following a clear strategy aimed at appealing, as it does, to a specific type of customer, who enjoys the adventure of grocery shopping at Trader Joe's, means that the company has carved a unique niche with no direct competition.

4 An attitude to people (in the workforce)

In response to the question "Is organisation culture important to you?", a senior operations manager says:

> Yes, the organisational culture is important to me. I am always reacting or adapting to it. There have been times when the adaptation required from me was too much. In those instances where running against the grain of the culture is not an option, I have made the decision to leave.

> Before joining a new organisation or switching jobs within one, I ask questions like does the culture grow me? Does it benefit me? Is it able to nurture me? Can I adapt to it? Will I be comfortable, and safe? Will I be making money in a role that matches my values? A culture is right for me if I can work around some stuff and still do the best I can do. There are certain companies I would not work for.

Organisations have distinctive attitudes to the people in their workforce. Theory X and Y, developed by Douglas McGregor in 1960,[10] describes two ends of a continuum where Theory X is an attitude of control, management by fear, underpinned by a belief that people are inherently lazy when it comes to working productively. Theory Y, however, develops from the perspective that given the right conditions workers are self-motivated, keen to do a good job and happy to work hard. In the day-to-day life of an organisation the attitudes are more nuanced than either X or Y, but the theory remains as relevant now as it did when it was first proposed.

Kenneth Roman, a former employee of Ogilvy & Mather, tells a delightful story of the attitude of the founder, David Ogilvy, to his workforce. One day, at a meeting, directors found at each place around the table a set of nesting Russian dolls. In every "layer" of his doll each director found the same message typed on a piece of paper:[11]

> *"If you hire people who are smaller than you are, we shall become a company of dwarfs. If you hire people who are bigger than you are, we shall become a company of giants."* Russian dolls became part of the culture.

Another former employee of the company commented:[12]

> *The agency's commitment, loyalty, and compassion towards its employees were rare; in turn, it reaped the benefits of a workforce that believed in the firm's purpose, practiced a business philosophy based on honest client service, and delivered outstanding work.*

This example illustrates a Theory Y attitude to the workforce that has served the company well. That this story reflects the firm's attitude to its people and that it had a clear purpose and business philosophy illustrates the relationships among the characteristics that contribute to an organisation's culture.

5 A global mindset

Whether they acknowledge it or not, all organisations are inextricably linked to the global economy in all manner of ways beyond their presence in or absence from another country. For example, their goods are sourced from elsewhere – a particularly sensitive area for many companies (see the Gap example on page 66); their customers' spending power is tied to what is going on in the global financial markets; the regulatory framework within which they operate is tied to global agreements.

Organisations entering international markets need a global mindset to get a harmonious interface between the national cultures and their organisational culture. An example of a company that did not have that is Walmart, the world's largest retailer, which has found it hard to enter new markets and decided in 2006 to pull out of its eight-year operation in Germany. An article in the UK *Times* in July 2006 reported that this was partly because of:

> *... troubles on the culture front for the chain's notoriously conservative management, which, back in America, is used to hiring and firing at will and having the company line totally*

obeyed. Last year [2005] a court ordered Walmart to drop key parts of its employee code of conduct in Germany, including a ban on flirting between supermarket staff. The court in Wuppertal ruled that the provisions were in breach of worker rights. In 2000, Metro's (a rival supermarket chain) chief executive, Hans-Joachim Koerber, predicted that Walmart would not succeed. "The company's culture does not travel, and Walmart does not understand the German customer," he said.

6 A relationship network

One view on organisation culture is that it is essentially about:[13]

... the relationships among individuals within groups, among groups, and between ideas and perspectives. Culture is concerned with identity, aspiration, symbolic exchange, coordination and structures and practices that serve relational ends, such as ethnicity, ritual, heritage, norms, meanings and beliefs. It is ... a set of contested attributes, constantly in flux, shaping and being shaped by social and economic aspects of human interaction.

How these relationships are "allowed" to function is an important determinant of an organisation's culture. The well-documented case of the disastrous Challenger spacecraft mission illustrates a set of faulty social relationships where (among other issues) hierarchy, self-protection and management power over professional knowledge – all cultural indicators – played a significant part in the mission's failure. Below is a telling extract from the testimony of Roger Boisjoly to the Presidential Commission investigating the disaster:[14]

Those of us who opposed the launch continued to speak out ... we were attempting to go back and re-review and try to make clear what we were trying to get across, and we couldn't understand why it [the recommendation by the engineers not to launch] was going to be reversed. So we spoke out and tried to explain once again the effects of low temperature ... After [we] had our last say, Mr Mason said we have to make a management decision. He turned to Bob Lund and asked him to take off his engineering hat and put on his management hat. From

> *this point, management formulated the points to base their decision on. There was never one comment in favour, as I have said, of launching by any engineer or other non-management person in the room before or after the caucus ... I felt personally that management was under a lot of pressure to launch and that they made a very tough decision, but I didn't agree with it.*

At this point it is evident that the voice of professional expertise was outweighed by the requirement for a management decision, which was taken in the context of not only the costs of deferring the launch but also the presidential State of the Nation address which was to be given the day after the scheduled launch and in which the expected triumph of the mission would feature. Another indicator of the fractured relationship between engineers and managers that emerged in the commission hearings was that people were precluded from speaking to those not in their chain of command.

In this instance there was no evident network of relationships. Compare this with the Grameen Bank example mentioned earlier where the success of the bank is built on developing networks of relationships:[15]

> *To become a borrower, you need to find four friends or acquaintances in your community who are also interested in getting loans. Every prospective borrower participates in a week-long training before they are eligible for a loan. The training session weeds out those who are not determined or sincere. At the end of the training, each group decides who among them will receive the first loan. That borrower must start repaying their loan before the next member of the group can receive one.*

7 A digital presence

A relatively new cultural characteristic is a "digital presence" that is an expression of the culture and operation of the organisation on its own websites and on social networking sites, for example Twitter and Facebook. Many companies also have a digital presence that reflects other people's views of their culture and operation. The organisation does not authorise or manage these postings but has to monitor them as a precautionary measure and in order to respond if necessary. The IKEA Fan Community is one such site (www.ikeafans.com). It has the "look and feel" of the IKEA official website but states:

> We are not affiliated with IKEA in any way; we are not IKEA co-workers, partners, affiliates, sales representatives, nor are we sponsored, financially or otherwise, by IKEA – we do this for fun! We're just regular folks who were looking for more IKEA information than was available on the internet.

For organisations to get their digital presence right – in a way that reflects their culture accurately – it is not just a matter of colour, language, semantics, and other visual and usability considerations. Trust (for example, if buying something or receiving messages), accessibility, company reputation, customer service expectations, usage patterns and brand expectation are just some of the things that have a bearing on the user's online experience of the organisation.

In this excerpt from an interview with Vitor Lourenco, a US-based Brazilian who is the designer of Twitter's user interface, he comments on the cultural base needed to design a site with global reach, that is, having the ability to attract and keep customers in many different parts of the world:[16]

> Q. You're quite the all-round talent, possessing skills in user interface design, visual design, usability, accessibility, client-side development (XHTML, CSS and Javascript). Do you think it's necessary for a designer to possess all these skills, or can a designer stick to design skills alone?
>
> A. These are basic requirements for a good web designer, and if you want to be successful, it will depend on how you've mastered them. User interface design is not a science, and no one will ever have 100% proficiency on it. It really depends on the media and contexts you're dealing with. For that matter, it's more important to have a solid cultural base and be able to put yourself in your user's shoes all the time.

Here is a further thought on some web-sensitive areas:[17]

Close your eyes. Envision a succulent two-inch slab of drip-ping-rare prime rib. Is your stomach rumbling, your appetite piqued, or are you offended since your fundamental belief system precludes harming animals? A single image or idea can create many different feelings or interpretations. Consider the diversity within your own organisation ... Does everyone agree on what is appropriate, acceptable, appetising, or attractive? An image pleasing to one group of people may alienate or even seriously offend many others. Something as simple as colour may elicit dramatically different mental images. For example, in the US, white is generally associated with purity, but in Japan it represents death.

These two examples suggest that getting the alignment right between the online environment and the live encounter makes a significant difference in achieving cultural consistency and appeal. An organisation's digital presence (via corporate website, Twitter, Facebook, blogs, and so on) has to attract and hold users, from anywhere in the world, who have myriad motivations for being interested in that organisation, in a way that is very different from conventional face-to-face, voice or static print mediums. The digital arena is also one where rapid technology development requires an organisation to keep up to date with what is going on and make strategic and investment decisions on whether and when to enter any new dimension.

Trader Joe's, for example, has made a decision not to offer online shopping. The company gives the reason (reflecting its culture) in the general FAQs on its website:

We're just old-fashioned. We set up our stores with care, finding just the right crew and adding a flavor of paradise. After con-sidering the options, we're still just big 'ole fans of the neigh-borhood grocery store where we can say hello when you're looking around wondering – what's for dinner?

8 A reputation

An organisation's reputation among its stakeholders (employees, customers, suppliers, investors and the general public) is crucial in building and sustaining its culture and its performance. It is also one of its most vulnerable areas – a good reputation can take years to build and then be lost or seriously damaged dramatically quickly. Stakeholders use various criteria, economic and non-economic, to arrive at an overall general assessment of the reputation of a business that is:[18]

> ... a perceptual representation of a company's past actions and future prospects that describes the firm's overall appeal to all of its key constituents when compared with leading rivals.

They get this "perceptual representation" from:

> ... the bedrock of its [the company's] identity – the core values such as credibility, reliability, trustworthiness, and responsibility that shape its communications, its culture, and its decisions.

Gap, a clothing retailer, prides itself on its corporate social responsibility and sustainability standings. In 2009 it was one of the world's most ethical companies as judged by *Ethisphere* magazine and was listed as one of the 100 best corporate citizens by *Corporate Responsibility Officer* magazine. So stories like the one reported in the UK *Sunday Times* on August 1st 2009 could have a significant negative impact on Gap's reputation:

> A factory that makes jeans for Gap and Levi Strauss is illegally dumping chemical waste in a river and two unsecured tips [landfill sites] where it poses a hazard to children ... Gap, which has a public image of environmental awareness, put the factory "on notice" to improve ... "While we're very proud of the progress we've made to date, we also understand that conditions are not perfect and that there is still a great deal more to be done to improve both environmental and factory working conditions in developing regions like Lesotho," said Glenn Murphy, chairman and chief executive of Gap Inc.

EcoTextile News (www.ecotextile.com) commented:

> However, despite the quick reaction from Gap, the news will still come as a blow to the retail giant along with Levi Strauss, both of whom have been investing significantly to build brands based on social responsibility. Both US brands will now be

under severe scrutiny, from the media and consumers alike, as to how the investigations progress. Both will need to show the results and, at a later date, discuss the safeguards that they've put in place.

9 A customer proposition

National cultures and organisational cultures meet either smoothly or jarringly at the point of marketing products and services. Consumer attitudes towards patriotism, credit use, preference for local brands, price sensitivity, acceptance of new products, or packaging/marketing message and delivery channels are all major aspects for marketers to get right. Here is an example of getting it right:[19]

> In 1997 Procter & Gamble's Crest entered the Chinese market with a green-tea flavoured toothpaste that built on the traditional Chinese belief that green tea is healthy and particularly good for teeth. With Chinese packaging, a Chinese name that translates as "clean better" and a price point that would attract mass consumers, Crest's revenues increased 24% per year between 2002 and 2006, and by 2006 it held 19% of the Chinese market for oral hygiene products. Crest's success in China is predicated upon understanding the Chinese consumer, and pricing its product appropriately to the market.

Alan Lafley, P&G's former CEO and president who stood down in 2009, implies how this type of success is achieved:[20]

> Everywhere I go, I try to hammer home the simple message that – in our fast-moving consumer goods industry – the consumer is boss. We have to win the consumer value equation every day. Almost every trip I take includes in-home or in-store consumer visits. Virtually every P&G innovation centre has real consumers visiting every day. Our employees spend days living with lower-income consumers and working in neighborhood stores.
>
> We have other important external relationships – with retail customers, suppliers, and, of course, investors and shareowners. But by defining consumers as our most important stakeholder, we clarified that every other relationship is subordinate

to the relationship with the women and men who buy and use our brands and products every day.

10 A horizon-scanning ability

Predicting the future is difficult to do. Who can be sure what the next big thing will be, or how the business environment will change, or which new opportunities or challenges may arise? But a characteristic of predicting or preparing for the future brings a necessary (for survival) adaptation benefit. Predictive skill comes in a variety of forms, through research and development labs, through scenario planning (developed by Shell in the 1970s), through employing "futurologists" to predict technology trends – as BT, a UK telecoms company does, through systematic assessment of changes in, for example, demographics, societies, economies and medicine. Perhaps remarkably, given its importance, horizon scanning is a characteristic many companies do not have.

Nokia is a company that is an expert horizon scanner, tracing its roots to a paper mill founded in 1865. In 1967 three companies – Nokia, Finnish Cable Works and Finnish Rubber Works – merged to form Nokia Corporation. At this point there were five businesses: rubber, cable, forestry, electronics and power generation. But in 1992 the company decided to focus on its telecommunications business. By 2008 Nokia was the 88th largest company in the world by revenue, with more than 1.1 billion customers in over 150 countries. During that year it sold 472m phones, generating $70 billion in revenue and earning $7 billion in profit. Its share of the global cell-phone market was greater than that of its next three competitors combined.

However, resting on its laurels is not a Nokia trait. In September 2009, Nokia's CEO, Olli-Pekka Kallasvuo, said:[21]

> *We are not a cell phone company … We now think of ourselves as a devices-and-services company that is deeply involved in media, music, gaming, and navigation.*

Nokia is developing new technologies and services that support this thinking. It does this partly through its ten worldwide research labs:

> *Each [lab is] based on an open innovation philosophy and affiliated with a local university ... From these labs researchers learn what different people's needs are – and what they can afford – by immersing themselves in locales that cover the widest spectrum of the human condition.*

They do this because the company believes that there are three reasons why people adopt new technology: survival, social, and entertainment. The common thread among the three:

> *... can be loosely described as culture, and Nokia has worked hard to develop a deep understanding of all the cultures in which it operates.*

Supporting the research labs is a website, Nokia Beta Labs, with the byline "Shaping the future together" (http://betalabs.nokia.com/), which solicits user input to developing products and services:

> *We built this website to share some of the exciting new ideas that we at Nokia have been working on. What we wish in return is of course your valuable insight of how to further improve the products. So please, be active in giving feedback!*

The Nokia example illustrates a more general point: organisations that have the cultural receptivity to think about, research and then adapt themselves appropriately to take advantage of the opportunities that they see in the future are more likely to have a competitive edge over those organisations that stick with what they know. Peter Drucker, a leading management thinker, advocated the discipline of "planned abandonment" to keep an organisation thriving. By this he meant freeing resources from being committed to what no longer contributes or will soon stop contributing to performance. To prompt abandonment he suggested regularly asking the question: "If we didn't do this already, knowing what we now do, would we still do it?" If the answer is no in regard to any particular aspect then it is time to stop doing it.

How the characteristics add to the culture's asset value

All organisations that care about their culture and are truly focused on success will pay attention to the ten characteristics listed above. But in different organisations (or indeed in different parts of an organisation) these attributes may look and feel different, and cluster and interact in different ways, depending on other factors in the whole system. The point is that each has a part to play but they cannot be treated independently – they are all contributory parts to the culture and operation of the organisational system.

From the examples it is evident that a bundle of cultural characteristics play a significant part, but not the only part, in making the culture distinctive to a specific organisation. Because the culture is dynamic and continuously forming, adapting and reconfiguring in response to conditions and mediating factors, it is impossible to quantify a level of significance for a named characteristic because it is not an independent variable.

However, it is possible to see whether or where there is a clash or dissonance between the characteristics. A commonly quoted example is speaking of a culture of "teamwork" but having an attitude (and an incentive scheme) that favours "winners and losers". For the most part, the characteristics add to the asset value of the culture when they are mutually supportive and diminish value when they are not.

Recap points

▶ The mix of characteristics that matter to an organisation's culture is organisation-specific.

▶ The characteristics that contribute to making an organisation's culture matter are difficult to value independently.

▶ Characteristics that matter greatly in one part of an organisation are reflected at different "strengths" in different parts or at other levels of the organisation. The point to remember is that it should stay recognisable as the same culture. (An analogy is an apple pie: it can be made with more or less sugar, with added spice, with brown or white flour, but it is still an apple pie.)

▶ Characteristics that matter at one point in time may matter less at another point in time.

▶ Cultural characteristics are not discrete variables that can be manipulated independently of each other.

▶ How characteristics are mediated by other factors affects employees' and customers' experience of the culture of the organisation.

▶ Problems arise when an organisation's members or stakeholders see cultural disconnections – usually between what is said to be required and what is seen in practice to be required.

What matters in one company's culture: IKEA

Shopping at IKEA, a global furnishing company, at weekends has been likened by some past customers to "penance – the retail equivalent of preparing to enter a monastic order" and "an ordeal somewhere between a trip to pre-*perestroika* Russia and the early stages of paranoid schizophrenia".[22] This is a strikingly common IKEA customer experience. IKEA's success in realising good design at low prices has created a demand for products that is difficult to meet in many stores. Take this UK example. IKEA's group chief executive told the *Daily Telegraph*:[23]

> We haven't been able to live up to the demands of our customers who shop with us at the weekend, especially the queuing. Every time we manage to fix something, we get another 20% more sales.

Perhaps surprisingly, customers are willing to put up with the frustration and difficulties of negotiating the ultimate in-store self-service experience – locating the item in a bewildering store layout, checking whether it is in stock, collecting their purchases from the warehouse, driving the goods home and assembling (often accompanied by cursing) the furniture themselves – because the company invests heavily in the characteristics that matter to its success. These make it easy for customers to make the trade-off between shopping discomfort and the outcome of their owning what they perceive as value for money, attractively designed, "green" items, purchased in a slightly quirky "Swedish" environment where each item has a Swedish name. IKEA stores feature the blue-and-yellow national colours, serve Swedish meatballs, and sell blond-wood Swedish designs and books about Sweden. As Olle Wastburg, director general of the Swedish Institute, says: "To visit IKEA is to visit Sweden."

Nurturing the characteristics that distinguish the culture has made IKEA a financially successful company. It has 296 stores in 36 countries, and sales have been rising steadily over the past decade, demonstrating the skilful inculcation of a global mindset and a clear business strategy (based on relatively few but enormous stores, positioned outside city centres). In 2008 – a dismal year for most retailers – IKEA's sales increased by 7%.

The start point for the business is the explicitly stated vision:

> To create a better everyday life for the many people. Our business idea supports this vision by offering a wide range of well-designed, functional home furnishing products at prices so low that as many people as possible will be able to afford them.

The vision drives the way the IKEA culture operates. For example, it is explicitly cost-conscious. June Deboehmler, IKEA product developer, says:

> When we decide about a product, we always start with the price. Then, what is the consumer need? ... So, when we start in the development process, we say, for example, we'd like to have a cabinet to hold a large screen TV that's 42 inches, and priced out to come in at X dollars ... what can you design, to make it at that price?

Because price comes in at a number of points in the design-to-shop-floor chain, there is a team of people involved in the development process from the start. This includes a field technician, who determines if IKEA has already designed something similar that can be mined for parts or design inspiration, and a packaging technician, who helps "find the smartest way to do something so that it can be flat-packed to minimise waste of space when transporting".

In designing the Lillberg chair, for example, technicians and designers noted that by making a small tweak in the angle of the chair's arm they could get more of the chairs in a single shipping container, and that, in the end, meant a lower cost to the consumer. "The arm (change) meant huge savings."

Acute price consciousness spills over into a general attribute of reducing waste. Marty Marston, IKEA public relations representative, says:[24]

> The whole idea of waste is very much embedded in our culture, not only in product development, but in all the various functional areas of IKEA. We are so against wastefulness. It's very much a Scandinavian thought behaviour.

This approach to waste management can be seen in IKEA's response to environmental issues; for example, the company has partnered with the World Wildlife Fund and Greenpeace in response to critics' concerns over its wood policy.

The alignment between the statement of vision and values (the values are togetherness, cost consciousness, respect and simplicity) extends into the clearly enacted business strategy, the explicit customer proposition, the day-to-day design of its products and the operation of the company. The company aims to develop a family-like quality where people support each other and have strong and open working relationships (following the dictat of founder Ingvar Kamprad, who said "We must take care of each other, inspire each other.")

IKEA's reputation rests not only on its quirkiness and Swedishness – both distinctive attributes – but also on its awareness that good stories are valuable. In an article in the *Times* on June 13th 2009, journalist Kate Muir reports going to an opera at IKEA's Wembley, London, store:

> The performance was, inevitably, titled Flatpack Opera. Opera is the only art form, with its capacity for high-camp histrionics, that can truly express the agony and ecstasy of visiting the world's favourite furniture store. It was awesome. The sopranos and tenors disported themselves around the IKEA room sets, with their Klippan sofas and Grimstad beds.

In the United States Mark Malkoff, a New York comedian, called the IKEA store in Paramus, New Jersey, and asked if he could stay there while his apartment was being fumigated. They said yes. He stayed in the store living in one of the room sets for a week. On January 17th 2008 the *Washington Post* reported:

> IKEA was dubious at first, but once they got to know Malkoff – realised what squeaky, G-rated videos he made and what a good, unpaid spokesman he'd be – they opened the doors and made a

little placard reading "Mark's Apartment" to go outside his living space.

Both of these were significant PR events – neither of which was initiated by the PR department – that also exploited digital presence via YouTube, blogs and non-IKEA websites (although neither stunt appears on the corporate website), as well as more traditional channels such as TV shows and newspaper reports. IKEA thus benefited from the digital capability of its customers and the relationship network attached to this. The spillover from these types of activity affects IKEA's corporate reputation positively, thus detracting from the more negative impacts of long queues, furniture with built-in obsolescence and complaints from environmental groups over the company's wood policy.[25]

This snapshot of IKEA illustrates the range of characteristics that contribute to its distinctive culture, which customers shopping in the stores and staff working for the company experience. The value of the culture shows in the financial results, in employee productivity and commitment, and in customer affection for the brand. It also illustrates the point that the characteristics are part of a dynamic culture – the "Swedishness" cannot be valued separately from the PR approach. If there were an attempt to increase the Swedishness, for example by requiring the store assistants to wear Swedish national dress, this would have an impact on and consequences for all other aspects of the culture.

Learning from IKEA

Three lessons come out of IKEA's approach to the factors that help make its culture distinctive:

▶ **Recognise what contributes to making the culture matter.** IKEA has a strong vision and a well-told story of how it grew from its founder's dream of putting low-cost, well-designed household items into the homes of many people. Recognising which attributes contribute and which are peripheral is easier if there is a strong vision, mission and purpose and a set of values. These do not necessarily have to be explicitly written down but they do have to be implicitly understood and subscribed to, and they have to be "lived" in the day-to-day operation of the company.

▶ **Invest in and nurture what matters to the culture.** For IKEA it is evident that the things that contribute to the culture – beyond the purpose and values – are a business strategy, Swedishness, customer proposition, reputation, quirkiness, marketing/PR and global mindset. In relation to the last point, talking about IKEA's success in the UK, Anna Crona, acting marketing director for the UK and Ireland, explains:[26]

> *Consumers have always been at the heart of our success, embracing the brand and its love of design. We've always been about functionality and high design, but we've always tried to make that in tune with the British and their way of life.*

▶ **Maintain cultural distinctiveness and competitive edge.** IKEA has successfully developed a unique market position with few competitors and an almost cult following. (There are IKEA hackers, that is "people who go online to share the process of re-purposing IKEA products to create personalised objects",[27] an IKEA fan club – www.ikeafans.com – and a professor at University College Dublin who "wrote some Ruby scripts to scrape the IKEA product catalogue to look up prices for common product codes across 12 stores – Ireland, UK, Italy, Netherlands, Finland, Sweden, Germany, Spain, France, Austria, US and Canada" in order to make cross-country price comparisons of IKEA products.[28]) Assuming it can maintain this distinctive cultural edge, IKEA has a valuable intangible asset working in its favour.

Summary

▶ Answering the question "Does culture matter?" is straightforward. Yes it does matter because culture is an intangible asset that is both distinctive to that organisation and adds value to it (or diminishes value).

▶ Delving deeper into the question is more problematic as organisation culture emerges from interacting and dynamic clusters of a range of characteristics (among other things).

▶ Focusing on these characteristics on a one-by-one basis does not give the answer to what culture is and thus how to increase its asset value.

▶ However, working to recognise which characteristics contribute to a specific organisation's culture does pay off, in the same way that recognising which combinations of elements contribute to a particular climate enables nurturing, care and respect, which in turn foster adaptation and sustainability.

Exercise 3: The characteristics that make a culture distinctive in Appendix 3 gives insight and practice in recognising the characteristics that contribute to making a specific organisation's culture distinctive and of value – that make the culture matter in terms of the asset value it can add.

Is culture related to business success?

Dick Clark, CEO of Merck, when asked about his strategy for restoring the pharmaceutical company to greatness in the face of lawsuits over its painkiller Vioxx, expiration of patents and a weak product pipeline, said his strategy was to put strategy second and focus on changing the company's culture. He explains:[1]

> The fact is culture eats strategy for lunch. You can have a good strategy in place, but if you don't have the culture and the enabling systems that allow you to successfully implement that strategy, the culture of the organisation will defeat the strategy.

Clark makes a clear connection between culture and strategy, and the underlying assumption is that a good strategy will result in business success. This is somewhat oversimplifying the link, but it is a starting point for the debate on the relationship between culture and business success.

What is business success?

The term "business success" is almost as slippery a term as "culture", because success for one organisation may not be success for another. For listed companies, business success is almost invariably taken to mean making a good financial return according to a variety of measures. Analysts comment on business performance each quarter, and there is always pressure on senior managers to meet market expectations – which is another measure of success, often regardless of how the results have been achieved. According to the CFA Institute Centre for Financial Market Integrity and the Business Roundtable Institute for Corporate Ethics, the consequences of complying with short-term thinking aimed at making the expected numbers are:

> *Loss of sight of longer-term value creation for all stakeholders leading to the unintended consequences of destroying long-term value, decreasing market efficiency, reducing investment returns, and impeding efforts to strengthen corporate governance.*

Reinforcing this perspective in a 2002 article in Fortune magazine, Daniel Vasella, CEO of Novartis, a pharmaceuticals company, weighed in saying:[2]

> *The practice by which CEOs offer guidance about their expected quarterly earnings performance, analysts set "targets" based on that guidance, and then companies try to meet those targets within the penny, is an old one. But in recent years the practice has become so enshrined in the culture of Wall Street that the men and women running public companies often think of little else. They become preoccupied with short-term "success", a mindset that can hamper or even destroy long-term performance for shareholders. I call this the tyranny of quarterly earnings.*

> *Let me say straight off, there is nothing inherently wrong with delivering consistent results, quarter after quarter – that is the mark of a great company, after all, when it is done over time. (And to be sure, one cannot achieve substantial long-term rewards for shareholders without delivering many, many short-term periods of outperformance along the way.) But tyranny is a slippery thing. Rarely does it make itself known for what it is right from the start. Once you get under the domination of making the quarter – even unwittingly – you start to compromise in the grey areas of your business, that wide swathe of terrain between the top and bottom lines. Perhaps you'll begin to sacrifice things (such as funding a promising research-and-development project, incremental improvements to your products, customer service, employee training, expansion into new markets, and, yes, community outreach) that are important and that may be vital for your company over the long term.*

The elements that Vasella believes are sacrificed to the tyranny of quarterly earnings correspond to several of the cultural characteristics referred to in Chapter 3 – including the horizon scanning, the global mindset and the relationship network. So returning to the climate analogy, its constituents individually and collectively adapt and adjust to a certain level of environmental change and are resilient enough to produce predictable weather within the normal boundaries. But if the change load on one part of the climate system is too great it taxes the whole beyond its tolerance to adapt, usually with negative consequences, as this example illustrates:[3]

> Volatile petroleum prices, along with federal policies aimed at reducing US dependency on oil imports and mitigating climate change, have sparked rapid growth in biofuel demand. In response, production of agricultural commodities that serve as feedstock for biofuels has increased ... The share of total domestic corn production supplying the ethanol market grew from 7.5% in 2001 to 22.6% in 2007 ... While biofuels have been viewed as an environmentally preferred alternative to fossil-based fuels, there is growing concern about the potential effects of feedstock development on resource use and environmental quality.

The effects of this lead to some scientists pointing out:[4]

> There is strong evidence that the results of deforestation and ecosystem degradation can be non-linear, ie, that both agricultural intensification (based on large-scale monocultures and high fertiliser and pesticide inputs) and expansion could trigger large-scale, irreversible ecosystem changes and possible collapse which could then trigger equally irreversible climate feedbacks.

Like the demand for meeting quarterly expectations, the decision to plant vast acres of corn to solve a pressing need has a negative impact on both resources and environmental quality. In the short term, corn for fuel might solve a problem; in the longer term the result is not success but an unhealthy and eventually unsustainable ecosystem and potentially irreversible climate changes.

Similarly, long-term business success is not achieved by an unremitting focus on short-term profitability. Organisations that work for success in several dimensions will develop and reinforce cultures that support longer-term profitability, more diverse value creation, and attitudes and aptitudes that are adaptive and resilient to changes in their operating contexts.

The ability to act on a broader range of success factors rather than just quarterly earnings targets is one of the cultural characteristics of Caterpillar, a heavy machinery manufacturer. Jim Owens, the company's CEO, interviewed in June 2009, talked about business success in terms of collaboration with all stakeholders, involving a wide range of people in strategic planning, and getting to a vision of Caterpillar that would energise and enthuse the workforce. (Again all corresponding to the common cultural characteristics mentioned in Chapter 3.) He noted:[5]

> We hit the buzz saw of the global recession that has been pretty cataclysmic for the drop in demand in our business, and we're now thinking of how to reposition, resize, recompete, regroup, and stay profitable at this lower volume level. But I tell my people that the top line sales and revenue targets are the least important as a goal. It's the safety – about how we take care of the people, it's the product quality, it's the supply chain, it's the global market share, we have to pay attention to.

The balanced scorecard, the Malcolm Baldrige National Quality Award (see Figure 4.1) and the European Foundation for Quality Management Excellence Award are examples of business results models that help companies achieve success in multiple dimensions. Two of Caterpillar's subsidiaries have won Malcolm Baldrige Awards (Solar Turbines in 1998 and Caterpillar Financial Services Corporation in 2003), demonstrating that the 80-year-old company has a commitment to success in more than the financials.

Solar Turbines, a wholly owned subsidiary of Caterpillar, was a Malcolm Baldrige Award winner in 1998. Receiving the award, Wendy Swanson said:

> Our business results are certainly up but it's not why we won. They're looking at the whole (company) effort ... how our values and mission are deployed throughout the manufacturing process.

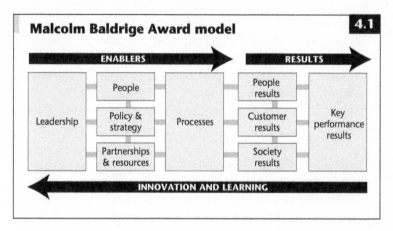

Malcolm Baldrige Award model 4.1

Eleven years later, continuing the trend of success in more than the financials, Shandong Jinneng Coal Gasification Co, one of Solar Turbines' customers in China, was the first company outside the United States to win the US Environmental Protection Agency (EPA) International CHP (combined heat and power) Award for its use of a Solar turbine to create electricity from burning coke oven gas at an operation in Shandong province. Steve Gosselin, Caterpillar vice-president with responsibility for Solar Turbines, said:

> Using Solar turbines in a coke oven gas application not only makes commercial sense, but as this award demonstrates, it also benefits the environment.

The EPA estimates that the Solar-based CHP system at Shandong Jinneng Coal Gasification reduces CO_2 emissions by 40,000 tons per year, the equivalent of removing annual emissions from approximately 6,600 automobiles. Here the success relates to an interest in environmental protection and an effective customer/ supplier relationship.

What constitutes success for Caterpillar is not necessarily what constitutes success for another organisation, even one in the same industry, because each organisation is unique. The choices and decisions on what specifically constitutes business success must be organisationally determined, and how such choices and decisions are made depends on complex interactions among all the elements of an organisation in its operating environment.

In general, however, a business strategy that measures success in more dimensions than simply quarterly profit improvements and recognises the value of the cultural assets in contributing to business performance suggests an ability to keep the organisation aligned, adaptive and healthy.

The connection between success and culture

If the assumption is made that business success is the result of successful execution of a "good strategy" (back to Clark's comment at the beginning of this chapter) that is measured by more than financial results, the connection between culture and business success may seem obvious, because this shifts the focus from strategy formulation to strategy execution, and culture is all about execution – how well the characteristics comprising the culture are used, or are able, to facilitate value delivery.

Southwest Airlines is an organisation where the links between strategy and its execution are related to its culture. The culture is strong – there is consistency in what people (inside and outside the organisation) see, hear and feel about it, and employees are clear how things are done and are willing and able to help the airline achieve its goals. The strategy is "good" – in that it is stretching and addresses short-term and longer-term goals – and clearly articulated. The result is business success. For example, year-end results for 2008 marked the company's 36th consecutive year of profitability.

A year later, in 2009, Southwest's CEO Gary Kelly made the following statement:[6]

> In second quarter 2009, we reported a profit. In, without a doubt, one of the worst revenue environments for the airlines, ever, this is an enormous achievement by the employees of Southwest Airlines. I am exceptionally proud of them, their warrior spirits, and their terrific operational and customer service results. We continue to stay focused on weathering this economic storm and managing alarming jet fuel price volatility.

But, as stated, business success should also be judged on factors other than financial performance and in Southwest's case customer satisfaction is another important success measure. Since 1987, when the US Department of Transportation began tracking customer satisfaction statistics, the airline has consistently led the industry with the lowest ratio of complaints per passenger boarded. Southwest also measures success on the management of its fleet of aircraft and the management of its people.

Kelly knows that the strong culture contributes to business success and is instrumental in some of the strategic decisions. He can take this into account when making a business decision. For example, in August 2009 it was reported that Southwest had failed in its bid to buy Frontier, a competitor, because the SWAPA (Southwest Airlines Pilots Association) did not see the acquisition as something that would add value. Kelly says:

> We said all along that we would only move forward on this deal if it proved to be the right decision for our employees and financially prudent for our company. We have a mission to preserve and protect our culture and the best interests of our employees, customers, and shareholders. This was a great opportunity that required us to act fast. A lot of people worked very hard with every intention of making this work. We were fortunate to be in a position to examine the acquisition to see if it was the right decision for Southwest Airlines.

In recognising that one of the cultural characteristics is employee participation in decision-making and in holding a belief that the culture is instrumental in the airline's strategy and success, Kelly himself took a culturally consistent course of action.

There are many books and articles, both popular and academic, that tell the story of the connection between the airline's culture and its business success. Figure 4.2, developed for a case study on Southwest Airlines, summarises the link between the two.

The examples of Merck, Novartis, Solar Turbines and Southwest Airlines all point to a connection between culture and the ability to execute the business strategy. But the inference is that only when an organisation's culture is both strong (that is, consistent) and

Southwest Airlines: culture and strategy link 4.2

Culture ──────► strategy ──────► business success

Core purpose and values	▶ What is our purpose? What are our principles and core values? ▶ What do we believe in?
Design management practices that reflect and embody these values	▶ What policies and practices are consistent with the purpose, values and principles?
Use these to build cultural intangible assets	▶ What can we do for the customer better than our competitors?
Plan a strategy that is consistent with the intangible assets and uses these to compete in innovative ways	▶ Given our capabilities, how can we deliver value (EVA) to customers in a way our competitors cannot easily imitate?
Business success judged on several criteria	▶ What criteria constitute success beyond growth and revenue?

Source: Adapted from a presentation on Southwest Airlines by Barry A. Macy, Texas Tech University, 2006

healthy (that is, employees are engaged and committed, customers are satisfied and other stakeholders are included in organisational discussions) will it be capable of executing its strategy effectively.

Intriguingly, one researcher[7] into the culture/business performance link found that strong cultures were able to deliver the business strategy in fairly stable operating conditions and achieve business success, but when the conditions became more turbulent or volatile they were less able to deliver and tended to be less successful. Reasons suggested for this were that firms with strong cultures:

▶ are good at exploiting known competences but are less good at quickly developing new competences suited to the new and/or changing context;

▶ have well-established systems and processes that people understand and that have become the accepted way of doing things – they are less susceptible to rapid change;

▶ have people with consistent views of the world who may be less likely to tolerate or accept different views of the organisational goals and ways of achieving them – thus they are less open to preparing for or adapting to a changing environment.

Other researchers have found links between culture and business success, but because the research has been conducted in various ways, using different methods, variables, definitions, measures and analysis there is little agreement on the effect of culture on the firm-level performance of an organisation.[8] But many business leaders are convinced that culture does have a substantial influence on performance, and research in 2007 by McKinsey, a leading management consultancy, highlights the way initiatives to boost talent, strengthen values and reinforce corporate culture appear to directly improve the bottom line.[9]

The business model

As one manager asked:

> How is it that companies with radically different cultures can be massively successful, and yet companies in the same industry with similar cultures – for example HSBC and Barclays – may have different levels of success? And how come some companies can expand successfully internationally and others can only be successful in their home markets?

The answer to such questions lies in the business model – the "what and how" of a business. A company's business model is a simplified representation of its business logic (see Figure 4.3). "It describes what a company offers its customers, how it reaches them and relates to them, through which resources, activities and partners it achieves this and, finally, how it earns money."[10] In a sense a business model is what someone seeking investor support to set up a company would describe in the business plan.

The business model is the terrain of the organisation. It is analogous to the topography (mountains, plains, and so on) which is one of the factors that affect the climate in a particular zone. As the topography informs the climate (and vice versa) so the business model informs the culture. Although two companies, for example two

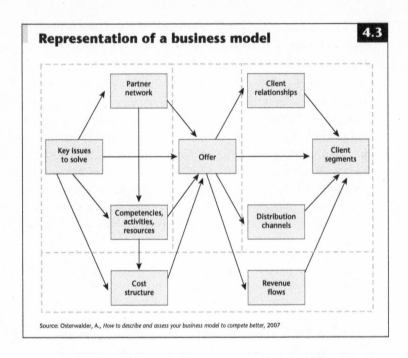

Representation of a business model   4.3

Source: Osterwalder, A., *How to describe and assess your business model to compete better*, 2007

banks, may be in the same industry, compete in similar markets and appear to have similar cultures, they are almost certain to have different business models. It is this difference, which affects the culture, that in part accounts for them having different success levels. (The business exists in relation to the environment in which it is situated and is not a self-contained system. It is subject to social, environmental, cultural and economic influences coming from outside its "borders".)

In Figure 4.3 the boxes represent the "what" of the organisation and require conscious choices and decisions to be made for each of them; for example, "competencies, activities and resources" requires choices and decisions on questions such as: What are the main activities we operate to run our business model? On which resources do they rely? To which value propositions, channels or relationships do they contribute?

The arrows represent the "how" of the organisation and include "hard" things like IT systems or explicit policies and "soft" things like leadership style or speed of decision-making. Members of organisations make choices and decisions based on these. For example, the arrow from "customer relationships" to "offer" requires choices and decisions based on soft questions – for example, How responsive will we be to customer feedback? Are we going to "tell" the customer or are we going to make choices and decision by involving the customer? Will we treat all customers equally? – and hard questions – for example, What IT system is the best customer relationship management system for our purposes? What packaging shall we offer our product in? What price point should we offer at?

Business-model decisions and choices are made in three dimensions that roughly relate to the three cultural perspectives described in Chapter 1, as Table 4.1 illustrates.

Each choice and decision has consequences that make for, or sustain, business model viability, as the example of Domino's Pizza illustrates. In July 2009 Domino's reported that international same-store sales (sales revenues of retail stores that have been open for a year or more) grew 4.1%. The international division continued its strong performance, posting its 62nd consecutive quarter of same-store sales growth. David Brandon, the company's CEO, says:[11]

> I'm putting this quarter in the "win" column for Domino's Pizza. I'm proud of my team and our accomplishment of emerging as a leader during tough times. The predictability of our [business] model continues to be a plus in an unpredictable landscape.

In this case the choice to be predictable yet remain competitive has a number of consequences, one of which is the requirement for continuous improvement. Brandon acts to develop the concept in his organisation, stating:[12]

> You cannot stay the same; you're either going to get better or you're going to get worse. One of the things that I do over and over again at my organisation is to reinforce the concept that we have to get better, that even during times of tremendous success, if we get complacent and start to read the press clippings and believe that we're better than we are, we're going to fall back.

Table 4.1 Dimensions of business model and cultural perspective

Dimension	Business model element	Service organisation example decisions and choices
Structural choices (integration perspective)	Offer Key issues to solve Revenue flows Cost structure	What services will we offer? How will we stay competitive during economic upturns and downturns? Where will we reinvest our revenue? What are our target clients prepared to pay for our services?
Situational choices (differentiation perspective)	Partner network Client segments Distribution channels	How will we extend our network of partners and develop relationships with partners in our different practices and locations? How different will our client segments be in our different locations? What channels will we use to market our services (will they differ by location/practice area)?
Functional choices (fragmentation perspective)	Client relationships Competencies, activities, resources	What types of relationships do we want with our clients (eg, collaborative, expert, trusted adviser)? What level and mix of people do we need? What will they be doing day-to-day? What resources do they need?

This is one soft (behavioural) example of activating the predictable business model. A hard example is a technology one:[13]

> Domino's, the pizza-delivery kingpin, on Wednesday [February 2008] will unveil a technology, Pizza Tracker, that lets customers literally track their pizza from the moment they place the order until it leaves the store en route to them. What's more, Domino's vows that its online tracking system – for phone or online orders – is accurate to within 40 seconds.

These two examples of continuous improvement relate to the business-model elements "client relationship" and "offer" and the arrow between them. Like all the other choices and consequences in Domino's predictable business model they both reflect and have an impact on the culture. Brandon reinforces the point:[14]

> One of the concepts that is truly essential if you really want to have a high-performance organisation is the concept of continuous improvement. It's almost a cliché, but it really is something that the culture has to embrace, and it has to manifest itself in everyday behaviour. The notion is, "I have to figure out a way to do something a little bit better today than I did yesterday." And if you can foster that in the culture of your organisation, great things happen.

Whatever the positive attributes of the culture, if the business model is flawed, success will prove elusive. Conversely, if the culture is good, a flawed business plan is much less likely. The example of Southwest Airlines deciding not to acquire Frontier (see page 83) illustrates making a business decision that is culturally right, rather than compromising the culture for a plan that might look good on paper but have unknown outcomes.

Even a successful business model must be adapted to meet changing circumstances if it is to stay successful. The print newspaper industry is one in which many companies are facing the need to adapt their business models. Used to a fairly stable circulation, newspaper companies are finding that a number of factors – predominantly technological, demographic and economic – are putting strong pressure on their finances:

▶ **Technological** pressures are cleverly illustrated in the film *State of Play*. It depicts the traditional newspaper industry culture coming up against the digital media news culture. As one reviewer notes:[15]

> Signs of technological change are everywhere in State of Play, which ultimately seems less interested in the intricacies of plot than with the romance of an almost-bygone medium. The Globe has just been sold to a media conglomerate with a lively interest in quarterly profits, and it's in the throes of a redesign

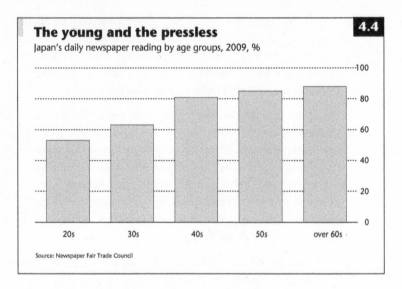

The young and the pressless   **4.4**

Japan's daily newspaper reading by age groups, 2009, %

Source: Newspaper Fair Trade Council

process that will look eerily familiar to loyal newsprint readers
(yes, both of you). Throughout the movie, tensions between
print and online journalism and the Web erupt into little turf
fights or larger arguments about ethics.

State of Play's final montage, a loving valentine to old-fashioned
newspapering, with its clanging presses and heaving, beeping
trucks, plays like a sepia-toned anthropological documentary
about a vanishing indigenous people.

▶ **Demographic** changes are reported in several countries –
younger people are less inclined to read print than older people.
Japan is an example (see Figure 4.4). As The Economist reported in
February 2010, its population is ageing and:

Its younger people do not appear to be growing into the [reading
print] habit as they age, says Takashi Kasuya, an executive at
Asahi, the second-biggest newspaper. Although Japanese newspapers have been careful not to put all their articles online free
of charge, a generation has decided that the news it obtains
from television, mobile phones and the internet is enough. The
young have also come to dislike newspapers' clutter.

▶ **Economic.** Tough market conditions in the United States have
meant many newspapers, including four of the 15 largest – Los

Angeles Times, Chicago Tribune, Star Tribune in Minneapolis and *The Philadelphia Inquirer* – are now in the hands of banks and other financial firms as a result of bankruptcy proceedings. As Michael Liedtke of the (online) *Huffington Post* remarks:[16]

> *The new owners face huge problems. Newspaper ad revenue, the industry's main source of income, is on pace to total around $27 billion this year, about $22 billion less than three years ago. Newspaper circulation is falling faster than ever. Finding solutions – such as mining websites for more revenue while newspapers protect what's left of their print franchises – will likely require a financial commitment that short-term owners might be reluctant to make.*

The combination of these three factors is commented on in a research report, *The How v Where of News Consumption*, by the US Pew Research Center's Project for Excellence in Journalism, which finds that in the United States:

> *The most compelling transformation in media consumption is not really where people are getting news but how ... People continue to want news from neutral non-partisan sources – by a margin of 66% to 23%. And the numbers on this remain rock-solid ... The significance of this platform shifting is economic, not a reflection of lost brand loyalty. The internet is not generating the kind of advertising revenue the old platforms did and increasingly appears as if it never will. The shift to online thus erodes revenue, but not because the audience is abandoning the values and practices of those traditional news operations.*

> *What's changing is how people interact with the news when they acquire it – and the old news deliverers certainly must adapt to these new expectations.*

> *A majority of Americans (51%) are now what Pew Research calls "news grazers", people who check in on the news from time to time rather than going at regular times. And those numbers are likely to grow. Nearly eight in ten (78%) of those under age 25 fit this description, hunting for news using search engines, customising your news front page, emailing friends with news, and setting up news email alerts – this is the consumer editing*

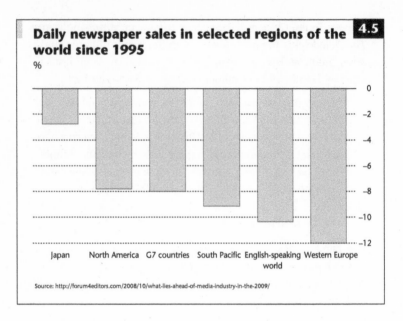

Daily newspaper sales in selected regions of the world since 1995 `4.5`

%

Source: http://forum4editors.com/2008/10/what-lies-ahead-of-media-industry-in-the-2009/

his and her own version of the news rather than passively accepting the news as it is delivered to them.

This mix of internal and external issues led, in the first half of 2009 in the United States, to 105 newspapers closing down, 10,000 newspaper jobs being lost, print advertising sales falling 30% (in the first quarter of 2009) and 23 of the top 25 newspapers reporting circulation declines of between 7% and 20%.[17] The drop is reflected in many regions, as Figure 4.5 illustrates.

Talking of the newspapers that closed, one commentator spoke forcefully about why this had happened:[18]

There were a number of things the papers plainly needed to do. Most of all they needed to stake their place in the new informational channel that was going to change our world. They had to shift their coverage to a new, tech-savvy generation. They needed new equipment to share in the experience of that generation, undergoing the biggest sociological shift since the 1960s. They needed to learn the new era's tools, experiment with and test a new medium, take advantage of its speed and immediacy to take their place in society even deeper into people's lives.

> *They needed to take a look at their work rules and union agree-*
> *ments to make sure they didn't hamper the evolution of their*
> *industry at a time when it could be facing mortal danger.*

In short, they needed to change their business model. But, in many cases, newspaper companies did not act to do this.

However, some did (and are). One example is the *New York Times* co-owned *Star-News:*[19]

> *The Star-News is putting out stories and discussion topics on*
> *15 Twitter feeds. Meanwhile, 30 of its staffers have their own*
> *accounts, which they use to promote their work, engage the*
> *community and mine story ideas. The paper (if one can still*
> *use the term) is also pushing out stories on its own Facebook*
> *page and encouraging reporters to do the same on their own*
> *pages. Many do. Says the web development manager, Vaughn*
> *Hagerty: "That conversation, that feedback, is key to a lot of the*
> *things we're doing."*

Failure to adapt the business model is a cultural decision, usually made unconsciously or by default. It relates to the cultural charac-teristics discussed in Chapter 3. Organisations willing and able to change their business model will inevitably nudge culture change (a topic discussed further in Chapter 7). Equally, the culture can nudge business-model change. Table 4.2 compares slow-footed newspapers with the fleeter-footed.

Table 4.2 Static culture versus changing culture

Cultural characteristics	What some newspapers did (static culture)	What other newspapers did (changing culture)
A story or stories	Stuck with the story "that the idea of accruing and catering to online followers and friends is strange – or worse, unbecoming"[a]	Told a story of a future of digital news fed through social networking
A business strategy	Kept on going down the same route	Changed the strategy to meet new circumstances

Cultural characteristics	What some newspapers did (static culture)	What other newspapers did (changing culture)
An attitude to people in the workforce	Patriarchal, top-down, "we (the leaders) know how to do things"	Encouraged staff to experiment, make suggestions, meet the changing circumstances head on and work with them collaboratively
Digital presence	Set up their digital presence as a sideline rather than as part of the mainstream offering	Made choices and decisions about committing resources, expertise and energy to converting the whole business model to favour digital
Reputation	Traded down the reputation (vested in intellectual capital) by making decisions for short-term profitability eg, on analytical content	Converted the intellectual capital into an online interactive rigorous debating forum
A customer proposition	Continued to try to play to the traditional reader without recognising the very different needs of tech-savvy people	Involved the tech-savvy people in developing content and an approach that met their needs without sacrificing the traditional, albeit diminishing number of print readers
A horizon-scanning ability	Kept their heads down and did not look towards the horizon	Anticipated or immediately examined and then embraced the emerging trends, taking innovative approaches to change their business model and culture
A purpose or set of values	Did not revisit the purpose and values and develop a new business model that reinterpreted them for changing circumstances	Reviewed the purpose and values regularly and changed the business model for a digital media world

Cultural characteristics	What some newspapers did (static culture)	What other newspapers did (changing culture)
A global mindset	Remained locked into their known market (geography and consumer)	Planned for a broader reach across or within geographies and internet span
A relationship network	Retained the cosy old-boy network	Embraced a wide network that involved citizen observers, industry analysts, volunteer reporters, etc

a Schulte, B., "The Distribution Revolution", *American Journalism Review*, December/January 2010.

The "edges", national culture and language

There are three other aspects to consider for an understanding of the connections between culture and business success.

The "edges"

Where are the "edges" between the organisation's culture and its business success? The culture of Walmart, one of the world's most successful companies in terms of financial performance, has been described as "frugal", aligning with its intention to offer customers goods at the lowest possible prices (the company's tagline is "Save Money. Live Better"). Walmart's success, however, depends on its suppliers being able to supply goods at a price that meets its demands. The success of Walmart's culture of frugality is predicated on the contractual conditions it imposes on its suppliers and the types and cultures of the organisations that they work in. For many of them – both within America (where Walmart has its headquarters) and outside – those conditions can impose extreme penalties, as the following story illustrates:[20]

> *The Lovable Company was founded in 1926 by the grandfather of Frank Garson II, who was Lovable's last president. It did business with Wal-Mart, Garson says, from the earliest days of founder Sam Walton's first store in Bentonville, Arkansas.*

Lovable made brassières and lingerie, supplying retailers that also included Sears and Victoria's Secret. At one point, it was the sixth-largest maker of intimate apparel in the United States, with 700 employees in this country and another 2,000 at eight factories in Central America.

Eventually Wal-Mart became Lovable's biggest customer. "Wal-Mart has a big pencil," says Garson. "They have such awesome purchasing power that they write their own ticket. If they don't like your prices, they'll go vertical and do it themselves – or they'll find someone that will meet their terms."

In the summer of 1995, Garson asserts, Wal-Mart did just that. "They had awarded us a contract, and in their wisdom, they changed the terms so dramatically that they really reneged." Garson, still worried about litigation, won't provide details. "But when you lose a customer that size, they are irreplaceable."

Lovable was already feeling intense cost pressure. Less than three years after Wal-Mart pulled its business, in its 72nd year, Lovable closed. "They leave a lot to be desired in the way they treat people," says Garson. "Their actions to pulverise people are unnecessary. Wal-Mart chewed us up and spit us out."

The question this story raises relates again to the connection between culture and business success. Can Walmart be truly described as successful in driving its culture of frugality for its customers' benefit when it has a company value of "respect for the individual" yet an outcome of success is the destruction of the culture (and business) of another company? Walmart did not respond to this when invited to do so.

The answer involves careful thinking about trade-offs, consequences, boundaries and interdependencies. Walmart, like most companies, has relationships with a web of employees, suppliers, customers, local governments and political systems, offshore workers, local communities, shareholders and "voiceless" stakeholders such as the environment. Walmart's large network of operations makes it impossible to show that there is a simple cause/effect relationship between a company's business success and its culture. Thinking about the network raises questions such as: Where does one organisation's culture and business success begin and end? What are the expectations and responsibilities of each set of stakeholders in relation to each other's success and culture? Again, the way they are answered reflects and reinforces the cultural aspects of the organisation.

National culture

What is the impact of national culture on organisational culture? Yongmaan Park, chairman of Doosan Corp., a South Korean conglomerate, observes:[21]

> Culture represents country, race, language, history, and such. But when you add "corporate" and make "corporate culture", that's almost identical in most of the successful conglomerates globally. The key processes of those companies – evaluation and control, strategic planning, HR – are all based on a performance-driven culture, meritocracy, transparency. We come from a different national culture, but successful corporations share a very similar corporate culture.

On one level that is true. Many companies use the same technologies to run their business processes (supplied, for example, by Microsoft, SAP, IBM or Cisco); they have similar approaches to performance management; business travellers experience the same hotel chains and airlines set up to meet their needs. This encourages a cultural dimension that transcends national boundaries. To what extent is difficult to quantify, but what is observable is that national cultures interact with corporate cultures in a way that can limit business success unless handled with great sensitivity.[22] As described in Chapter 3, for example, Walmart pulled out of Germany because its culture does not travel and it does not understand the German customer. Similarly, IKEA pulled out of Japan in 1986 because of poor sales. These are just two examples of a national culture rejecting a business culture that had found success in other countries. However, when IKEA returned to Japan in 2006 sales went well. The reason given in The Economist in September 2009 is that "the Japanese are finally, after an economic crisis that follows almost two decades of growing hardship, turning thrifty". IKEA had learnt from its previous experience. Spotting an opportunity afforded by a shift in national culture, it seized it to try again with its low-cost, good-design model and was successful the second time around.

Language

Within multinational companies, English is the language generally used for communication. Thus in any meeting several mother tongues may be represented, but everyone will speak (with more or less facility) English. Because "language is central to our experience of being human, and the languages we speak profoundly shape the way we think, the way we see the world, the way we live our lives",[23] the way the people in the room frame their thoughts and respond to each other's perceptions of issues, concerns, questions and decisions is likely to represent their mother-tongue ways of looking at the world.

This is often a recipe for miscommunication, misunderstanding and general lack of success. Deborah Tannen makes the point that "culture is constituted in part by ways of using language and, language exists only as it is shaped in particular cultures".[24] The way members of organisations manage the connections between languages, a diversity of perspectives and the national cultures they represent contributes to an organisation's culture and its business success.

Beyond the language that people normally speak is the more or less endemic language of business, which has been well lampooned by, for example, Scott Adams, author of the Dilbert books, Lucy Kellaway, a journalist who writes on management issues, and Ricky Gervais and Stephen Merchant, who wrote the TV series *The Office*. In the *BBC Magazine*, Kellaway says:[25]

> I wrote a fictional column in the Financial Times about a senior manager who spoke almost entirely in business clichés. Martin Lukes talked the talk. Or rather, he added value by reaching out and sharing his blue sky thinking. At the end of the day he stepped up to the plate and delivered world class jargon that really pushed the envelope. After eight years of being him I came to accept the nouns pretending to be verbs. To task and to impact. Even the new verb to architect I almost took in my

stride. I didn't even really mind the impenetrable sentences full of leveraging value and paradigm shifts. But what still rankled after so long were the little things: that he said myself instead of me and that he would never talk about a problem, when he could dialogue around an issue instead.

This follows Park's view that there is an overarching business culture, but in this case the business language is the contributory factor. Although it may sound bizarre to people who do not speak "business", it is a social construct that serves as a common language running parallel to all the varieties of English that are spoken (by both people who have English as a mother tongue and people who have learned it as a second language).

What this linguistic aspect of the culture contributes to business success is difficult to judge, but it is not too far-fetched to suggest that organisational members who "speak the same language" are likely to be collectively more successful than if they were all speaking different languages, variations of the same language, or did not understand the management language being spoken. (Changing the culture by changing the language is discussed in Chapter 7.)

Recap points

▶ Business success is more than meeting quarterly earnings targets. The ability to think about and act on a broad range of success factors rather than just quarterly earnings targets is a cultural intangible asset.

▶ There appear to be some links between culture and business success but these are difficult to prove.

▶ The business model – the logic of the business – forms the "terrain" of the culture. The choices made in relation to operating the business model and the consequences of these choices influence and are influenced by the organisation culture.

▶ A fundamentally flawed business model cannot result in business success even if the culture is strong and healthy; but where the culture is strong and healthy there is less likely to be a flawed business model.

▶ Failure to adapt the business model to changing circumstances appropriately is often a cultural decision that has a damaging effect on business success.

▶ Organisations make cultural choices about their boundaries, where the "fences" are located around the organisation, and about their responsibilities to stakeholders. These choices help define business success.

▶ National cultures and the languages present in an organisation influence its culture. Sensitivity to these aspects may foster business success, though again this is difficult to prove.

One company's way of getting to business success: W.L. Gore

Privately held companies are not under direct scrutiny from analysts on a quarterly basis and are not obliged to publish their financial results. W.L. Gore & Associates is a product company with global reach – that is, it supplies customers around the world. Virtually all its thousands of products are based on just one material, a versatile polymer called ePTFE (expanded polytetrafluoroethylene), which the company engineers to perform a wide variety of functions. It is financially successful and does not release detailed figures:[26]

> But it is no secret that the balance sheet is strong and the company has been in the black every year in its history. It doesn't lack opportunities, whether geographical or technical, nor is it constrained by ability to invest.

Since 1998 the company's revenues have grown by 7–9% each year (2008 revenue was $2.5 billion).

What makes Gore special and distinctively different is its culture. CEO Terri Kelly is convinced that it is the culture and practices, variously described as "unusual", "radical", "humanistic" and "innovative", which drive business success. The culture derives from the thinking of the company's founders, Bill and Vieve Gore, who felt that culture was a critical link to driving innovation and success. Bill Gore had the vision right from the beginning (1958) "that everyone participates in the growth of the company, everyone's a shareholder of the company ... it's a partnership, and you are part of that enterprise". Steve Shuster, a member of Gore's enterprise communications team, who has worked for the company for 27 years, talks about his experience of the culture:[27]

> You feel like you're part of a family. I have been working at Gore for 27 years, and I still get excited coming to work each day. There is a sense of being among family, and this creates a special bond between associates and a connection with the company.

> Everyone is an owner in the company and shares in the good times and in the bad times. Everyone works in teams, and there is very little hierarchy at Gore.

> The company culture at Gore gives people a sense of belonging and gives us a sense that we are making an impact on society via our products.

> There are four principles that are the foundation of Gore's culture: fairness, freedom, commitment, and waterline. The waterline principle means that it's ok to make a decision that might punch a hole in the boat as long as the hole is above the waterline so that it won't potentially sink the ship. But if the decision might create a hole below the waterline which might cause the ship to sink, then associates are encouraged to consult with their team so that a collaborative decision can be made.

> Our culture is based on integrity and a high level of ethics. The organisation operates as a flat, or "lattice", organisation, where all employees are referred to as "associates". There are no bosses, only "sponsors" who are similar to sports team coaches. Sponsors are responsible for leading the teams and are mainly focused on their team members' growth and development. The process of becoming a sponsor is through followership, and each group chooses their own sponsor.

> Gore's lattice, team-based organisational structure and the opportunity to provide feedback about other team members are two of our innovative work practices. Associates get to manage what type of projects they are working on. Also, associates' compensation is based in part on their contribution to the enterprise. All associates rank each of their colleagues according to what they feel their contribution has been to the enterprise.

But Kelly does not believe in culture for culture's sake, stating firmly that the culture should be driving the strategic intent of the business, which, for Gore, is to be a highly effective enterprise that delivers a continuous stream of innovative products. The business model is set up to do this. As mentioned, its core technology is ePTFE fluoropolymers and the company makes five types of products: fibres, sheets, tubes, tapes and films. These are organised across four divisions: medical, fabrics, industrial products and electronic products. There are some practices (the "how" of the business model) that Kelly says are critical to the adaptation of the business model as circumstances change (see Table 4.3).

Table 4.3 **Gore's key practices for operating the business model**

Small plants in clusters	Self-contained, relatively autonomous business units
	Typically fewer than 250 associates per plant
Project teams organised around passionate champions	Emphasis on face-to-face communication
	Lots of internal selling
	Strong collaboration across functions
High expectations for networking	Enabled by formal and informal mechanisms
	Functional and cross-functional project teams and groups
	Monthly technology tradeshows and presentations

Source: Kelly, T., "Nurturing a Vibrant Culture to Drive Innovation", MIT/Sloan Dean's Innovative Leadership Series, December 9th 2008

Kelly also notes the disciplined methodology with which they approach innovation and bringing a project to market. It has several elements:

▶ Innovation within boundaries – using the core technology.

▶ Focusing on best-in-class product concepts, Bob Henn, who oversees R&D at Gore, says that the phrase "the only" has special power:

> It's how we review product concepts. We give you those two words – "the only" – and then we say, "Now, fill in the rest." If you can fill in that blank and validate it without resorting to marketing gimmicks, then you're onto something.

▶ Rigorous, transparent peer reviews.

▶ An ever-evolving portfolio of tools and best practices.

▶ Relentless protection of intellectual property.

▶ A product specialist committed to each product line.

▶ Peer-reviewed ranking and compensation process.

The launch of Glide Floss is an early example of the innovation discipline in action:[28]

> *In 1991, six months after joining the company and on his first week in a new division, John Spencer heard about the stalled floss project. He quickly proposed a radical new plan: stop chasing other producers and market the product directly to consumers. Spencer's proposal quickly aroused opposition from some of the company's most successful operations. The loudest objections came from Gore's medical-technology group, which had built up a profitable business manufacturing such sophisticated products as vascular grafts and artificial heart valves. "They voiced major concerns that putting the Gore name on a string for teeth would hurt the company's image as a medical-technology leader," Spencer says.*

> *Spencer's response: use a clinical trial to validate the product in a way that the medical-technology group would respect. It was a simple test, pitting Gore's PTFE floss against standard nylon floss and asking consumers which they preferred. Most picked Gore – and those who didn't said that they doubted that the new floss worked, because it didn't hurt their gums.*

> *The clinical trial was a breakthrough. The American Dental Association conferred its seal of approval on Gore's floss, which Spencer named Glide Floss. The loudest critics inside the company quieted down. And Spencer had his marketing hook: he would position Glide as the product for people who didn't like to floss – in other words, almost everybody.*

Kelly believes that putting in disciplines where it matters and minimising bureaucracy is an effective way to business success. This includes minimising hierarchy, where people are led by those they agree to follow – leaders must be comfortable working through influence not hierarchical power. This model of distributed leadership means that one of the roles of leaders is to invest time, energy and commitment in shaping, living, and modelling the culture to drive the strategic intent of the business. Kelly declares:

> *Although I'm a business leader for military fabric, I'm a leader only if there are people who are willing to follow me. A project doesn't move forward unless people buy into it. You cultivate followership by*

> *selling yourself, articulating your ideas, and developing a reputation for seeing things through ... It's a very chaotic environment.*

But she follows up by noting that the company's growth plans will largely be dictated by its ability to assimilate new people:

> *It's all about how we bring new folks in, get them to understand our values and focus leadership on fitting it all together. For our associates to know we aren't constrained by markets or finance, just by our own culture – that's a good problem to have. It's all in our own hands.*

Learning from Gore

There are three lessons in Gore's approach to making the connection between culture and business success:

▶ **Recognise that the business model and the culture are parts of an interdependent system.** Gore's rigorous technical disciplines result in high-value products, but it is not only the technical disciplines that matter. Products are developed by small teams working collaboratively with minimal bureaucracy, in an entrepreneurial atmosphere where diverse perspectives are valued and the creative spark is given free rein. The whole system is aligned in a way that to an outsider appears chaotic but is, in fact, systematically assessed and carefully managed, including through the language of the organisation, to keep the culture thriving and the business model adaptive to deliver business success.

▶ **Have disciplined methods for nurturing the culture and enabling it to drive the strategic intent of the business.** Gore's culture functions well partly as a result of paying attention to it in a number of dimensions. Kelly talks of it in terms of "what we believe": in the individual, in the power of small teams, that everyone is in the same boat, and in the long-term view. There are also the four cultural guiding principles of freedom, fairness, commitment and waterline. These are supported by a set of core values, key disciplines and business practices (such as profit sharing, commitment rather than job titles and a compensation process based on peer-reviewed compensation). Leaders are expected to invest time in nurturing the culture and ensuring that it is responsive and adaptive to external influences that include customers, economic climate, local cultures, globalisation, government, suppliers, technology, competition, labour market and environment.

▶ **Make it plain that business success is not measured only by short-term quarterly financial results.** Gore takes the long-term view, not just in getting to business results. The collaborative process for product development requires long-term co-operation between individuals and teams. This requirement to nurture working relationships is supported by the flat structure and the flexible lattice arrangement. Collaborative decision-making also takes time, but the feeling is that "time spent in the beginning tapping into the best ideas and gaining consensus pays off in the implementation". Success is measured in each aspect of Gore's mission to "nurture a vibrant culture that engages talented associates who deliver innovative products that create extraordinary value for all of our stakeholders".

Summary

▶ Connecting business success and culture seems to make intuitive sense, and many people believe that the connection is strong. However research suggests that the links are not that easy to make.

▶ Taking a systems approach that involves knowing the business model, making informed choices about the elements of it, and determining how it should be operated are good beginnings for understanding where and how the culture is or can be connected to business success.

▶ Even with this knowledge there are some intervening factors that can act to disrupt any connection, mainly deriving from the external environment. But developing a business model and an aligned culture that have the attitude and aptitude for adaptation to changing circumstances will reinforce the connection between culture and business success.

Exercise 4: Connecting business success and culture in Appendix 3 is a two-step exercise that helps make the connection between business success and culture.

Culture: creation, accountability and responsibility

Robin Bidwell established ERM, a global provider of environmental, health and safety, risk and social consulting services, in 1973. Asked about the culture he says:

> I didn't set up the organisation with a culture in mind. What I did was set up ERM in a certain way and then waited to see what worked and how things got done. The culture comes from the way the leaders of the organisation do things – the decisions they make, the things they pay attention to, the way they incentivise people, the way they deploy resources – these things lead to a distinctive way of behaving in the organisation.

He then observes:

> We now operate in 40 countries – in the different geographies the culture can reflect differently. We don't all have to believe exactly the same thing as long as everyone is aware of the sort of overarching culture. Wherever possible we employ local rather than expat staff and they take the culture in an appropriate direction for their country of operation.

Bidwell's experience is that leaders can and do set the culture's tone and groundwork – they "create" the culture – and other people have a specific stewardship role in relation to it (in ERM's case these are the local managers). Beyond that, everybody in the organisation has an ownership stake in its culture (illustrated by the point that he "waited to see what worked").

Culture creators

Edgar Schein of MIT Sloan School of Management believes that the "only thing of real importance that leaders do is to create and manage culture".[1] In developing his thoughts on how they do this, he identifies five ways:

▶ What they pay attention to in terms of measures and organisational controls.

▶ How they react to the crises and critical incidents that dog organisational life.

▶ How much they deliberately role-model, teach and coach.

▶ Their choice of criteria for rewards and status allocation.

▶ Their support for criteria for recruitment, selection, promotion, retirement and excommunication (that is, when someone is shunned and/or encouraged to leave by sometimes underhand methods).

Meg Whitman, formerly CEO of eBay, an online auction company, reinforces Schein's view of the crucial role leaders play in creating the culture of an organisation:[2]

> Leadership entails painting a vision of where you want to go, establishing priorities for getting there, building the right team, aligning the organisation, and holding people accountable for results. It also requires an ability to communicate effectively so that everyone is on the same page. In addition, effective leaders create cultures where mistakes are acceptable.

Anand Mahindra, CEO of Mahindra & Mahindra Group, which comprises 98 companies (as of April 2008) grouped in eight sectors, endorses this with an analogy:[3]

> We have defined our core values, and there are the annual retreats (a conference for senior executives where the priorities for the organisation are presented and discussed). These mechanisms help me compose the music so that many soloists can play in my orchestra. The players know what's not negotiable: the pace, the tempo, and the traditions. I have to write the music and then stick to my role of conducting the orchestra rather than trying to play the music myself.

Often new leaders are explicitly charged with changing the culture, which implies creating a new one. But even when this is not the case – in instances where they are expected to maintain the status quo – almost all new leaders put their distinctive stamp on the existing organisational culture, thus creating a new form of it.

At AIG Financial Products (UK), for example, Joe Cassano created a culture very different from that which had existed under the previous CEO, Tom Savage. Cassano's "reign of terror of 400 employees", according to one investigator, "brought the company, the US economy, and the global financial system to its knees". One London trader says:[4]

> AIG F.P. became a dictatorship. Joe would bully people around. He'd humiliate them and then try to make it up to them by giving them huge amounts of money.

Another says:

> The culture changed. The fear level was so high that when we had these morning meetings you presented what you did not to upset him. And if you were critical of the organisation all hell would break loose.

And a third says:

> Under Joe, the debate and discussion that was common under Tom [Savage] ceased.

However, culture creation is not necessarily a one-person diktat or as straightforward as the AIG example suggests. For the most part it is a subtle and continuously evolving process that takes place in various ways and at various speeds in the different parts of the organisation. What is worth remembering is that:[5]

> Stability and change can both be part of culture. Like weather "you will never find cultures that move at the same rate over the whole front" … at any given moment, culture is changing only in parts; other parts remain stable.

Furthermore, from the moment that people join an organisation they inevitably bring their biases, values and expectations to it, thereby influencing and helping to shape or create the culture. In these respects organisation culture is beyond single-person creation. Nevertheless, a leader's task is to set the direction and tone – essentially, compose the music – and then let others not only interpret and play, but also model and reinforce what they, the leaders, are looking for.

Culture stewards

While the CEO or leader creates the culture there are others – specialist cultural champions or stewards – who explicitly act to support it. The three categories of people who generally have that specialism as part of their role are described below. A fourth category comprises the leadership team members and organisational managers who act to support the cultural direction the CEO or leader sets. This role may or may not be a specified part of their job description but it is an implied part of every management role.

Human resources staff

Dave Ulrich, professor of business at the Ross School of Business, University of Michigan, has, over several years of research (still continuing), identified competences needed by HR people. One of the six he identified (in 2007) was:

Culture and change steward. The HR professional appreciates, articulates, and helps shape a company's culture ... As stewards of culture, HR professionals respect the past culture and also can help to shape a new culture. They coach managers in how their actions reflect and drive culture; they weave the cultural standards into HR practices and processes; and they make culture real to employees. Additionally, successful HR professionals facilitate change in two ways. First, they help make culture happen. Second, they develop disciplines to make changes happen throughout the organisation. This may include implementation of strategy, projects, or initiatives. They help turn what is known into what is done.

Organisation development consultants

This means organisation development consultants directly employed by the organisation and not hired external consultants. Richard Beckhard, formerly adjunct professor at Sloan School of Management, gives a classic definition of organisation development:[6]

> Organisation Development is an effort (1) planned, (2) organisation-wide, and (3) managed from the top, to (4) increase organisation effectiveness and health through (5) planned interventions in the organisations "processes", using behavioural-science knowledge.

People who do this type of work are often also called "change agents" or "culture champions" and frequently have a background in behavioural science and/or psychology. One organisation development consultant describes the work she does:

> I describe myself as an advocate for difference. What I mean by that is that I am helping people in the organisation interrupt the cultural legacy – doing things the way we've always done them. I find single instances of where things are going well and differently, and I work out why this happens and how to do more of it. From this I am teaching people new stories about the way we do things that are more in line with the future our CEO is seeing for the company, and the strategic plan he has for it. I help orchestrate a lot of stuff that aligns the culture with the strategy. Because we're a big company – 92,000 people – we have a lot of different cultural challenges: for example, international acquisitions can be problematic, and our products and service lines tend to work as subcultures which can take things off in a wrong direction, particularly where there are clashes. My role is really to articulate and steward the culture to harmonise with the tone the CEO sets.

Chief culture officers

One organisation that has made culture management an explicit executive role is Google, which appointed Stacy Savides Sullivan in 2007 as its chief culture officer. She describes her brief as follows:[7]

To work with employees around the world to figure out ways to maintain and enhance and develop our culture and keep the core values we had in the very beginning – [supported by] a flat organisation, a lack of hierarchy, a collaborative environment – to keep these as we continue to grow and spread them and filtrate them into our new offices around the world.

We want all of our employees to play a part in being involved in keeping our culture the way it is today but also growing and developing it. So some of my role is coming up with different programs or processes, and some of it is just being there to talk with people when they have issues ... in their [sub]culture and [help them with] ideas on how to improve it.

Through the work that they do these designated stewards are constantly nudging and/or reinforcing an organisation's culture – as one HR champion talking about an organisational development and transformation project he was leading explained:

"The new CEO [brought up through the company's ranks] has involved me in a very wide-ranging business transformation, involving significant restructuring, a large reduction in workforce numbers, and a shift from what he believed was a too complex, too consensus-oriented organisation, with too much of an internal focus, and too little emphasis on project execution. He hasn't explicitly said he wants a culture change but that is implied in all the changes he is making. My accountability is to ensure that the culture does change in line with the new strategy and I am doing things like changing the incentive schemes to align with a performance culture, helping people make decisions in a different way, and so on. I haven't heralded a 'culture change programme' as my own bias is that we should not aim at changing culture per se, more that we should recognise it as an output of other things we change in the system and use the cultural assessment we already have in place to check that we are indeed making the changes we wanted. If nothing in our culture changes through this transformation, then nothing really happened!"

Culture owners

All the examples so far indicate the part that all employees (including those in the categories already discussed) play in creating, co-creating, fitting into and working with their organisation's culture. Everyone, to a greater or lesser extent, has that role, whether it is conscious or unconscious, and positive or negative in its outcome.

One manager spoke for many when asked the question: who owns and shapes the culture? His unhesitating response was:

> *Everybody does. We all have to be able to shape it. People can influence it by the way they behave. Individuals can make a difference. In my case I was told "you can't grow in this company because you haven't been in sales". I proved this wrong. By getting a leadership role without going through the sales route I shaped the culture a bit. Now I'm an example for others. Intelligent people sense what's going on – they see things changing as the behaviour of the group changes. Informally everyone has ownership and shapes it.*

In the AIG example on page 108, the traders were at least complicit in the creation of a culture of fear and could be said to be joint creators of it. Simply by virtue of working together, each in their own way and in line with their background and experiences, people have an impact on the culture and it has an impact on them – collectively they are de facto "owners" of it. How much they feel a sense of ownership or a pride in ownership depends on a number of factors. Generally, where people feel encouraged or able to take responsibility for the culture there is a greater sense of ownership of it. This is one of the hallmarks of a healthy culture,

Cultural accountability

Accountability and responsibility are often used interchangeably, but it is useful to distinguish them. Accountability means an employee's obligation to report progress, at the request of a third party, of agreements and expectations. In a hierarchical organisation, those held accountable can identify their own subordinates and hold them accountable for partial results. Responsibility means owning, or feeling a sense of ownership of, tasks and situations for which a person is accountable. Thus someone takes responsibility and is held accountable.

Christopher Avery of Responsibility Redefined, a consultancy, offers the following as a clarification of the two words:

> *If you have a manager and aren't clear about what you are held accountable for, you might want to take responsibility for finding out.*

Culture creators and culture stewards are accountable for the culture; in other words, they have a formal obligation to report on it to a third party. (This may not apply to the general stewardship of the culture by line managers.) The leader or chief executive's accountability is usually to a board of directors and the shareholders; the culture steward's accountability is to the CEO, often through a hierarchical chain of command.

Those able to give a good account of their nurturing of the culture recognise how and in what aspects it is of value and instigate actions to develop it. This means looking for opportunities to increase the cultural worth and being alert to potential damage in order to mitigate this. Those who have to report (or are called on to report) any cultural shortcomings and failures "take the rap" for this. Commenting in 2009 on the AIG case mentioned earlier, US Senator Charles Grassley, the top Republican on the Senate Finance Committee, said in an interview:[8]

> *AIG executives should perhaps "resign or go commit suicide", adopting what he called a Japanese approach to taking responsibility for their actions.*
>
> *[Later ...] Grassley retreated from those comments, but urged the executives to express regret, and perhaps to resign.*
>
> *"What I'm expressing here, obviously, is not that I want people to commit suicide," Grassley said ... "but I do feel very strongly that we have not had statements of apology, statements of remorse, statements of contrition on the part of CEOs of manufacturing companies or banks or financial services or insurance companies that are asking for bailouts, that they*

understand that they are responsible for running their corporation into the ground."

In this example, Grassley, in his role as a member of the Senate Finance Committee, is the third party to whom AIG executives are held accountable. And he makes the point about their need to take responsibility for their actions.

Typically, those accountable for the culture put in place explicit yardsticks that support the direction in which they want it to go. These are mostly in the form of measures, organisational controls, rewards, incentives and various criteria that allow or restrict access to recruitment, promotion, and training or development. But there are also implicit aspects that are more difficult for people to understand; for example, there may be unstated rules about the dress code, acceptable behaviour, or how quickly a response to an e-mail is required.

These yardsticks give people the information they need to make choices about how much they want to comply with the prevailing culture and how much they want to challenge it. Most people actively or tacitly agree to accept the written and unwritten requirements, norms and practices with which those accountable for the culture expect compliance. If people choose not to fit in (or simply do not) there may be consequences, such as formal and informal penalties or sanctions.

A well-publicised case in the UK illustrates the consequences of choosing not to fit in with the organisational culture. In October 2009, David Nutt was asked by the home secretary, Alan Johnson, to resign as chairman of the Advisory Council on the Misuse of Drugs (ACMD). In a letter, Johnson said to Nutt:[9]

> As home secretary it is for me to make decisions, having received advice from the [council] ... it is important that the government's messages on drugs are clear and as an adviser you do nothing to undermine the public understanding of them ... I am afraid the manner in which you have acted runs contrary to your responsibilities.

Taken at face value, this example can be summarised as shown in Table 5.1, leading to the conclusion that a clash was almost inevitable.

Table 5.1 **Accountability and responsibility**

Home secretary	Accountable to the prime minister. Responsible for giving the public clear messages about drugs.	Feels ownership in a culture where certain protocols, norms and behaviours must be followed if changes in established policy are to be explored or recommended.
David Nutt, chairman of the ACMD	Accountable to the home secretary. Responsible for giving honest and informed scientific opinion on drugs.	Feels ownership in a culture where opinions and policy are based on research evidence rather than political or moral positioning.

In the corporate world, compliance with and conformance to cultural norms usually mean an individual's participation is "tallied" in some form of regular and formal accounting process, for example performance appraisals. In these manager/employee discussions, the employees have to demonstrate that in the course of their work they have conformed to cultural expectations. In the following extract from a spoof performance appraisal of Albert Einstein (written by Peter Norvig, director of research at Google), it is evident that Einstein's manager feels that he falls short of the cultural expectations (of the patent office where they worked) around collaboration and teamwork:[10]

> Regrettably, I had to put you down as "poor" for "works well with others" and "shares credit appropriately". You had no co-authors on the five papers you published this year and you wrote that your special theory of relativity came to you after a discussion with your friend Michele Besso. But you didn't even acknowledge him in your June paper. This is an area for improvement.

The conversation as Einstein tried to account for his lack of conformance can only be imagined.

This example illustrates the point that an employee who wants to succeed (in this performance appraisal Einstein was not recommended for promotion) must make finely tuned judgments on what is culturally acceptable in relation to the immediate manager, the work group, the wider organisation and the external context. Employees are by regulation and by default accountable to the culture, and if they do not meet cultural expectations they are unlikely to stay with the company for long.

Cultural responsibility

In most organisations, the requirement to take responsibility for the role they play in the culture is an implied part of every employee's contract with the organisation. That is why, for example, Zappos looks for "cultural fit" in new staff and Gore takes the view that everyone is an owner of the company. Companies are looking for people who will support, protect and develop their culture.

However, the extent to which people feel or are able to exercise that ownership varies from organisation to organisation. At AIG, for example, people felt terrorised and fearful; because they felt no ownership in the culture they made no effort to change it. Conversely, Nutt believed that "policy should be based on evidence", saying "it's a bit odd to make policy that goes in the face of evidence". He was prepared to vigorously defend that view and take the consequences of doing so.

His being asked to resign illustrates the point that taking active responsibility for the culture, particularly if it involves a challenge to the established order, can be a minefield. As Robert Kennedy noted in 1966 when he was a US senator:[11]

> Few men are willing to brave the disapproval of their fellows, the censure of their colleagues, the wrath of their society. Moral courage is a rarer commodity than bravery in battle or great intelligence. Yet it is the one essential, vital quality for those who seek to change a world which yields most painfully to change.

Organisational life is hard on people who are at odds with its dominant culture. Typically, they have to tread a fine line between fitting in without compromising their values, or being extreme and strident, as Debra Meyerson, professor of education and organisational behaviour at Stanford University, who studies conditions and change strategies that remove inequities and foster productive intergroup relations, has found. She has written extensively about people she calls "tempered radicals": people who are both insiders and outsiders, working to fit in with what is culturally acceptable and to change the norms of acceptability. "It's about rocking the boat, but not so hard that you fall out of it."

She documents many success stories of these tempered radicals who are able to take responsibility for aspects of the culture because:[12]

> They have legitimacy and appreciate the mindsets the organisations work under ... They understand the culture and what it means to fit in. They do not undermine themselves or try to threaten the people in power.

By being what she describes as "cautious and committed catalysts" they create cultural change by "subtly calling into question taken-for-granted beliefs and work practices".[13]

This method of taking responsibility for the culture can have powerful effects, as illustrated by the story Meyerson tells of an employee in the HR department of Hewlett-Packard, a technology company, who, in the late 1990s, was interested in diversity. Her manager did not consider this a pressing issue but was happy for her to look at disability:[14]

> [The employee] organised a local network of employees with disabilities and then used their numbers to convince a small group of managers to declare a disability awareness day.

> "They didn't realise what I was going to do," the employee said. What she did was bring in people from 30 non-profit organisations to educate employees. She also borrowed 100 wheelchairs so that people at HP could feel what it was like to work in one. She got 100 sound-blocking devices so that people could experience deafness. She blindfolded employees and sent them on an obstacle course.

"That made all the difference," the employee said. "It trans-formed the worksite."

Over several years she won the confidence of senior managers and, with their support, began to produce workshops on a range of diversity topics, educating thousands of employees. In 2009 Hewlett-Packard was listed in *Diversity MBA Magazine* as one of the top 50 companies in diversity leadership:

Today, a global diversity division supports business success worldwide at the corporate level, and a diversity council of senior leadership from each HP business develops, directs and champions diversity initiatives. The company has several diversity-friendly policies and practices, including employee network groups and, since the '90s, domestic partner benefits.

Matthew Crawford's experience as a writer of abstracts of articles was quite different from that of the HP employee:[15]

My job was structured on the supposition that in writing an abstract there is a method that merely needs to be applied, and that this does not require understanding ... My starting quota after finishing a week of training was 15 articles per day. By my eleventh month at the company, my quota was up to 28 articles per day ... The quality standards were the generic ones of grammar ... which could be applied without my supervisor having to read the article ... the metric to which I answered ... was purely quantitative.

So the job required both dumbing down and a bit of moral re-education. [I] felt trapped in a contradiction. The fast pace demanded absorption in the task, yet that pace also precluded absorption, and had the effect of estranging me from my own doings. Or rather I tried to absent myself, the better to meet my quota, but the writing of an abstract ... cannot be done mind-lessly ... To not do justice to an author who had poured his life into the subject at hand felt like violence against what was best in myself.

Over lunch Mike (a work colleague) would recount the outra-geous things he had written in his abstracts ... I could see my own future in such furtive moments of sabotage.

Rather than rock the boat, Crawford went along with what was asked of him, essentially "checking his values at the door". After 11 months he left the job to take a doctorate in political philosophy and followed this with a job as executive director of a think-tank. Five months later he decided to open a motorbike repair shop, where he has been working as a craftsman mechanic for over ten years.

Cultural accountability and responsibility

In an ideal world there would be complete clarity about who has cultural accountability and how much and what type of cultural responsibility is encouraged or can be taken. Some organisations, such as Zappos (see Chapter 2) and Gore (see Chapter 4), have that high degree of clarity; but in others it is more opaque and results in one or more of five situations. In each of these, many of the ten characteristics that typically comprise a healthy culture and make it a valuable intangible asset are missing (see Chapter 4).

Accountability takes precedence over responsibility

In this case the formal systems to evaluate performance are given more weight by the individual and/or the organisation than taking responsibility for a sensible outcome. Whether or not the following story is true, it reflects the kind of "jobsworth" behaviour that is common today:[16]

> Agatha Christie [a thriller writer] was the guest of honour at a Foyles literary luncheon. The doorman asked her for her invitation and refused to admit her, even though she told him she was the guest of honour, when she couldn't produce it. She didn't make any fuss and just went home.

This is an example of someone (in this case the doorman) who feels that the thing he is being held accountable for is more important than taking responsibility, showing initiative, or even acting sensibly. This type of behaviour is common in organisations where the culture is tightly controlled and those who step out of line are penalised.

119

In the United States and the UK television programmes have shown CEOs of companies going *Back to the Floor* (UK) or being the *Undercover Boss* (United States). The intent of both programmes is similar: to enable company executives to experience what it is like at the front line of their organisation. Several of the scenarios presented suggest that line managers are being held accountable for getting virtually unachievable results, and in pursuit of these they put extreme pressure on the workforce.

Larry O'Donnell, CEO of Waste Management, spent one of his days as undercover boss on an assembly line picking cardboard and other recyclables off a fast-moving line of rubbish. The *Baltimore Sun* reported:[17]

> At the end of his day on the line ... he can hardly believe how mentally and physically exhausted he feels. He also vows to find out which middle manager is responsible for a policy in which workers like the one who generously showed him how to work the line are docked two minutes' pay for every minute they clock in late.

As his experience progressed:

> O'Donnell has had a lot of epiphanies about how hard-pressed some of the workers are – and how some of the policies that come out of his big office are responsible for their pain. He works on a two-person crew on a garbage truck in upstate New York, and the woman who drives the truck explains that they are under such a tight quota for the number of garbage cans they must empty in each shift that there is no time for bathroom breaks. She shows him an empty coffee can she uses instead. She also points out the company truck parked in the shadows that "spies" on her and other drivers. O'Donnell looks as if he can't believe it.

In this instance what can be judged as a "culture of results", or "getting more with less", where targets are unrealistic, has a demoralising effect all round and squashes possibilities of taking responsibility for making the culture healthier.

Confusion over who should take cultural responsibility

In many organisations it is not clear who should take cultural responsibility or what it would look like. There are many reasons why this might be the case. The following example relates to the investigation of the Ponzi scheme operated by Bernard Madoff, which swindled investors out of what was estimated at around $65 billion.

The US Securities and Exchange Commission, whose mission is "to protect investors, maintain fair, orderly, and efficient [financial] markets, and facilitate capital formation", received many tips and warnings about Madoff's business operation in the years preceding his arrest. After this, a ten-month investigation conducted by the SEC's inspector general, H. David Kotz, revealed chronic ineptitude to deal with the warnings, as the *New York Times* reported:[18]

> The newly public documents [late 2009] do not add fresh charges to the official findings, but they do provide a vivid sense of the tensions, confusion and petty squabbles that derailed a half-dozen failed inquiries.

> Some interviews describe a culture where understaffed investigations languished for months before sputtering out, unresolved. Others evoke an environment that became openly dismissive of anonymous tips, like some of the early Madoff warnings.

> In one e-mail message, a senior lawyer in the agency's New York office said he thought "we should get out of the business of burning resources to chase Ponzi schemes".

> He later explained in an interview that he thought investigations of Ponzi schemes should be left to other agencies with criminal jurisdiction. Several young staff members said those views had shaped their own misguided decisions in the Madoff inquiries.

Clearly it is difficult to say how this situation arose or what it was like working in it, but the example touches upon a number of cultural factors including: the possibility that employees do not recognise the choices they have; a possible lack of organisational purpose or established values; the examples the leaders were setting; a shrugging off of responsibilities; a lack of clarity on accountability; an inability to collaborate or share information.

To change a culture in which people are confused about when and how to take responsibility is clearly difficult. Mary Schapiro was appointed chair of the SEC on January 20th (sworn in on January 27th) 2009 – soon after Madoff was arrested for running the scheme (December 11th 2008) – with a brief to reform the commission. She commented on the task a year later (February 2010):[19]

> Reform can take more time than one might have thought at the outset. We have to understand the real-life implications of what we're doing, the unintended consequences. We need to digest all the comments and all the economic analysis. And that leads us down a path that sometimes isn't 100% predictable at the beginning.

(Chapter 7 discusses the question of whether culture can be changed.)

Not taking responsibility

In some cases employees appear not to be in a position to want to take cultural responsibility. The assembly-line workers at Waste Management mentioned earlier may well feel that way. Similarly, Alain de Botton, a British philosopher and writer, takes a tour of the United Biscuits factory in Lambermont, Belgium, and observes the production line:[20]

> Two middle-aged women in hairnets sat facing each other over a moving rubber carpet, looking out for the smallest fault in the texture of dough, and occasionally reaching over to pick out an offending biscuit, their concentrated stares suggesting that they were engaged in a tense game of draughts.

It might be that they enjoy their work, but it does make de Botton wonder. Dilbert, the cartoon character created by Scott Adams, appeals to all workers who, like him (Dilbert), experience, in the analysis of Pamela Johnson and Julie Indvik, both professors at California State University:[21]

> The basic disregard to his dignity as a human being, which is the biggest problem in workplaces generally. People, plagued by abusive bosses, pointless rules and meaningless strategies, live for the weekend, doing as little as possible to get through the workweek. The result is a workplace that is very much like that of a Dilbert cartoon – but a heck of a lot less funny. And what is particularly sad is that most people do not expect anything better.

> Plagued by a heartless boss, confined to a featureless cubicle and forced to endure the Great Lies of Management ("Employees are our most valuable assets"), Dilbert is a bespectacled engineer who ventures through corporate Wonderland. The comic strip is also about human rights, human purpose, the human potential. Yet, the popularity of Dilbert reflects the fact that many people find their jobs futile, boring and non-productive.

When people feel they are powerless, why would they want or venture to take responsibility? In Dilbert-like situations, the ten characteristics that comprise a healthy culture are nearly all missing or not felt and experienced by workers, who thus have no sense of ownership of the culture.

Taking responsibility from outside the system

A visitor walking into an organisation might have a hard time working out who are direct employees and who are indirect employees, such as contractors, temporary workers or consultants whose work contributes to the performance of the company but who are not usually included in its performance-appraisal system, training courses, staff events, internal communication network and other aspects of the formal framework that supports the culture. Their status is simultaneously insider and outsider. In a sense they are tourists in the organisation with restrictions attached to their stay. Nevertheless, they have to fit in with and get on in the culture, take appropriate responsibility for it, and be accountable to it.

If managed poorly there may be frictions, but if managed well these "outsiders" can bring a different and perhaps welcome perspective. A website-design contractor describes her experience:[22]

> *Firstly you really do have to hit the ground running. You're there as a temporary (highly skilled) worker, and you don't have time to settle in. The company you're working for doesn't have time to introduce you to everyone or take you through a long-winded explanation of their systems or the way they work – you're there to do a job, and you're expected to pretty much get your head down and get on with it.*

> *You go into a new company knowing maybe one or two people there – but the rest of the employees don't know you from a bar of soap – and you have to prove to them on a daily basis that (a) you know what you're doing, (b) you don't need much help from them, and (c) you're worth the money.*

> *To me, this means working with 150% effort the whole time – and it also means being infinitely flexible. I'm there to make everyone else's job easier, which means when they say "jump", I really do have to ask "how high?".*

Just as tourists, in having their expectations met in return for contributing to the economy, influence a nation's culture, so indirect employees influence the culture of the organisation. Depending on what they are in the organisation to do and their level of skill and expertise, contractors, temporary staff, consultants, suppliers, analysts who comment on the organisation all play a part in the culture dynamic that cannot be ignored.

Accountability is diffused

If it is not possible to see a direct connection in accountabilities – from the CEO and executive levels down the organisational chart to where value is created at the interface with a customer or client – then they are diffused. This happens where people are aiming at more than one target. Take the case where some people in an organisation may be held accountable for increased customer satisfaction, some for sales growth and others for introducing new product lines, with little connection between them. This makes for confusion, which is compounded if those held accountable have no control over the mechanisms that will help them achieve the target. In this instance a customer relationship management (CRM) system may be crucial to all three targets, but because they are not all aimed in the same direction the system is producing information that meets no one's needs. The managers who need the information do not "own" the CRM system and thus cannot either individually or collectively make it work effectively for them.

Aligned accountabilities are essential to a healthy culture. A company that appears to have now got it right is Unilever, a consumer-goods company. Paul Polman was appointed CEO in January 2009 with a clear brief to galvanise the company. In his first nine months he earned a reputation for delivering results, and Unilever posted four quarters of volume growth that year. According to an article in the *Daily Mail* in February 2010, he "sent a lightning rod through sleepy Unilever".

In an interview in 2009, Polman described the "performance culture" he and his leadership team were aiming for. It is based less on strategy and more on execution:[23]

> We make it very clear that execution is important here. Supporting the performance culture are discipline, accountability, reward structures, measurements, and rigorous follow through – all focused on delivering high performance ... You have to walk the talk here as well. So, when we go to store visits or in-home visits, we do roll up our sleeves. We talk to consumers, and we put the products on the shelf that are needed.

Under Polman's direction Unilever aligned the ten characteristics of an organisation culture so that they were all focused on delivering the performance culture he wanted to create. Employees were held accountable to clear targets and objectives.

Recap points

▶ Assign a single point of accountability (usually the CEO) whose job is to define, model and nurture the culture through various rewards and sanctions and make clear to members of the organisation what the cultural expectations are.

▶ Have specialists (human resources staff, organisation development consultants and chief culture officers) who are responsible for stewarding, supporting and directing the culture.

▶ Make it clear to all members of the organisation that everyone is responsible for the culture, has an ownership stake in it and is accountable to it. (Those who "check their values at the door" are still making cultural statements.)

▶ If a number of people have a measure of delegated accountability for the culture – through job performance objectives or suchlike – make sure that they are all working in the same, agreed cultural direction.

▶ Indirect employees such as contractors and commentators on an organisation's culture have an impact on it and should be included in cultural discussions.

▶ People have different perspectives on what taking responsibility for the culture is in practice. Getting a good balance between fitting in and rocking the boat is both an individual and an organisational trade-off.

▶ Formal systems such as pay systems and job titles for supporting the culture should be aligned with the informal systems, practices and ways of doing things.

One company's way of owning the culture: Toyota

The early 2010 recall of more than 8m Toyota vehicles because of possible problems with unintended acceleration, and then thousands of the latest model Prius because of the momentary loss of braking capacity in some environments, has severely stressed Toyota's market reputation and credibility. In the words of Jeffrey Liker, professor of industrial and operations engineering at the University of Michigan and author of several books on Toyota:[24]

> There is a lot of speculation of what Toyota did and did not do right in the past that allowed these problems to occur and we will probably never get all the facts ... I think it is more useful now to focus on what Toyota can learn for the future. Toyota Business Practices would say:
>
> 1. Brutally confront the actual facts of what happened.

2. Find the root cause through five-why questioning, going deeper than this particular problem to identify system causes.

3. Diligently put in place countermeasures.

4. Monitor the results to continue learning.

... It would be tragic if organisations that have looked up to Toyota as a model of a lean enterprise suddenly concluded that lean does not work. I believe the success of Toyota over the last six decades has proved the principles of lean regardless of what happens to Toyota going forward. I would certainly hate to see other companies give up their pursuit of excellence because Toyota was found to be human and less than perfect.

The success of Toyota up to that point was phenomenal. In 2008 it had surpassed General Motors (GM) to become the number one car manufacturer in the world. This was the first time in 77 years that an automaker other than GM had been top dog in global auto sales. During 2008, Toyota sold 8.9m vehicles worldwide compared with GM's 8.35m. In his first communication after his appointment in June 2009 as president of Toyota, Akio Toyoda, the grandson of the founder, outlined the secret of the company's success to that point.

Toyota has overcome many challenges during its seven decades of business. What has made this possible is the way we make our cars under our "customer first" and "genchi genbutsu" [go to the source and see for yourself] principles. Furthermore, all Toyota companies around the world have risen to the challenge each time to engage in technological innovation and increased productivity.

The principles Toyoda mentions are part of "The Toyota Way", which, in the words of Steven Atkins (a pseudonym), a 16-year veteran of Toyota, has its roots in the work of W. Edwards Deming, who was invited to Japan after the second world war by the Japanese government. He had a group of students from Toyota who embraced his teachings on the 14 points for transformation of American industry and adopted them into the company. The 14 points listed below apply equally to any size or type of organisation and/or to a business unit within an organisation.[25]

1 Create constancy of purpose toward improvement of product and service, with the aim to become competitive and to stay in business, and to provide jobs.

2 Adopt the new philosophy. We are in a new economic age.

Western management must awaken to the challenge, must learn their responsibilities, and take on leadership for change.

3 Cease dependence on inspection to achieve quality. Eliminate the need for inspection on a mass basis by building quality into the product in the first place.

4 End the practice of awarding business on the basis of price tag. Instead, minimise total cost. Move towards a single supplier for any one item, on a long-term relationship of loyalty and trust.

5 Improve constantly and forever the system of production and service, to improve quality and productivity, and thus constantly decrease costs.

6 Institute training on the job.

7 Institute leadership (see point 12 and Chapter 8). The aim of supervision should be to help people and machines and gadgets to do a better job. Supervision of management is in need of overhaul, as well as supervision of production workers.

8 Drive out fear, so that everyone may work effectively for the company (see Chapter 3).

9 Break down barriers between departments. People in research, design, sales and production must work as a team, to foresee problems of production and in use that may be encountered with the product or service.

10 Eliminate slogans, exhortations and targets for the workforce asking for zero defects and new levels of productivity. Such exhortations only create adversarial relationships, as the bulk of the causes of low quality and low productivity belong to the system and thus lie beyond the power of the workforce.

▶ Eliminate work standards (quotas) on the factory floor. Substitute leadership.

▶ Eliminate management by objective. Eliminate management by numbers, numerical goals. Substitute leadership.

11 Remove barriers that rob the hourly worker of his right to pride of workmanship. The responsibility of supervisors must be changed from sheer numbers to quality.

12 Remove barriers that rob people in management and in engineering of their right to pride of workmanship. This means,

inter alia, abolishment of the annual or merit rating and of management by objective (see Chapter 3).

13 Institute a vigorous programme of education and self-improvement.

14 Put everybody in the company to work to accomplish the transformation. The transformation is everybody's job.

These principles were codified as "The Toyota Way" in 2001 under Fujio Cho, the company's president from 1999 to 2005, who was concerned about the global expansion. He felt that the wisdom and principles would not be accurately transferred from location to location without a standardised guide. Underpinning the principles are a number of quotes from previous patriarchs of Toyota, including several by Taiichi Ohno on the Toyota production system (TPS) and one that is particularly relevant now: "Costs do not exist to be calculated. Costs exist to be reduced."

The point is that there is a standard way of operating that has been codified and that all employees are taught from day one with the company. Specifically, company employees are expected to:

▶ base their management decisions on a long-term philosophy, even at the expense of short-term financial goals;

▶ generate value for the customer, society and the economy;

▶ align the organisation towards a common goal that is bigger than making money;

▶ be responsible;

▶ strive to determine their own fate;

▶ accept responsibility for their conduct.

Beyond these precepts there is a shared vocabulary related to the continuous improvement process and a reflective approach. Thus people in the company are familiar with the concepts of, for example, *muda* (waste), *muri* (overburden), *mura* (unevenness), *jidoka* (standardise tasks), *andon* (signal for help), *genchi genbutsu* (go to the source and see for yourself), *hansei* (relentless reflection) and *kaisen* (continuous improvement). The common vocabulary, the standardised processes and the constant reinforcement of the Toyota mindset (embodied in the principles) helps to integrate people from many nationalities and backgrounds into a distinctive culture that has been a powerful force in driving the company's success.

Conformance to the culture is the price of entry. Atkins confirms that:

> Everyone has to have the attitude of hansei, which requires an admission that there are always better ways to do things. The better way becomes a standard until the new better way is found. An example is the way a horn is tested. In America a machine tests a horn a hundred thousand times – a high level of testing given that Americans outside of cities like New York sound their horns relatively rarely. But in India people use their horns all the time so a different testing standard is required, and we've had to find a better way of horn testing using our principles of genchi genbutsu.

Having said this, Atkins noted wryly that the Toyota Way of constructive criticism to reach a better way of doing things "is not always received in good spirit at home".

Asked who is responsible for the culture, Atkins replied:

> Since President Cho's time no one person has been designated as the champion, but the Way has been continuously reinforced through the training and development function and through on the job training. New hires are taught the Toyota Way and it is reinforced on the job. Everybody is engaged in the Toyota Way and is responsible for it. Its principles are reinforced on a daily basis in every place of work by everyone from top to bottom starting with the president – I can't point to any designated champions of it.

The reinforcement is not only through teaching, social pressure and example but also through rigorous monitoring, control and feedback systems. Many of these are simple visuals but they alert the teams to areas for investigation, hansei [relentless reflection], problem solving and improvement. Liker, author of *The Toyota Way*, commenting on the control tools and the people, summarises as follows:[26]

> The more I have studied TPS and the Toyota Way, the more I understand that it is a system designed to provide the tools for people to continually improve their work. The Toyota Way means more dependence on people, not less. It is a culture, even more than a set of efficiency and improvement techniques. You depend upon the workers to reduce inventory, identify hidden problems, and fix them. The workers have a sense of urgency, purpose, and teamwork because if they don't fix it there will be an inventory outage. On a daily basis, engineers, skilled workers, quality specialists, vendors,

team leaders, and – most importantly – operators are all involved in continuous problem solving and improvement, which over time trains everyone to become better problem solvers.

Although Toyoda may not be champion of the culture any more than anyone else in the company is, he is a prime example of a leader who walks the talk. Atkins says:

Wherever he goes he engages with people on the plant floor. Last summer [August 2009] he made his first speech to senior automotive industry leaders at a conference in Traverse City. At the airport there were four cars waiting for him including the Lexus with the security personnel and driver and a Venza developed at the Tech Centre which he'd seen in the previous year. He surprised everyone by not getting into the Lexus to be driven to the office, but walking straight to the Venza. He gave it a thorough inspection and then asked if he could drive it. He took the keys and drove himself to the office in it. He's a very hands-on person. His philosophy is a practical one of "I need to be engaged in this". He does it. He doesn't just speak it and that sets the tone for everyone.

Leading by example – behaving the way they expect people to behave and doing what they are trying to encourage in others – gives clear signals from leaders to employees. (Toyoda's grandfather Kiichiro Toyoda showed his belief in both his principles and his leadership style, resigning as president of the company in the 1950s when his company was forced to reorganise and lay off a large number of people, undermining the firm's value of giving someone a job for life.) Atkins reinforces the fact that leaders encourage people to go beyond their immediate environment to learn how to improve their products:

A lot of engineers try driving competitor vehicles, speak with dealers, and design stuff in line with what they're hearing and learning about. We're encouraged by the company to minimise the gap between the customer and the designer.

The attitude of continuous learning is also ingrained in the culture. Atkins observes:

The chairman's father travels the world (he's 86) constantly talking with people on site and asking questions. We are a learning organisation. There's an expectation that people who are properly engaged in reflective thinking will suggest changes as it's only by thinking that products get changed and improved. I can't emphasise it enough, the learning process is the cultural process. We are a culture of learning. Toyota is a company not satisfied with "good enough" – everything can get better. Toyota is raising the bar from one generation of products to the next. For example, we are now on the eighth version of the Camry and each version is a significant improvement on the previous one. We are all responsible for keeping that culture alive.

It is hard to tell at this stage whether Toyota's culture will prove its salvation or its downfall as it struggles to get to grips with the harsh conditions faced by the car industry as a whole and its own specific difficulties. If it truly is a learning organisation, it may well learn to learn differently with a good outcome. If the strength of the culture has locked people into learning a specific way, the mindset and processes may not be flexible enough to meet the different challenges it now faces. The cultural asset may turn into a liability for which the leaders are more likely to be held accountable than the employees.

Learning from Toyota

Three lessons come out of Toyota's approach to cultural account-ability and responsibility:

▶ **Having a clear set of consistent instructions, the Toyota Way, about how things are done in the organisation makes it easy for employees to understand what they are responsible for and who they are accountable to.** In Toyota it is clear that every employee must be an active participant in maintaining and living the Toyota Way. Although there are aspects of it that reflect differently in different countries, for the most part all employees either conform to this expectation and work with it or do not join the organisation. There is little room for hangers-on.

▶ **Having leaders who demonstrably "walk the talk" and take the responsibility and accountability they expect from others sends clear signals on expectations to the whole organisation.** From the president down, all leaders and managers role-model the behaviours and practices embodied in the Toyota Way. It is seen as a positive attribute by staff and observers of the company. The fact that Toyoda will crawl under a car to inspect it in the middle of an official visit to a factory may be surprising to some, but it indicates his passion to stay close to what is going on.

▶ **Achieving a culture that is both tightly controlled and flexible enough to adapt to changing circumstances is a fine line to tread.** In Toyota's case, having processes and systems that look for continuous improvement in all things is admirable, and has been the envy of many companies. However, overcontrol, even of a continuous improvement process, brings its own pitfalls. On October 9th 2009 the New York Times reported that Toyoda said:[27]

> His company was shamefully unprepared for the global economic crisis that has devastated the auto industry, and is a step away from "capitulation to irrelevance or death". The company, he added, is "grasping for salvation".

At the time of writing (April 2010) the jury is out on whether it will survive or die.

Summary

▶ Owning the culture is part of every employee's role. Everyone can and should take responsibility to fit in, meet cultural expectations and/or develop the culture. People who choose to abdicate that responsibility may suffer sanctions.

▶ Accountability for the culture – defining or reinforcing the norms and expectations – is primarily the role of the CEO with the support of other champions.

▶ Where accountability for the culture is assigned to several people they must all be aligned on what they are accountable for and how this will be measured. It is better to have fewer people accountable for the culture than many.

Exercise 5: Determining accountability and responsibility in Appendix 3 is an exercise to create discussion about the clarity of accountability and responsibility for the culture of an organisation.

6

What is the right organisation culture?

In the chapter "Learning to Love Your Corporate Culture" in his book *Liar's Poker*, Michael Lewis gives an account of his time as a trainee in the mid-1980s at Salomon Brothers, a Wall Street investment bank:[1]

> The man was telling us how to survive. "You've got to think of Salomon Brothers as like a jungle," he said ... "and the guy you end up working for is your jungle leader. Whether you succeed here or not depends on knowing how to survive in the jungle. You've got to learn from your boss. He's key."

He reports that:

> Life as a Salomon trainee was like being beaten up every day by the neighbourhood bully. Eventually you grew mean and surly ... The firm never took you aside and rubbed you on the back to let you know that everything was going to be fine. Just the opposite, the firm built a system around the belief that trainees should wriggle and squirm.

And he goes on to note that the relevant bits of his training:

> ... were the war stories, the passing on of the oral tradition of Salomon Brothers. Over three months leading salesmen, traders and financiers shared their experiences with the class. They trafficked in unrefined street wisdom: how money travels around the world (any way it wants), how a trader feels and behaves (any way he wants), and how to schmooze a customer ... All the while there was a hidden agenda: to Salomonise the trainee.

Although the book was written over 20 years ago, the lessons that can be drawn from the extract still stand: the purpose of any induction process is to develop in new employees a basis of language and experience about the organisation to a point where they are sharing "systems of meaning that are accepted, internalised, and acted on at every level of the organisation"[2] so that employees are then able to operate effectively within the organisation and create value for it.

At a practical level, shared systems of meaning come down to learning and understanding the purpose of an organisation's explicit rules, policies and procedures and through conversations and other means, such as discovering the implicit rules that govern the way the organisation works. It is these implicit and explicit aspects of the way work gets done in an organisation that both inform and are informed by the culture. According to Lewis, the shared systems of meaning at Salomon Brothers involved "understanding that the unbridled pursuit of perceived self-interest was healthy. Eat or be eaten". (Chapter 8 discusses whether culture can be learned.)

Lewis then had to make sense of the myriad rules behind Salomon Brothers' systems of meaning, and determine how to fit them into his frame of reference and act in accordance with them. It was not easy:

> There were a million little rules to obey; I knew none of them. Salesmen, traders, and managers swarmed over the floor, and at first I could not tell them apart ... Most of the men stared at small green screens full of numbers. They'd shout into one phone, then into the other, then at someone across the row of trading desks, then back to the phones, then point to the screen and scream.

Lewis did his job well for three years before deciding to leave because for him:

> The belief in making the dollars crumbled; the proposition that the more money you earn, the better the life you are leading was refuted by too much hard evidence to the contrary. And without that belief, I lost the need to make huge sums of money

... It is a small piece of education, but still the most useful thing I picked up at Salomon Brothers.

One way of defining organisation culture is as an "active living phenomenon through which people jointly create and recreate the worlds in which they live";[3] in other words, they are able to make sense of their organisation's systems of meaning and believe in them. When, as Lewis did, they lose faith in the meaning, they generally take one of three routes: they leave the organisation voluntarily; they become "presentees" (being physically at work but mentally elsewhere, doing the minimum needed to avoid any penalties); or they become actively antagonistic to it (and may then be forced out).

In every culture there is the drive to share meaning and make sense of things. In the book *Good Work*, Mihaly Csikszentmihalyi points out:[4]

> *Every culture that has endured and that has advanced the human condition ... has had a coherent view of the universe. The cosmologies that the Chinese, the Indians, the Aztecs, or the Judeo Christian West invented may appear inadequate or even bizarre in hindsight. But they did provide direction to people's actions and a justification for their lives.*

Often it is stories, myths and legends that help generate shared meaning and making sense of things, as was the case at Salomon Brothers. This is also illustrated in the explanations people have for natural phenomena. For example, stories explaining thunder, or lightning, or the existence of stars are told in many cultures and take many different forms, but all are based on developing a shared system of meaning and sensemaking. In Norse legend thunder is made sense of through the explanation that it is caused by the war god Thor's chariot wheels.

Taking the drive to share meaning and make sense of things into the realm of work, Alain de Botton asks: "When does a job feel meaningful?" He answers it saying: "Whenever it allows us to generate delight or reduce suffering in others." He goes on to say:[5]

> *Though we are often taught to think of ourselves as inherently selfish, the longing to act meaningfully in our work seems just*

as stubborn a part of our make-up as our appetite for status or money.

This view implies that the right organisational culture is one where people feel they are doing meaningful work and can make sense of it in their scheme of things. This view also underlies what is covered in this chapter, even though the resonance that Scott Adams's Dilbert cartoons and the TV programme *The Office* have with so many people indicates that organisations with truly "meaningful" cultures are very much the exception.

Culture and good work

Research and experience suggest that most workers aspire to do "good work", defined as work that is of high quality (excellent), socially responsible (ethical) and meaningful to the worker (engaging).[6] This notion of good work brings into play the idea that the right organisation culture is one that supports the well-being of those who work for it and of society as a whole.

Marriott Hotels International, a hotel group established in 1927 by J. Willard and Alice Marriott, is an example of a company where this is the case. It is now run by their son, Bill Marriott, whose blog gives a flavour of the way the company is run. His entry for June 25th 2009, for example, has the title "Embracing Marriott's Extended Family". The final paragraph reads:[7]

> *My dad was an incredibly smart businessman, but first and foremost, he was a family man and instilled those family values in our company. That's why, at Marriott, we take so much pride in our associates, our owners and our guests and care for them as if they were a part of our extended family.*

The company ethos is one of paying close attention to the well-being of its employees and franchisees around the world. It scores well on the Ethical Score awarded by Corporate Critic (www.corporatecritic.org) and is a regular award-winner on various "good company" lists. For example, in 2009 Marriott Hotels International ranked number 4 in the *Sunday Times* 20 Best Big Companies to Work For list.

This ranking is derived from statistically analysed, valid and reliable surveys sent to UK employees, so it reports on quantitative data only. The methodology is clearly explained in *Best Companies Methodology* (www.bestcompanies.co.uk). An organisation's score depends on how highly its employees rate it according to the eight factors the survey measures:

▶ Leadership. How employees feel about the head of the organisation, senior managers, and the organisation's values and principles.

▶ My manager. How employees feel about and communicate with their direct manager.

▶ Personal growth. What employees feel about training and their future prospects.

▶ Well-being. How employees feel about stress, pressure at work and work–life balance.

▶ My team. Employees' feelings towards their immediate colleagues and how well they work together.

▶ Giving something back. The extent to which employees feel their organisation has a positive impact on society.

▶ My company. The level of engagement employees have with their job and the organisation.

▶ Fair deal. How happy employees are with their pay and benefits.

The instructions for companies participating in the process make the point that each organisation should look only at its own data and determine what, in the results, is important to its performance. The report on Marriott Hotels International, relating only to its UK operation, commented:[8]

> There is a culture of respect and recognition, and there is training specifically on teamwork, a quality prized by the company ... Staff say that senior managers truly live the values of the organisation (71%), help them fulfil their potential (71%) and motivate them to give their best every day (70%). Furthermore, 69% of Marriott UK staff thought senior managers were excellent role models and 75% said that they regularly show appreciation.

Comments by individual employees in other countries where Marriott Hotels operates put flesh on the UK survey facts, suggesting that there is an integrated, overarching culture.

For example, an employee in India (who is also an Indian national) made the point:

> A unique thing in this place is the work culture. I think all associates are treated equally. At an individual level there are differences but no one turns their back when someone actually needs help.

While Mohammad Karzai, an American employee originally from Afghanistan, has worked for 27 years for the company as a restaurant server. He comments:[9]

> I remember Mr Marriott and his family coming into the Kona Kai and we reserved them the same table every Sunday for the brunch. He knew us by name and remembered our stories, so whenever he came in, he'd ask about my family.

Karzai, an immigrant from Afghanistan, credits Marriott Hotels for helping him get started in the United States:

> I didn't have much when I came here. Marriott gave me a job that entitled me to wonderful benefits: a credit union where I could get a loan to buy my first car, a flexible schedule and other things. No wonder I've been here so long.

Alice Rodriguez, a senior programmer/analyst at Marriott Hotels' head office, says:[10]

> After 30 years, I still look forward to coming to work because my team is great to work with. We each have our individual assignments, but everyone instinctively pulls together when the need arises.

However, it is important to note that individual employees pick different aspects of what makes their work meaningful. In this respect, the integration, differentiation and fragmentation aspects of culture, discussed in Chapter 1, are evident at an individual level:

▶ Integration – employees share what it means to work in an

Table 6.1 **Cultural framework for good work**

Integration	The organisation has: ▶ a clearly defined direction focused on profitability, people, places and purpose; ▶ stated it that will do more good than harm through its products, services or other outputs; ▶ a leader who leads in a consistent way, setting an example of the behaviours and values he wants to see demonstrated throughout the organisation.
Differentiation	Employees: ▶ have opportunities for learning and development socially, cognitively and emotionally (and are encouraged to take them); ▶ do work that supports their well-being and is on balance enjoyable, although it may be hard; ▶ find their work meaningful and are clear about the contribution they make and where it fits in. One person described it as having "work that's real, that counts, that matters for people, and to be in a place where you care about the folks around you and know that they care about you".[a]
Fragmentation	Each employee: ▶ feels that their skills and capabilities are sufficiently recognised and deployed; ▶ gets timely, detailed and constructive feedback, and feels trusted and respected, whatever their position.

a Csikszentmihalyi, M., *Good Business*, Penguin Books, 2003.

international hotel chain. At a simplistic level it is serving the guests/customers.

▶ Differentiation – employees have different roles, each of which has its own system of meaning within the overall Marriott systems of meaning.

▶ Fragmentation – employees make sense of their roles in terms of what they most get out of them at an individual level whether it be good benefits or working in a team.

These three aspects, here exemplified by Marriott, can be used to develop a cultural framework that enshrines the concept of "good work" (see Table 6.1).

Right culture versus wrong culture

Given that company cultures should enable and encourage good and meaningful work it is naive to assume that this can be accomplished only in a specific type of organisational culture or that one type of culture is right for all organisations.

Rex Tillerson, CEO of ExxonMobil, describes his company's top-down command-and-control culture of consistency and discipline as "the source of our competitive advantage", and has made it a priority to reinforce it. But different cultures suit different companies. When Disney acquired Pixar, an animated film production studio, in 2006, Steve Jobs remarked:[11]

> Most of the time that Bob [Iger] and I have spent talking about this hasn't been about economics, it's been about preserving the Pixar culture (of collaboration) because we all know that's the thing that's going to determine the success here in the long run.

Ed Catmull, one of the founders of Pixar, comments on the collaborative aspects of the culture:[12]

> Of great importance – and something that sets us apart from other studios – is the way people at all levels support one another. Everyone is fully invested in helping everyone else turn out the best work. They really do feel that it's all for one and one for all. Nothing exemplifies this more than our creative brain trust and our daily review process. [Both these are methods of getting immediate and constructive feedback on the progress of productions.]

Given Pixar's and Exxon's different cultural styles, it is interesting to note that managers often discuss organisation culture in terms of polarities, with "collaborative" being felt to be the right type

Table 6.2 **Collaborative versus controlling**

Culture	Characterised by	"Right" when ...	"Wrong" when ...
Collaborative (focused on relationships)	"Mutually beneficial relationships between two or more parties who work together toward common goals by sharing responsibility, authority, and accountability for achieving results ... to address concerns that go beyond [those] of any particular party."[a]	People talk to each other about the actions that should be taken. The organisation's infrastructure hierarchy or chain of command facilitates such discussions. There is a common pool of reliable data and information that people can draw upon.	What is professed is not done – people say they are collaborative but there is little evidence of this. People are unwilling to learn from others or give up their way of doing things. Collaboration means different things to different people.
Controlling (focused on monitoring)	A combination of: – formal systems that pay close attention to outcomes; – finely tuned social systems that govern attitudes and behaviour.[b] Both involve the monitoring and correcting of any deviations from norms, expectations and requirements.	There is a clear chain of command. Individuals are respected and trusted regardless of their rank in the hierarchy. There is rigorous adherence to standards.	People feel manipulated or coerced and micromanaged, and are afraid to speak out.

a Chrislip, D.D. and Larson, C.E., *Collaborative Leadership: How Citizens and Civic Leaders Can Make a Difference*, Jossey-Bass, 1994.
b O'Reilly, C., "Corporation, culture and commitment: motivation and social control in organizations", *California Management Review*, Vol. 31, No. 4, 1989.

of culture and "controlling" the wrong type of culture, and that leaders tend to talk of a desire to change their organisation's culture "from" something "to" something else.

One danger of such polarised thinking is that it does not allow for:[13]

> The great likelihood that there are multiple organisation subcultures, or even countercultures, competing to define the nature of situations [that is, shape the culture and behaviour] within organisational boundaries.

It is normal for the overarching cultural statement to be reflected differently in different parts of the organisation.

Another danger is that it excludes the possibility that people can do meaningful, good, enjoyable work and make sense of the part they play in the organisation in a culture that might be considered "wrong". To illustrate that cultures are more nuanced than right or wrong, Tables 6.2–6.5 outline cultures commonly paired as opposites, the first in the pair being "right" and the second "wrong". The tables and the examples that follow demonstrate that cultures are rarely pure "either/or" (which is why a cultural label can be misleading) but are much more likely to be "both/and".

Example: The Royal Marines

Both controlling:

The Royal Marines like other military organisations have a clear and well-established hierarchy and chains of command. Deference to authority is a matter of habit. Yet:

> The Royal Marines are a peculiar military organisation. While a chain of command is clear and respect for rank is evident, a unified spirit infuses the Royal Marines.

And collaborative:[14]

> Those who do not contribute to the collective good are criticised and ultimately ostracised. ... Recruits are, for instance, encouraged to assist each other in preparing themselves for drill, even though the presentation of oneself for drill seems a

Table 6.3 **Open versus secretive**

Culture	Characterised by	"Right" when ...	"Wrong" when ...
Open (focused on transparency of information)	Organisation-wide disclosure of reliable, timely, comprehensive, relevant, comparable and material information that enables its users to make an accurate assessment of business conditions, activities and performance relative to their work.[a]	People have: – access to forums for sharing information and assessing it; – opportunities to convert information into actions they can practise and apply; – the freedom to ask questions, debate, and discuss the information.	Information is: – filtered on untested assumptions of "need to know"; – prized over knowledge (vested in people who are valued for what they know, and how they come to know it); – presented in a misleading or partial way.
Secretive (focused on hoarding information – "knowledge is power")	A belief that the intellectual property within the organisation should be protected from outside threat and/or leakage. Failure to do this would expose the organisation or its members to harm. Secrecy is seen to be a sensible adaptive behaviour. (Some organisations have membership groups with specific powers and responsibilities that exclude others; eg, promotion committees.)[b]	The risk of sharing information outweighs the benefits. Proprietary or competitive information would be compromised. Regulatory or ethical requirements mandate it.	People feel powerless and demeaned when information is withheld. Information is used against people who have no access to it. People are forced into difficult positions to guard someone else's secret.

a http://riskinstitute.ch/145360.htm
b http://jmi.sagepub.com/cgi/content/abstract/17/2/107

wholly individual task. On parade, drill leaders stress to new recruits the requirement to help each other with the cleaning of their boots, checking each other off, even suggesting that if one recruit is particularly good at something, he should be tasked to perform that role for all his colleagues while they repay his help by assisting him in other ways.

Example: Apple

Both secretive:

Many articles, books and blogs have been written on Apple's secretive culture. Here is one example:[15]

> Secrecy is one of Apple's signature products. A cult of corporate omerta – the mafia code of silence – is ruthlessly enforced, with employees sacked for leaks and careless talk. Executives feed deliberate misinformation into one part of the company so that any leak can be traced back to its source.

And open:

Apple designers come up with ten different mock-ups of any new feature and give themselves room to design without restriction. Later they whittle the number down to three, spend more months on those, and then end up with one strong decision:[16]

> Every week, the [Apple design] teams have two meetings. One is to brainstorm, to forget about constraints and think freely. As Michael Lopp [senior engineering manager] put it: to "go crazy". Then they hold a production meeting, an entirely separate but equally regular meeting, which is the other's antithesis. Here, the designers and engineers are required to nail everything down, to work out how this crazy idea might actually work. This process and organisation continues throughout the development of any app, though of course the balance shifts as the app progresses. But keeping an option for creative thought even at a late stage is really smart.

Table 6.4 **Innovative versus risk-averse**

Culture	Characterised by	"Right" when ...	"Wrong" when ...
Innovative (focused on bringing new products and services to market)	Evidence of questioning, constructive challenges, risk-taking, openness, patience and a future-looking orientation throughout the entire workforce.	There is tolerance for uncertainty and ambiguity. Learning is more important than success or failure. There is respect for diverse perspectives.	It is not linked to the business strategy. It is seen as dispensable in a downturn. It is seen as a responsibility belonging to only one department or role; eg, to an R&D department.
Risk-averse (focused on maintaining or developing the tried and trusted products and services)	The desire to protect what is rather than explore what could be. The belief that the costs of failure are higher than the rewards of success.	People clearly understand the risk profile of the organisation and why it is important to the organisation's success. People are equipped with situation-specific risk-assessment tools to help them make better risk-related decisions. People who take thoughtful, well-considered risks within the stated parameters are applauded regardless of the outcome of the risk.[a]	Fear of making a mistake gets in the way of making improvements or taking initiative. The risk/reward balance is not regularly examined (risks change). Unwillingness to present new ideas results in corporate paralysis and inability to adapt.[b]

a www.takerisks.com/innovationarticle.html
b www.jstor.org/pss/3867695

Example: Mozilla Firefox

Both innovative:

The Mozilla Firefox open-source free web browser was launched in 2004. Since then, Firefox has captured nearly a quarter of the browser market by focusing on speed, security and innovation. The browser was built by a dispersed community of mostly volunteer programmers, testers and fans co-ordinated by the non-profit Mozilla Foundation, which works on the principle:

> The Mozilla project is a global community of people who believe that openness, innovation and opportunity are key to the continued health of the internet.

To this end the focus is on user choices rather than market dominance. As Mitchell Baker, "chief lizard wrangler" for Mozilla Corporation, puts it:[17]

> Firefox, with its large community of add-on developers, can provide thousands of features that are "killer" for scores of niche audiences which can really help in attracting all the users in the long tail, while the basic Firefox can attract a large number of users at the top of the curve.

It was then marketed through an innovative interactive marketing campaign. A website (www.spreadfirefox.com) provided a forum to establish, vitalise and organise a community of at least 63,000 volunteers with the single-minded objective of increasing the adoption and usage of the Mozilla Firefox browser.

And risk-averse:

Web users have to know that their browsing is secure. As Sandeep Krishnamurthy points out in his article on Mozilla:

> The web browser is central to the security of the online experience. A poorly designed browser might not be able to detect malignant software applications compromising the data stored on the computer ... browser providers must make considerable investments to protect the security of users from viruses and malignant websites.

The advertisement for general counsel by Mozilla Corporation (a

Table 6.5 **Group versus individual**

Culture	Characterised by	"Right" when ...	"Wrong" when ...
Group (focused on collectively achieving a common goal)	Clear goals on what the group is to achieve by when. Shared understanding of the scope and method of completing the tasks. Processes and systems that support the completion of the tasks and activities.	Groups have clear boundaries Group members are interdependent and their roles are differentiated. Group members are held collectively responsible for the output of their work.[a]	Group values are espoused but rewards are linked to individual performance. Conflicts between group members are not resolved. Norms and expectations about behaviour are not shared by group members.
Individual (focused on individual achievement of a goal)	Experts working on individual achievement of tasks.	Individual members of the organisation respect each other. Individuals get clear, timely and constructive feedback on their performance. The tasks individuals are expected to do are appropriate for their knowledge and skills and are sufficiently challenging.	Individuals put their self-interest above the interests of the organisation. Individuals are unable to work effectively because they lack resources and/or support. Individuals are unclear about what their aims should be and what their contribution is to the overall process.

a Carlson, M., "A Model for Improving a Group's Effectiveness", *Popular Government*, Vol. 63, No. 4, Summer 1998.

wholly owned subsidiary of the Mozilla Foundation) highlighted the need for the successful applicant to "have an exceptional understanding of software and Internet business transactions, intellectual property issues, and the trade-offs between legal and business risks".[18] Harvey J. Anderson was appointed to this role in February 2008 and his blog (http://lockshot.wordpress.com/) provides insight into the many types of risks Mozilla faces and why it cannot afford to take some of them. In February 2010 he said that about 30% of Mozilla's legal matters are trademark enforcement related. Other issues relate to bogus sites that ask for subscriptions to use Firefox (it is a free service) and patent protection.

Example: Wikipedia

Both group:

Wikipedia is a freely licensed encyclopedia written by volunteers in many languages. It is a top-ten global website available in 70 languages. In his book *The Wikipedia Revolution*, Andrew Lih notes:[19]

> The power of Wikipedia's model is that it is free-form – anyone can edit any page at any time. Contributors work on a micro-level, adding a fact here, changing punctuation there. The community trusts individuals to behave responsibly.

To achieve quality of entries the contributors are working to three simple directives that are clearly understood (although there is an increasingly formal organisation emerging to ensure these are adhered to, for example assigning editors to some of its entries):

▶ Maintain a neutral point of view

▶ Verifiability

▶ No original research

Beyond these directives are operating principles:

▶ Assume good faith

▶ Be bold

▶ Sofixit

▶ "Don't bite the newbies"

And individual:

In 2002 Derek Ramsay developed a software robot (bot) that enabled census data to be linked to specific cities and towns. At the time the English Wikipedia had just over 50,000 articles. With this bot Ramsay would be adding:

> 33,832 more, all in one shot. He would instantly be responsible for 40% of all the Wikipedia articles. But in the spirit of Be Bold … he hit the start button.

Inevitably, there was a community response to his boldness. Some members thought it was a great deed while others thought it was an abomination. However, on balance Ramsay said that he had no regrets, particularly since his action had two effects: it spawned debate on what became bot policy; and it led to the introduction of bots to do other mundane and repetitive tasks. Lih concludes the Ramsay story with a further observation:

> The side effect … was that Rambot's [Ramsay's] additions did not just sit there gathering digital dust, entertaining occasional visitors. The base county and town articles inspired others.

Cultural clashes

The preceding sections highlight the points made in earlier chapters that organisations are culturally nuanced and extends this by suggesting that cultures are "right" if they enable people to do high-quality work in conditions that mean something and make sense to them, and where the work is engaging and ethical.

It sounds much easier to achieve this set of conditions than it is in practice. This is partly because there is no "right" culture to aim for. Most cultures can be right or wrong depending on the circumstances. Furthermore, organisations are not identifiable as purely one type of culture or another. Rather they are collections of subcultures within the overall culture, and to complicate things further people's individuality affects whether they feel they are in the "right" culture.

Muddying the search for the right culture are the inevitable cultural clashes that occur when the culture is right for one group but not for another. Edgar Schein of MIT Sloan School of Management notes:[20]

> Perhaps the biggest insight from years of consulting with DEC was the discovery that with success and growth, subsystems develop and these, in turn, develop cultures of their own. What is even more dramatic is the discovery that these subcultures may conflict with each other, making the managerial process inside organisations comparable to what it might be like to be managing in the United Nations.

Examples of six typical types of clashes are given below.

1 Mergers and acquisitions

Some analysts are surprised that the acquisition of Pixar by Disney has worked successfully:[21]

> How Disney and Pixar are making the integration work holds lessons for other executives faced with the delicate task of uniting two cultures. Tactics that have served the companies well include the obvious, like communicating changes to employees effectively. Other decisions, including drawing up an explicit map of what elements of Pixar would not change, have been more unusual.

Robert Iger, CEO of Disney, agreed to an explicit list of guidelines for protecting Pixar's creative culture. For instance, Pixar employees were able to keep their relatively plentiful health benefits and were not forced to sign employment contracts. He even stipulated that the sign on Pixar's front gate would remain unchanged. Richard Cook, chairman of Walt Disney Studios, says:

> None of this has been easy but it helps when everyone has tremendous respect both professionally and personally for one another.

2 Generational

This example appeared in an article in Fast Company:[22]

Deloitte & Touche USA, the accounting and consulting firm with 32,000 employees, heard from its gen-Y workers (ie, those born in the years 1976–95) that brutal audit schedules, in which teams had to camp out at client companies for weeks or months at a time, seemed superfluous in an age when client records are digitised. They felt they could get the same work done remotely. Deloitte's clients told the firm that they didn't care whether auditors were on-site or not, as long as the quality of the work didn't suffer. After a successful test in its New York office in which employees had the choice to work off-site, the firm rolled the programme out nationally.

3 National

Lih discusses the issues of taking Wikipedia international:[23]

A decision was made early on ... to allow the language culture to come through. Consider the article [[dog]], for example. In English the main picture is one of a yellow Labrador. Simply using the main picture for other languages wouldn't make sense if they don't have Labrador dogs in those countries ... In Asian languages, the article may talk more about dogs in the lunar calendar zodiac, something you wouldn't necessarily find in the Swahili or Finnish wikipedia.

4 Professional and/or special interest

A dispute between the Communication Workers Union and the Royal Mail in the UK exemplifies cultural differences between two parties. Announcing a 24-hour strike, Dave Ward, the union's deputy general secretary, said:[24]

There are serious and growing problems in the postal sector which urgently need resolving. We have renewed our offer of a three-month no-strike deal to Royal Mail in return for meaningful talks over modernisation. The current cuts, bullying managers and ever-increasing workloads on a shrinking workforce cannot continue. Pressure and stress is at breaking point for postal workers.

A Royal Mail spokeswoman said:

> *Strike action hurts both businesses and individuals and our customers will not understand how the CWU leadership can keep saying it backs modernisation while constantly resisting the introduction of new technology and more efficient working practices on the ground.*

5 Departmental

John Chambers, CEO of Cisco Systems, talks about the company's old "cowboy culture", where strong personalities were rewarded for jostling one another out of the way to get his approval. After he launched the company's reorganisation into boards and councils, he admits "there were times when everyone, even the CEO, was very uncomfortable". The internal economy of the old Cisco was very much market-based. Chambers chose to redistribute the wealth. Executives are now compensated on how well the whole company performs, rather than their individual product units. There was strong cultural resistance to these changes, Chambers says, and some 20% of the executives left the company. "Explaining to people why we needed to change things was the hard part."

6 Strategic or leadership change

A British Airways executive comments on the appointment of Willie Walsh in May 2005 to succeed Rod Eddington as CEO:

> *Bringing in an outsider as leader brings specific cultural risks. Rod Eddington's entry was low risk, Willie's is not. Rod was chosen in order to re-stabilise, Willie to de-stabilise. The current atmosphere in BA is one where the management has no idea of how the leadership will respond to the changing fortunes ahead. This disempowers people as they will increasingly refer everything upwards. In very large companies this is very dangerous and highly inefficient, but may bring short-term benefits. Wrong decisions will be made on important issues, and the company as a whole will not respond quickly enough. There could be significant cultural clashes between supporters of stability and supporters of change.*

Willie Walsh has, since joining BA, faced a tough job in driving the airline to success and profitability. But as one commentator says "he is no pushover" and, so far, he has stayed in post.

"Cultural fluency"

Cultural clashes are an inevitable part of organisational life and resolving them can be difficult. It requires "cultural fluency" – that is, in any interpersonal interaction the appropriate application of respect, empathy, flexibility, patience, interest, curiosity, openness, the willingness to suspend judgment, tolerance for ambiguity and sense of humour[25] – in the workforce. This can be developed by taking the following six steps:

▶ **Appreciate the difference that culture can make.** Accept that culture plays a fundamental role in the way that individuals, groups and organisational functions interact. Identify cultural similarities in order to build upon them and develop strategies that will help to bridge differences.

▶ **Develop awareness of how cultural differences influence ways of seeing the world.** The things that members of any culture have to do are often similar: making sure they have housing and food, obtaining work and dealing with people. However, the meanings and importance that members of a culture place on particular activities in particular circumstances may vary tremendously. This causes problems when people from diverse cultures attach different meanings or importance to similar situations, so it is important to develop an understanding of people's varying views on a given situation.

▶ **Provide forums for education about different cultures.** Read a variety of books, magazines, newspaper articles and internet sources that discuss different organisational cultures. Compare and contrast the views of different writers. Novels often reveal the most about cultural differences.

▶ **Be flexible in meetings with people.** Take a flexible approach in meetings with other parties in problem-solving, negotiations or culture-clash resolution efforts. Be aware of the needs and interests of the different people involved.

▶ **Recognise when something different appears to be happening.** Put up antennae to observe possible cultural differences that might result in a cultural clash and take steps to reframe the situation in a way that makes it less threatening or antagonistic. Adopt a different perspective. (Re)-establish common ground as a basis for agreement. Develop options and alternatives.

▶ **Be willing to adapt.** Determine the willingness or ability for each party to adapt to the other's culture. Make appropriate decisions on whether and how to do this.

Recap points

▶ The "right" culture is one where:
  - people are able to do work that is meaningful to them and they can make sense of;
  - there are stated (and demonstrated) purposes beyond making money;
  - the work is high-quality, ethical and engaging.

▶ Individuals experience the culture in very different ways. What is right for one person may be wrong for another.

▶ Labels of culture, such as a collaborative culture, are shorthand for the predominant and recognisable characteristics of that type of culture.

▶ Cultures are not pure or consistent throughout, rather they are "both/and" – as in open and secretive, or collaborative and competitive – depending on circumstances and the various subcultures.

▶ Cultural clashes are inevitable. One way of handling these constructively is to develop cultural fluency in the workforce.

One company's experience: Reckitt Benckiser

The Reckitt Benckiser group was created in 1999 after the merger of Reckitt & Colman of the UK and Benckiser of the Netherlands. Bart Becht, a Benckiser man before 1999 when he took over as CEO of the merged company, has presided over Reckitt Benckiser's yearly performance improvement. Even during the global recession that started in 2007 the company performed well, and in the full year 2008 sales rose by 13% at constant exchange rates to £6.56 billion, whereas net income rose by 12% to reach £1.14 billion. Its product lines are predominantly household and over-the-counter health care, focused on 17 "power brands" (see Appendix 1) including Dettol, Airwick, Clearasil, Finish and Nurofen.

Although the company is financially successful it keeps a low profile, which a commentator who had had a hard time getting an interview with Becht described as "a bizarre level of paranoia from a company with such a proud record of achievement". When he finally got his interview, Becht explained that "what shareholders basically judge us on is how the business performs, not how we function in the limelight".

Becht believes the company's success is due to a strategic focus on market leadership and product innovation:[26]

> We focus disproportionately on categories where we have strong leadership positions and where we can have good margins ... Out of £5 billion in total turnover, £2 billion comes from products that have been launched in the past three years.

When in 2009 Reckitt Benckiser won *The Economist*'s Innovation Award in the category Corporate Use of Innovation, one of the judges commented:[27]

> The company has demonstrated strong sales and profit growth, in large part because of the strength of its innovative and entrepreneurial corporate culture. Controversy is encouraged, bureaucracy avoided and performance rewarded. A diverse multinational workforce provides a wealth of perspectives on consumer behaviour. The company has a talent for dreaming up products that consumers did not realise they wanted (and for giving them crazy names). Some 35–40% of its sales come from products launched in the past three years, which is a clear indication of its continued ability to dream up winning new ideas.

Becht gave his perspective on the innovative and entrepreneurial corporate culture in response to the question "How much of your success is due to your unique business culture?":[28]

> A lot. We try to give our people considerable responsibility from virtually day one so that they develop a sense of ownership. We also try to develop a spirit of entrepreneurship unlike a lot of other big

companies where it gets stifled. We actively encourage people to come up with new ideas. We are very focused on achieving results, but we don't punish people for failure just because a new idea doesn't happen to work.

Although entrepreneurs tend towards individualism, Becht made the point:

We also work in groups all the time, so team spirit is also very much part of our culture ... we fight as hard internally for the best ideas as we fight externally to achieve results for the company. We do indeed have many heated debates, but we also try to accommodate minority ideas by trialling and testing them as these can sometimes be the best ones.

In another interview Becht elaborated further:[29]

We are definitely more of a go-getting, action-oriented culture. We are aggressive in terms of achieving targets, no question about that. We are not focused on endless debates to make sure everybody is aligned. But I wouldn't say it is not a caring place. Key to growth is innovation and that comes from people. We have a different style culturally from other companies. We are more multicultural. We firmly believe that by having people from different backgrounds we get new ideas on the table much quicker than other companies.

He says he encourages staff to fight their corner, make mistakes and be entrepreneurial:

If I have ten people with different backgrounds in a room they're not going to agree. So, as long as I have constructive conflict, by the end of the discussion they're going to come up with a perspective which is very different. That's what I want.

Other aspects of the culture are reflected in the search for continuous efficiency gains, notably through two dedicated teams. Becht explains that one team, "Squeeze", is looking constantly at the detailed design of products and finding ways to trim the amount of materials used to manufacture them. Its recommendations could be down to minutiae such as changing the design of bottles to cut out a few grams of plastic per item, which across millions of products has a surprisingly big impact on spending. The other team, "Extrim", focuses on the efficiency of the rest of the operation, including everything from cheaper sourcing to the speed and layout of factories. It may also include closing plants.

This illustrates a point made earlier in the chapter: that an overall label of the culture, in this case entrepreneurial and innovative, is not the whole cultural story. Reckitt Benckiser's culture is also described as team-based yet with individual "fighters". One ex-employee described it as a "brutal", not consensus-driven, multicultural environment where constructive clashes are encouraged.

With this rich culture comes evidence of an organisation that has a social conscience and is thinking sustainably. In 2009 the company entered the Dow Jones Sustainability World Index (DJSI World) – as one of the top 10% in the world – and has been ranked among the top 12 performers in the world in the Carbon Disclosure Leadership Index. It has pledged continuing support for Save the Children, a UK charity, and in 2009 paid flights, basics expenses and time off work for 61 staff to participate in a challenge hike. On this trip Paul Woodward, a logistics team member at the firm's Nottingham base, rubbed shoulders with senior colleagues he would never ordinarily meet. He says:[30]

> I found it quite daunting at first as I think I am one of only three people from the shop floor being sent over. But we will all be in the same boat at the end of the day. I can't honestly believe I'm going. I am just your normal, average Joe, now I am going to travel to India and help people. It's just an amazing opportunity!

Reckitt Benckiser has the attributes of the right culture in that people are encouraged to do high-quality work, in an ethical environment, where the nature of entrepreneurship and innovation requires engagement. Beyond that its innovations are driven from constructive conflict, implying cultural fluency. What it means to work at the company is perfectly clear: people work at high pressure in a demanding environment, where team work is valued and conflict is part of the norm; the sense individuals make of this is more difficult to assess. The ex-employee who found the environment "brutal" could not make sense of it. The company's employee turnover rate is comparable to that of other fast-moving consumer goods and pharmaceutical companies at approximately 10%; alongside this there is also a great deal of rapid upward mobility for those who deliver results.[31]

Learning from Reckitt Benckiser

Three lessons come out of Reckitt Benckiser's approach to culture:

▶ **Make it clear what the culture is and what is expected from people.** A variety of approaches can be used. Reckitt Benckiser's careers website, for example, invites people to take the Core Values Challenge (an interactive quiz) and the Virtual Career game. Becht is consistent in his descriptions of the culture, how it plays out and what he expects from people. The point is to make it easy for people to share systems of meaning and make sense of these.

▶ **Align all aspects of the organisation in support of the culture.** The career and performance management systems, the formal communications forums, the various business metrics used to track targets and the way teams are structured are just some examples of the alignment of the organisational elements:[32]

> The structure is designed to encourage the entrepreneurial spirit. Rather than endless layers of management that tend to plague large organisations, the company has small teams and few processes, with just two people between the marketing director in a country and the chief executive.

▶ **Be aware that subcultures, and cultural clashes, are normal in any culture.** No culture is entirely uniform and consistent. The tension lies in managing the various subculture interests and conflicts in a way that benefits the whole organisation and keeps the culture thriving. One way of doing this is through developing cultural fluency in the workforce. Reckitt Benckiser encourages staff:[33]

> to move around the world regularly, often doing different jobs in the process. The reasoning is that they become better and more rounded managers, more capable of managing an international business with a portfolio of global brands.

Summary

▶ Most organisational cultures can be labelled as one type or another, for example entrepreneurial. However, this serves only as a high-level descriptor. Organisations are not purely one culture but rather exhibit characteristics of several, partly because there are numerous subcultures, each with its own characteristics.

▶ Even at the label level there is no one right organisation culture, but there are conditions that can apply in every type of culture that make it right. Briefly, the right culture is one where people share systems of meaning and are encouraged to do high-quality, engaging work within an ethical framework. Such a culture should also value and respect an individual's contribution and allow for capability and cultural fluency development.

Exercise 6: The two swords in Appendix 3 is an exercise in cultural fluency taking the analogy from Miyamoto Musashi, a 17th-century Japanese *samurai*, who learned to handle two swords at one time.

Can culture be created, changed, or protected?

Lou Gerstner, chairman and CEO of IBM from 1993 to 2002, said:

> Until I came to IBM, I probably would have told you that culture was just one among several important elements in any organisation's make-up and success – along with vision, strategy, marketing, financials, and the like. I came to see, in my time at IBM, that culture isn't just one aspect of the game; it is the game. In the end, an organisation is nothing more than the collective capacity of its people to create value.

This quote puts him straight into the theoretical camp of academic researchers who take a "cognitive or symbolic perspective on the study of organisations". That means:[1]

> [They leave] behind the view that a culture is something an organisation has, in favour of the view that a culture is something an organisation is.

And they experience organisations as:

> Networks of subjective meanings or shared frames of reference that organisation members share to varying degrees and which, to an external observer, appear to function in a rule-like or grammar-like manner.

The main alternative theoretical camp views culture not as what an organisation "is" but something it "has" (as Gerstner did before joining IBM; during his time there he changed camps). The "has" camp considers culture as a variable that can be identified and relatively easily changed in the same way that a strategy or a marketing approach can be changed.

Theories of organisation culture may not appear to have direct day-to-day relevance to a manager, but reflecting on the "is" or "has" perspective is helpful. A manager who thinks the organisation is the culture will understand that changing the way something "is" is an extremely difficult, time-consuming, skilled process that cannot be forced. It is akin to trying to change the personality and characteristics of an individual, something most people in a relationship know is complex to say the least.

Alternatively, a manager who thinks that an organisation has a culture – that culture is a variable that can be isolated and changed as a product's packaging might be – will try to change it in the same way, expecting it to happen in the same timescales.

Rather than being a purist about this, a better approach is to understand organisations as both being and having a culture, which the description of an organisation's culture as an "active living phenomenon through which people jointly create and recreate the worlds in which they live"[2] implies. Students moving into shared housing are an example of where this happens. The individuals jointly work out, for example, how much tidiness/untidiness they can tolerate in common areas and establish "ways of doing things round here". When a member leaves and another joins the ways of doing things change (sometimes subtly and sometimes dramatically). This concept of creating and recreating culture is reinforced in the view that:[3]

> Culture is highly mutable, flexible, open to shaping from many directions at once in its changing environments, and most importantly, a result of constructions continuously debated and contested among its highly independent, even unruly membership.

Taking the "is" and "has" views together serves as a reminder of two things.

1 Organisation culture is not an entity or a thing, independent from the business strategy, that can be manipulated by pulling levers

Rather:[4]

> Organisations with a clearly articulated strategy that engage and energise employees appealing to their higher ideals and values and rallying them around a set of meaningful, unified goals have the platform for creating the shared "systems of meaning" and experience that create the culture.

Zain is a Kuwait-based telecommunications company. It was initially a small local player, but in 2003 a new strategy was introduced and by 2009 it was operating in 24 countries across Africa[5] and the Middle East, with a dedicated workforce of 15,000 serving 69.5m customers. Saad Al-Barrak, Zain's CEO, is clear that his business's success is due partly to having clarity on the mission and values aligned with the way they are enacted from day to day. He says:

> We are ... defined by our commitment to delivering excellence, living by our core values and strengthening our culture of corporate social responsibility.

Of course this could be dismissed as a leader's rhetoric, but one young Jordanian speaking about her experience working for Zain says:

> Like all the people I work with I feel motivated, supported and have the freedom I aspire to with opportunities to learn and expand. It has a family-like feel – our employees are part of growing a very distinctive culture formed around the goal of growing the business and the values of heart, radiance and belonging.

2 An organisation's culture, like a society's culture, changes continuously regardless of any formal or informal efforts to change it

The changing factors in the external environment that touch or involve an organisation will have an impact on its culture. Some that organisations have had to grapple with over the past decade are flexible information technologies, various historical and political events, regulatory changes, demographic changes, the 2008 financial crisis and recession, and increasing discussion about climate change. If responded to with foresight, sensitivity and skill the result can be an extraordinarily beneficial cultural transformation, as the Cisco example illustrates.

The rapid changes in technology caused John Chambers, CEO of Cisco, to change his thinking and the way he leads the company. In this extract from an interview he explains why:[6]

> I had to change. And I'm a command-and-control guy. But that's not the future. The future's going to be all around collaboration and teamwork, with a structured process behind it. That's the key ... especially during major, violent economic or market disruptions, you've got to move fast. And you've got to be willing to listen and try new things. And I realise that you can be part of the solution, or you can be part of the problem. If you think that you cannot be left behind, you're wrong – regardless of what position you're in.

Aiming to be part of the solution and keep Cisco successful:[7]

> [Chambers] has been taking Cisco through a massive, radical, often bumpy reorganisation. The goal is to spread the company's leadership and decision-making far wider than any big company has attempted before, to working groups that currently involve 500 executives. This move, Chambers says, reflects a new philosophy about how business can best work in a networked world. "In 2001, we were like most high-tech companies, with one or two primary products that were really important to us," he explains. "All decisions came to the top 10 people in the company, and we drove things back down from there." Today, a network of councils and boards empowered to launch new businesses, plus an evolving set of Web 2.0 gizmos – not to mention a new financial incentive system – encourage executives to work together like never before. Pull back the tent flaps and Cisco citizens are blogging, vlogging, and virtualising, using social-networking tools that they've made themselves

and that, in many cases, far exceed the capabilities of the commercially available wikis, YouTubes, and Facebooks created by the kids up the road in Palo Alto.

The bumpy part – and the eye-opener – is that the leaders of business units formerly competing for power and resources now share responsibility for one another's success. What used to be "me" is now "we". The goal is to get more products to market faster, and Chambers crows at the results. "The boards and councils have been able to innovate with tremendous speed. Fifteen minutes and one week to get a [business] plan that used to take six months!" As storm clouds form for the rest of the business community, he says, "We're going to gain market share." Rain? What rain?

Chambers is changing Cisco in response to changing conditions in the external environment and in doing this he is working with both what the culture is and what it has. So, for example, it is a fast-paced, adaptive, collaborative culture that has experience in managing downturns and emerging successfully. Chambers points out:

This is my fifth downturn over the last 20 years. In each of those, we went into them with kind of a playbook, if you will, of what we run our plays on during economic tough times. We've always gained market share and emerged stronger than we went into it. Part of the reason that we did that is we don't look short term. No one knows for sure. But we're preparing ourselves for how we look, whether it's six months out or 24 months out.

An article in *The Economist* in August 2009 says that Tom Malone, a professor at MIT Sloan School of Management:[8]

... sees Cisco as a pioneer for a larger trend. Traditionally management was about command and control. Now ... bosses should move to a more flexible view, best described as coordinate and cultivate ... Cisco has a good chance of coming to exemplify [this] new world.

The two points discussed above are useful to bear in mind when discussing creating, changing, or protecting an organisation's culture. They serve as reminders that organisation culture is essentially about interrelationships between people, ideas, external circumstances and existing conditions. Culture change is related to elements that are "constantly in flux, shaping and being shaped by social and economic aspects of human interaction".[9]

This portrayal of culture reflects the climate metaphor presented in Chapter 1. Humans did not create climate but they have altered it (with potentially disastrous consequences), and they are now seeking to protect it. Similarly, members of an organisation cannot create culture from a "clean sheet", but they can change it and they can protect it. How successfully depends on numerous factors.

Creating a culture

Managers often talk about "creating a culture", for example:[10]

> The strategic global expansion IKEA is undertaking involves creating a global internal culture and business system that connects their brand and human resource strategies via shared democratic company values.

This sort of statement is confusing in that IKEA already had a culture and what the firm was seeking to do was to change it from a domestic to a global one.

The term "creating a culture" is more appropriately used in relation to only two situations:

▶ a newly created company;

▶ the merger of two or more companies with the aim of creating a genuinely new organisation as opposed to subsuming one into the other.

Even in these situations it is not a "greenfield site" (that is, an undeveloped site that is earmarked for development) because organisation culture does not explode from nothing into being. Even in a start-up, the attributes, preferences and experiences of the founder(s) and first employees, together with the business model and the underlying business strategy, already exist and play a part in the development of a distinctive culture.

A newly created company

Although Tata Group is not "newly created" – it was established in 1868 by Jamsetji Tata – the way it was originally set up and still operates now is a testament to the founder's beliefs and values. Tata was a member of the Parsi (also known as Zoroastrianist) community and was originally studying to be a priest. The underpinning belief of this religion is that a life well lived must dedicate itself to charity and justice. Since its founding:

> Tata has operated on the premise that a company thrives on social capital (that is the value created from investing in good community and human relationships) in the same way that it relies on hard assets for sustainable growth.

Today the group comprises around 90 companies in every major international market and in seven industry sectors: information systems and communications, engineering, materials, services, energy, consumer products and chemicals. Every Tata company or enterprise operates independently. Each has its own board of directors and shareholders to whom it is answerable. There are two decision-making bodies that define and direct the business endeavours of the Tata Group: the Group Executive Office defines and reviews its business activities; and the Group Corporate Centre is a forum where broad policy issues relating to the growth of Tata companies are reviewed and entry into new areas is discussed.

In conformance with the founder's wishes and ideals, each year all Tata businesses earmark part of their operating expenditure for social, environmental and education programmes, and more than 4% of their operating income for the 11 charitable trusts that own 66% of what is effectively the Tata Group holding company, Tata Sons. The Tatas regard this spending as an operating investment. "For us [community support] is a fixed cost of manufacturing," says Partha Sengupta, vice-president of corporate services at Tata Steel.

Again reflecting the founder's beliefs is the avoidance of any activities with even a tangential link to "sin" industries – a term that for the Tatas encompasses not only tobacco, liquor and gambling but also motion pictures. In the mid-2000s, the leaders of the group's publishing company tested this stance, asking for funding to start a film division. "The inner circle discussed it and decided it was not acceptable," recalls Jamshed J. Irani, vice-chairman of Tata Sons. The publishing company's management team made plans to go ahead anyway. Tata then sold its shares in the company and removed the Tata name.

R. Gopalakrishnan, an executive director of Tata Sons, says:

> We may be among the few companies around the world who think and act first as a citizen. In a free enterprise, the community is not just another stakeholder in the business, but is in fact, the very purpose of its existence.

This emphasis on the founder's values is a crucial aspect of the group's corporate culture. It is strong enough, Tata's leaders say, to hold the group together as it diversifies and expands outside India. In going global they have set themselves a goal not just to increase turnover but also "to go places where we could create a meaningful presence [and] participate in the development of the country".

As the group acquires companies – in 2007 Corus, a steel company, and the Ritz-Carlton Hotel, Boston, and in 2008 Jaguar Land Rover – the challenge is to transform the acquired companies' culture to a new one with the distinctive Tata stamp.

A merger of two companies

The received wisdom is that most mergers and acquisitions (M&As) fail to realise the hoped-for value. Regardless of the strategic merits, studies consistently find that 60–70% of deals diminish shareholder value. Among the reasons suggested is that the due diligence that takes place before the merger rarely includes an assessment of cultural fit. Building on the notion that an organisation both is and has a culture, trying to consolidate two organisations that have no shared history, systems of meaning, experiences, working patterns, values, and so on, is akin to trying to consolidate two nation states into one (or in the earlier analogy two climate zones).

Creating a new culture in this situation is exceptionally challenging as cultural differences are a double-edged sword. This can be valuable (for example, one company may learn new ways of doing things from the other to their mutual benefit) or it can be destructive (for example, when the two cultures clash and/or have conflicting approaches to things). The ability to manage the cultural integration process effectively appears to have an important influence on M&A outcomes, as this extract from the analysis of the split between Time Warner and AOL nine years after their merger (in 2000) illustrates:[11]

> *Jeffrey Brown (PBS interviewer): Even at the beginning, there were questions about it. There were questions about whether it was valued correctly, certainly. Wall Street didn't like it right away. There were a lot of questions clearly about the potential culture clash, right?*
>
> *Frank Ahrens (business journalist): Right. What happened was Time Warner had just gone through its own culture clash a few years earlier when Time and Warner Brothers merged. And you had the sort of pinstripe New York timing [business] people and the sort of open-collar LA Hollywood people. And they had just come through that.*
>
> *Now you bring in these deal-oriented folks from Dulles. Remember, AOL was an internet provider, but it was a dealmaker, a lot of business partnerships, a lot of advertising, a real go-go attitude.*
>
> *And so there was a clash, an immediate clash. The folks from Time Warner resented these go-go, young, hot-shot 20-something-year-old millionaires telling them how to run a business. And there were a number of concrete examples that came out of that that caused this thing to crash.*

Another example of a merger that did not work because of cultural mismatches and a failure to deal with them is that of Daimler-Benz and Chrysler Corporation, which were in 1998 two of the world's leading car manufacturers, and which in November that year combined their businesses in what they claimed to be a "merger of equals". Jurgen Schrempp and Robert Eaton led the merged entity as joint CEOs and joint chairmen.

However, analysts felt that to make the merger a success, several important issues should be addressed. The most significant of these was organisational culture. The company's success depended on integrating two starkly different corporate cultures. "If they can't create a climate of learning from each other," warned Ulrich Steger, a management professor at IMD, a Swiss business school, "they could be heading for an unbelievable catastrophe." Daimler-Benz was characterised by methodical decision-making while Chrysler encouraged creativity. Chrysler was a symbol of American adaptability and resilience, valuing efficiency, empowerment and egalitarian relations among staff; Daimler-Benz seemed to value respect for authority, bureaucratic precision and centralised decision-making.

These cultural differences soon became manifest in the daily activities of the company. For example, Chrysler executives quickly became frustrated with the attention Daimler-Benz executives gave to trivial matters, such as the shape of a pamphlet sent to employees. Daimler-Benz executives were equally perplexed when Eaton showed his emotions with tears in a speech to other executives. In May 2007 DaimlerChrysler sold the Chrysler Group to Cerberus Capital Management, a private equity company, for $7.4 billion, dissolving the 1998 merger that started with high hopes but failed to live up to expectations.

Given the intricacies of merging there are nine strategies that can help. Each is common sense and although there is no guarantee of success, taking action on all of them will produce better results than taking action on a few of them and/or ignoring them altogether. Reckitt Benckiser (see pages 155–9) is an example of a well-orchestrated, highly successful merger that took place in 1999. The strategies are as follows:[12]

▶ Consider and assess cultural compatibility using a variety of methods (several are discussed in Chapter 2).

▶ Think through how employees are likely to react to the merger news – most often they feel they are losing rather than gaining something – and be realistic about what it offers them.

▶ Plan for challenges in helping people work together in new ways. System incompatibility may make this even harder (look at the techniques for developing cultural fluency discussed in Chapter 6).

▷ Develop a flexible and comprehensive integration plan. Rather than trying to merge two cultures, aim to identify the best in both to create the way for a different culture.

▷ Share information and encourage communication. Keep information flowing through a variety of channels. Use methods that involve and engage people including social media.

▷ Encourage employee participation and involvement in voicing concerns, sharing what works and building the future.

▷ Enhance commitment to the new entity by leading by example and demonstrating the behaviours and characteristics required. Build networks and communities.

▷ Manage the transition (which can take several years) through training, support and dialogue.

▷ Be sensitive to individual and timing considerations. People react in different ways to major threats and changes.

Changing a culture

Any decision to try to make a planned change to an organisation's culture should derive from a perceived (and communicable) shortfall in business performance or change in business strategy. Because planned culture change is a slow and often painful process, it should not be undertaken without a compelling business reason. So, for example, Sony, an electronics manufacturer that was losing competitiveness, decided to invest more in specific global brands (one of which was Playstation) than in less well-known brands:[13]

> [This brand focus] forced the company to engage in culture change efforts that have had repercussions on the rest of the corporate strategy. As Sony CEO, Nobuyuki Idei, stated: "We have to change from a manufacturing industry culture to a knowledge-based global culture ... a reinvention of the business model itself."

This managed type of culture change is not straightforward and, as stated in previous chapters, is not a matter of manipulating organisational levers. Nevertheless, organisational cultures can change and, as observed above, are constantly evolving and adapting regardless of any specific intention that they should change. Ult-imately, most orchestrated, formal culture-change programmes are doomed to failure because the experts in charge of them fall into traps and the programmes themselves have unintended con-sequences. Take total quality management (TQM) and business process re-engineering (BPR) as two examples of programmes designed to get employees to "think, talk and act in new ways". The implicit aim of these was to create a "cultural revolution". Some organisations were successful in doing this, but about 70% of firms that "set off down this new path were unsuccessful".[14]

Expert traps

A paper by Edgar Schein of MIT Sloan School of Management dis-cusses five traps that are easy for culture-change consultants to "fall into because they do not take cultural and sociological factors into account when working with complex social systems".[15] The traps are to:

▶ begin a culture change with a diagnosis or assessment – this is a mistake because
a) people may have no motive to be honest or open in their responses
b) questions may trigger unknown consequences
c) a "diagnosis" implies that there is a "remedy" as in a doctor/patient relationship;

▶ assume that the owner (the person accountable for the culture) of a culture-change programme is an individual rather than a set of interconnected individuals and groups who make up a cultural unit;

▶ assume that the owner (and the consultant) knows what culture is and does;

▶ assume that individual assessments (through interviews, surveys, and so on) provide valid data for a group;

▶ assume that the consultant has and should use a standard method of working based on sound theory and past history of success.

The result of falling into any or all of these traps is, in Schein's words (quoted previously in Chapter 2 but repeated here as a reminder), that:[16]

> *Consulting goals get very fuzzy. In my work with organisa-*
> *tional culture, I frequently find that there are strong subcultures*
> *at work in the organisation, and that these subcultures have*
> *different goals. Is my job, then, from a systemic point of view*
> *to align them, to integrate them, or to let them fight it out for*
> *dominance?*

This quandary reinforces the crucial fact that cultures are complex. Hence a change programme that invariably takes a one-size-fits-all approach will not work and will certainly not be responded to in the same way throughout the organisation.

Culture-change programmes have unintended consequences

A study of culture-change programmes, conducted in 2002 by two professors at Cardiff Business School, outlined eight types of unintended consequences that typically occur in the wake of these (see Table 7.1).

Table 7.1 Unintended consequences of culture-change programmes

	Comment	Example
Ritualisation of change	The change programme is seen as a ritual (similar to the annual appraisal process) with objectives that have to be accomplished at specific intervals, rather than a continual integrated process.	A monthly customer service culture-change objective: "The one I remember most was the smiling service one. You were supposed to smile and greet the customer when they got within ten feet of you ... we don't really do [that] these days ... I think it's still in the rule book somewhere."

	Comment	*Example*
Hijacked intentions	The original intentions of the change programme get lost or diverted.	"We had different ideas on what 'customer first' meant in practice. At first it meant that we should do everything in our power to please the customer. Then the accountants realised that would cost money and we should only do what was reasonable and not too costly to do. That derailed some of the intent of the programme". (Manager, call centre)
Cultural erosion	The culture-change programme begins with good intentions, and people subscribe to the objectives and start working with them in mind. But over time people revert to the way they worked previously.	"When the programme began it was easier for managers to back things up, praise staff, etc. But after a while you just start forgetting things, other things take priority." "One thing slips then another, then another, and before you know it you're back to square one."
Cultural reinvention	The espoused "new" culture is little more than a repackaging of the "old" one.	"It's all very well blathering on about 'customers come first' and 'customers pay your wages' but in the harsh light of day it's sales. It's always been sales – today we hide that behind the customer culture stuff – and that's just a blind."

	Comment	*Example*
Ivory tower change	Head-office staff, often with the help of external consultants, develop a culture-change programme for the whole organisation without having real experience of what it is like working in the various departments or on the front line facing customers.	"I just got feedback from 100 colleagues, where they fill in forms … They've been drawn up and designed by somebody who has obviously had a personnel background, who has never run a company store in their life, and some of the questions are awkward for a colleague to answer, and unfair to take feedback on – such as, 'Does your general store manager communicate with you on a daily basis?' which is unfair to ask a checkout operator or a lady on the deli counter." (General store manager, six years' service)
Inattention to symbolism	Too little attention is paid to the things that get noticed, eg, retained perks and privileges and behaviour that runs counter to the new culture.	"Well, we're like every company – lots of malicious and salacious rumours. The one that amused us here came out smack-bang in the middle of the customer service culture drive last year. The word was a board member lost it with a customer and literally threw him out the door. It's become a saying here – I tell them to smarten up service standards and they start joking about slinging me out the door."

	Comment	Example
Uncontrolled efforts	Weak governance of a culture-change programme results in unco-ordinated efforts and confused accountabilities.	"One directive from personnel instructs me to empower my assistant manager, changing her job description to include balance checks. Another directive – from the audit department – lists all the balance checks I've got to do. What am I supposed to do? What do they want? I do one and I piss off the other." The conflict here lies in who does the balance checks – the manager or the assistant manager. In this instance, the HR and audit departments have different views and the manager is caught in the middle.
Behavioural compliance	People will change their behaviour if they know they are being monitored, but they do not change their underlying values and beliefs in line with that organisation's changes because their experience leads them to be cynical about the intentions and outcomes.	"When the guys are up from head office of course we do all the crap they tell us to. But when we're left alone we do things the way we've always done them – I've worked here for ten years – I know this place better than some suit."

Sources: Harris, L. and Ogbonna, E., "The Unintended Consequences of Culture Interventions: A Study of Unexpected Outcomes", *British Journal of Management*, Vol. 13, 2002; Ogbonna, E. and Wilkinson, B., "The False Promise of Culture Change", *Journal of Management Studies*, Vol. 40, No. 5, July 2003

The best way to change an organisation's culture successfully is by meeting the six conditions in Table 7.2.

Table 7.2 **Conditions for successful culture change**

Condition	Comment
Clear and well-articulated reasons for changing the culture that are inextricably linked to the business strategy	This requires an organisational ability to sense changes in the environment to which it must respond, such as a competitive threat. But it is usually only major changes or new problems that make a culture change desirable. Organisations should always bear in mind "the possibility that many elements of the culture will actually help to solve the problem, that culture is a source of strength, and that one does not change it without a great deal of effort and pain."[a]
Clear and well articulated principles for delivering the business strategy which are supported by values that are shared, and acted on by those working for the organisation – albeit in different ways in its different parts	The values, beliefs and assumptions of individual employees are at least in sync with the organisational ones, ensuring that challenges to them are constructive rather than destructive and that employees are not being coerced into working to a value system they do not subscribe to.
Alignment of such matters as language, policies, practices, processes and the physical environment with the principles for delivering the business strategy	If this alignment requires changes in one or more subsystems, eg, if new service standards need to be developed, if manufacturing processes need to change, or if refinancing is needed, can the system change in the appropriate direction? Is there systemic flexibility? Can the system innovate?
Overt leadership commitment through deeds as well as words to the desired/required "way we do things here"	Leaders trust and respect each other and work together to shape and demonstrate the desired/required culture. There is no subcultural ethos that cuts them off from the concerns of the workforce or that encourages them to make assumptions, judgments and decisions with inadequate information.

Condition	Comment
A recognition of what degree of change is possible given the constraints of history, legacy, the business model, resources, etc	In line with concepts of path dependence (which "in its loosest sense means that current and future states, actions, or decisions depend upon the path of previous states, actions, or decisions"[b]), organisations have only a certain cultural "range of movement" that is in line with their past path. Returning to the climate zone analogy, it would not be easy even if it were possible to change one climate zone into another.
Acceptance that planned culture change takes years rather than months, and that culture is in any case changing all the time irrespective of any plans to change it	Keeping planned and societal organisational culture change harmonised is tricky, as the consumerisation of IT (that is, giving corporate IT users access to the scale and innovation of the consumer market) issue illustrates. When Bob Nardelli joined Home Depot from GE he "adopted and adapted an array of specific tools designed to gradually change the company's culture". In 2006, Ram Charan, one of the consultants working with Nardelli, reported: "But the Home Depot culture today – with its focus on process, hard data, and accountability – is different from what it was five years ago. And there are concrete signs of its acceptance by employees."[c] In terms of business performance, "Nardelli's numbers were quite good," says Matthew Fassler, an analyst at Goldman Sachs. "Driven by a housing and home improvement boom, sales soared from $46 billion in 2000, the year Nardelli took over, to $81.5 billion in 2005, an average annual growth rate of 12%. Profits more than doubled, to $5.8 billion that year."[d] (But note that Nardelli abruptly resigned as chairman and chief executive of Home Depot in January 2007, suggesting that the culture change was not as effective as it was at first sight.)

a Schein, E., "Five Traps for Consulting Psychologists or How I Learned to Take Culture Seriously", Consulting Psychology Journal, Vol. 55, No. 2, 2003.
b Scott E. Page, "Path Dependence", Quarterly Journal of Political Science, Vol. 1, No. 1, 2006.
c Charan, R., "Home Depot's Blueprint for Culture Change", Harvard Business Review, April 2006.
d Grow, B., "Out at Home Depot", Business Week, January 9th 2007.

Protecting the culture

When questions about protecting an organisation's culture arise, they typically relate to perceived threats to a culture that works. There are two common instances:

▶ When one company buys another. Is the intention to form a new single company or is it to allow the acquired company to keep its own identity and operate independently in much the same way as it has in the past? When asked following the company's acquisition by Amazon (see Chapter 2) whether Zappos's culture would change, Tony Hsieh (CEO) answered:[17]

> Our culture at Zappos is unique and always evolving and changing, because one of our core values is to embrace and drive change. What happens to our culture is up to us, which has always been true. Just like before, we are in control of our destiny and how our culture evolves.
>
> A big part of the reason why Amazon is interested in us is because they recognise the value of our culture, our people, and our brand. Their desire is for us to continue to grow and develop our culture (and perhaps even a little bit of our culture may rub off on them).
>
> They are not looking to have their folks come in and run Zappos unless we ask them to. That being said, they have a lot of experience and expertise in a lot of areas, so we're very excited about the opportunities to tap into their knowledge, expertise, and resources, especially on the technology side. This is about making the Zappos brand, culture, and business even stronger than it is today.

▶ The undermining of an organisation's heritage or traditional cultural strengths, perhaps as a result of actions taken in response to market changes and threats. When this occurs and is seen to be damaging, there may be a drive to pull the culture back to its cultural heritage. Lockheed Martin's CEO Bob Stevens explains the need to reinforce the company's culture:[18]

> In each phase of our maturation as a corporation, we have set goals, developed strategies and assigned resources, just as we

do on all of our customer programmes. And that's the same approach we are now taking as we focus on establishing and reinforcing a common culture that permeates every corner of our organisation.

A strong, unifying culture is imperative for many reasons. For one, it increases our customers' confidence that they will encounter the same standards of excellence in every Lockheed Martin business. For another, it improves our agility in responding to opportunities that require teaming across business lines. It also allows our people to move easily throughout the corporation into jobs where their skills are most needed.

It is usually leaders who take a role in protecting the culture when it is under threat, as these examples show. On a day-to-day basis, in big organisations it is usually the human resources department that acts as cultural sheriff by virtue of the policies, practices and processes it introduces, perpetuates or mandates.

On visiting Ernst & Young's London office, philosopher Alain de Botton made the following observations:[19]

On entering the building, one encounters a lobby designed so that the head of any newcomer will ineluctably lean backwards to follow a succession of floors rising up to apparent infinity and in the process dwell ... on the respect that must be owed to those responsible for putting up and managing this colossus ... Quite what one should be honouring is unclear. Perhaps hard work, precision, a certain ruthlessness and the surprising intricacy of the audit process. A plaque affixed to a wall declares, "We like people who demonstrate integrity, energy and enthusiasm."

To help protect the culture implied in this paragraph, he notes how the HR department orchestrates the efforts. He comments:

Contrived as the strategies ... may seem, it is in fact their very artificiality which guarantees their success.

He suggests that these activities, including communication forums, training and development, induction processes and performance appraisals, are a "communal salve" necessary to sooth issues in an organisation that is dependent on thousands of people getting along with each other in order to meet client needs. But:

> [... which is vulnerable] to internecine fighting, to the petty with-holding of information between departments, to the nurturing of poisonous grudges over inequitable pay scales, to the appearance of dandruff on the collars of managers, to the splitting of infinitives in company releases, and to the offering of clammy hands to crucial contacts.

Recap points

▶ An organisation both "is" a culture and "has" a culture.

▶ Organisation culture is not an entity or a thing, independent from the business strategy, that can be manipulated by pulling levers.

▶ The culture of society, and thus by extension organisation culture, is changing all the time regardless of any formal or informal cultural transformation efforts.

▶ Creating a culture is never a "big bang". The attributes, preferences and experiences of the founder(s) and first employees, the business model and the strategy being brought to bear in the new entity all affect what will develop over time into a distinctive culture.

▶ The due diligence associated with mergers and acquisitions should include discussions of the cultural fit, compatibility and value that each culture brings.

▶ Any decision to try to make a planned change to the organisation's culture should derive from a perceived (and communicable) shortfall in business performance or change in business strategy.

▶ Success in culture change is more likely to be achieved not by announcing and trying to implement a culture-change programme but by meeting six conditions (see Table 7.2 on page 177).

One company's experience: Ford

Since coming to Ford from Boeing in 2006, Alan Mulally has

launched a dramatic turnaround effort at the company, which, although still very much a work in progress, has made Ford considerably stronger than its domestic rivals. On joining the company Mulally saw a dramatic drop in vehicle retail sales (18m units in 2005 to 8m units in 2008).

Presenting his business plan to the US Senate Banking Committee in December 2009, Mulally made the point that when he joined Ford he recognised that the business model needed to change and that he was changing it. His principal strategic decision was to focus on the Ford brand and dispose of other brands such as Jaguar, Land Rover and Volvo. He said in an interview with the *New Yorker* in July 2009 that his "going forward point of view" was that under the Ford brand the company needed "to be in every segment and best in class or best in the world". Mulally has not announced a culture-change programme – and he rarely mentions the word "culture" – but in making this strategic shift he has set about changing the culture.

Patty Flaherty, director, HR strategy and Ford learning and development, who has worked for the company since 1999, talks of her experience of Mulally's transformation:

> *I don't remember Alan stating that his aim was to change the culture. In one interview [with the* New Yorker*], he made the point "I would never be presumptuous enough to critique the past." He was very respectful of Ford. But he was eager to take the company to a new place, and he was explicit about that. Indeed, within a short period of joining, he articulated a four-point plan that in the fourth point implied significant culture change:*
>
> *1. Aggressively restructure to operate profitably at the current demand and challenging model mix.*
>
> *2. Accelerate development of new products that customers want and value.*
>
> *3. Finance the plan and improve the balance sheet.*
>
> *4. Work together effectively as one team.*
>
> *Up to that point, people focused on their own efforts, with little regard to the work of others or the success of the whole. So, although he did not specifically call out a culture change, Alan was wise enough to know that to achieve the other three points of the plan, people had to "work together" in a new way.*

To provide clarity of direction, Alan had the business plan printed on a "ONE Ford" pocket card, with one side of the card describing the plan under the headings: One Team, One Plan, One Goal, and the other side laying out the set of "Expected Behaviours" required to deliver the plan. The behaviours fall into four categories, utilising the word FORD as an acronym for the first word in each category. (See Figure 7.1.) Collectively, both sides of the card embody Alan's message of working together as "ONE Ford". Every employee carries this succinct and powerful message with them, attached to their Ford ID badge. And poster-sized versions of the card can be found on the walls of every conference room in every country in which we operate, translated into each of the local languages. The message is heard and clearly understood – everywhere!

But the words alone have not been the most powerful element in changing the culture. Alan has earned the people's trust, respect and credibility since he's been here by not only espousing all of the things he wants to have happen, but by bringing the words to life in our everyday experiences at Ford – and by reinforcing them himself through his own words and actions. Making real what the card represents has meant a shift in the way we do work at Ford, and this, in turn, has had the effect of changing the culture.

Seeing this happen, I believe that culture changes as an output or outcome of changing the way work is done and changing what people experience on a day-to-day basis, including the creation of new definitions of what success and failure are within a company. Many people try to change culture by simply espousing the kinds of things Alan did on the card, and by hoping that the words will come to life and how people do work will change. I believe culture change happens the other way around. First you change the way people work and their day-to-day experiences, and the outcome of that is culture change. Without making the words come to life in the people's shared experiences, I don't believe you have a chance of changing the culture. In our case, Alan specifically set out to change how people experienced "working together" at Ford.

When Alan came to Ford, he instituted a weekly, Thursday morning Business Plan Review (BPR) meeting with all of the key business leaders. Each week, they collectively review the business plan and they work together to resolve any issues that are taking us off plan.

During these meetings, some status is presented in terms of red (off-plan), yellow (marginal), and green (on plan). In the first few

---

One Ford: one team, one plan, one goal   **7.1**

ONE TEAM

People working together as a lean, global enterprise for automotive leadership, as measured by:

> Customer, Employee, Dealer, Investor, Supplier, Union/Council, and Community Satisfaction

ONE PLAN

▷ Aggressively restructure to operate profitably at the current demand and changing model mix

▷ Accelerate development of new products our customers want and value

▷ Finance our plan and improve our balance sheet

▷ Work together effectively as one team

ONE GOAL

An exciting viable Ford delivering profitable growth for all

Expected Behaviours

Foster Functional and Technical Excellence

▷ Know and have a passion for our business and our customers
▷ Demonstrate and build functional and technical excellence
▷ Ensure process discipline
▷ Have a continuous improvement philosophy and practice

Own Working Together

▷ Believe in skilled and motivated people working together
▷ Include everyone; respect, listen to, help and appreciate others
▷ Build strong relationships; be a team player; develop ourselves and others
▷ Communicate clearly, concisely and candidly

Role Model Ford Values

▷ Show initiative, courage, integrity and good corporate citizenship
▷ Improve quality, safety and sustainability
▷ Have a can do, find a way attitude and emotional resilience
▷ Enjoy the journey and each other, have fun – never at others' expense

Deliver Results

▷ Deal positively with our business realities; develop compelling and comprehensive plans, while keeping an enterprise view
▷ Set high expectations and inspire others
▷ Make sound decisions using facts and data
▷ Hold ourselves and others responsible and accountable for delivering results and satisfying our customers

Source: Ford Motor Company

---

meetings, status on all key metrics was presented as green. Finally Alan said, "Since we just lost $12 billion, isn't there something that's not going well?" At the next meeting, one of the leaders presented the status of a key metric as red. There was a moment of stunned silence in the room, and then Alan stood and clapped to show his approval of the honest portrayal of the true facts of the situation. In that one moment, Alan recreated the definition of failure or success in our culture. He didn't call the leader a failure for telling the ugly truth. Instead, he let us know that success would now mean leading with transparency and with real facts and data. It's not that Alan doesn't want us to be green in all categories. It's that he believes you "can't manage a secret" and that by putting the real facts on the table, you can "work together" as a team to "find a way" to resolve the issues and get back on plan. It was a very powerful meeting that made concrete, almost for the first time, the new way of working that Alan advocates. Those managers who do not want to be transparent, share facts, data, accountability, information, or work together, tend to self-select out of the organisation – indeed some have.

So, how is the culture changing? What has happened in the three *years Alan's been here is an increasing alignment between business and people processes and the plan and behaviours of ONE Ford. We are continuing to move from:*

Secretive	*Transparent*
Subjective	*Facts and data*
Siloed/chimneyed	*One team, working together*
Ford-led	*Customer-driven*

Clearly "moving the needle" (that is, making progress in the right direction) as we have is a huge shift. The success of the change is tested in the responses the leadership gives whenever it is called to task. This can be in major situations – a recall, for example – or in more minor everyday situations when someone acts in a countercultural way. There are three possible responses to countercultural action or behaviour: (a) ignoring it, (b) condoning it, or (c) calling it out as unacceptable. In terms of credibility and creating a new kind of shared experience, (c) is the only valid response. We can't allow disconnects between what we espouse and what we do and reinforce. That's one of the reasons we have integrated the expected behaviours on the ONE Ford card into the way we recruit, develop, and give performance feedback at our company.

Of course, this is a never-ending journey. The culture is being tested every day – every minute perhaps. In an organisation this size, there are subcultures, layered cultures and myriad cultural complexities – but one company culture transcends these and we are all currently gravitating steadily towards ONE Ford. Over the last three years we are showing in a new way how we take our legacy very seriously. In Alan's words, "We (and our customers) have a tremendous goodwill for the Ford Motor Company. This is Ford, this is Henry Ford, this is an American icon. (We represent) over a 100 years of innovation, safe and efficient transportation." We mean to continue that tradition as ONE Ford.

Learning from Ford

Note that in Ford's case the culture change meets all six conditions discussed, but three lessons are reinforced in Ford's approach to culture change:

▶ **Develop a clear business strategy and a strong set of corporate values or equivalent that transcend individuals.**

The simple-to-understand, clear and succinct pocket card that synthesises Ford's business plan and the way of realising it gives people the direction needed to work as one team in support of ONE Ford. The Thursday meetings mean that all functional heads are sharing the same data and talking to their own teams. The transparency of information means that there are no secrets – everybody knows the plan, and everybody works together to achieve it.

▶ **Ensure leaders role-model the behaviours and cultural norms they want employees to model.** Mulally role models, talks about and is consistent in demanding the way of working that he believes is in Ford's best interest. One interviewer described this as "good-natured but relentless insistence on following what he has determined to be the correct course of action".[20] His personal style has earned the trust and respect of the workforce, and he has successfully negotiated with unions and others to take what looks like being a successful business plan. (Unlike its traditional rivals, GM and Chrysler, Ford did not take the government loans that the other two companies accepted in the 2008 financial crisis.) The plan identified specific goals for the company, created a process that moves it toward those goals and installed a system to make sure it gets there. Mulally "watches all this with intensity – and demands weekly, sometimes daily, updates". Chief financial officer Lewis Booth, a 31-year Ford veteran, says:

> Alan's style is pretty relentless. He says, "If this is the reality, what are we going to do about it?" not "We're going to work our way through it."

But his style is one that works. Mulally's openness seems to have won him support throughout the organisation. Joe Hinrichs, head of Ford's Asia Pacific and Africa business unit, says: "Alan brings infectious energy. This is a person people want to follow."

▶ **Divide and do the work differently – change the way work is done (do not have formal culture-change programmes).** Having a clear plan and then ensuring that all processes in the organisation are aligned to achieve this has the effect of changing the culture. It is likely to mean that people who are unwilling or unable to work in the new way leave the organisation. Those that remain share experiences, successes and failures in the new paradigm, and over time the culture shifts. In Ford's case the method for achieving the business plan also involves inculcating the attributes of the "right culture" and "good work" discussed in Chapter 6. And, as noted, there is no end point – the culture change is a work in progress.

Summary

▶ An organisation's culture is in a continuous state of flux, responding to changes in the organisation's markets and in the wider society in which it operates. In these circumstances aiming to create, change or protect the culture is challenging and takes time.

▶ Rather than introduce culture creation or change initiatives it is better to look at what the business model and strategy are, the way work is done and the supporting infrastructures, and use these to change the culture over time.

▶ Credible leaders who role-model the characteristics they want to see in the organisation help reinforce the desired cultural attributes.

Exercise 7: Culture change in Appendix 3 provides a structure for planning for culture change in a non-programmatic way.

Can culture be learned?

More than 40 years ago Edgar Schein of MIT Sloan School of Management made the point that the process of learning about an organisation "is so ubiquitous and we go through it so often during our total career, that it is all too easy to overlook it".[1] He continued with the observation that "there are constant resocialisation pressures" and these have an impact on the whole workforce. The pressures relate partly to the changes in society and the external environment, partly to the flow of people into and out of an organisation, and partly to organisational decisions and choices.

This means that to function effectively within an organisation, all those who belong to it have to learn the culture and adapt their learning as it changes. This is not surprising as culture develops through the interaction of people making sense of their world (see Chapter 6). To learn the culture well enough to fit in and get on in it, individuals have to demonstrate certain attributes. The most important are:[2]

▶ a commitment to develop links with others in their organisation via the establishment of networks, coalitions and friendships;

▶ strong motivation and the appropriate skills to learn what is needed;

▶ astute situational awareness and responsiveness, which require insight, subtlety, intuition and an informed perspective;

▶ the possession of values that match those of the organisation or are adaptable to them;

▶ an ability to align personal knowledge, experience, values and sense of importance with the organisation's values, goals and plans.

Where these are not all present things can go wrong, as the following example illustrates.

Luke Maxwell (not his real name) was recruited to the role of assistant director in the planning department of a large transport company. Here he gives a bit of background:

> I work in this sector because I love transport. I love cities and the infrastructures that make them work effectively.

He had been with his previous company for five years, but for personal reasons wanted to relocate to the city where the new job was:

> Looking back, that was one in a series of mistakes I made. I shouldn't have taken the job just because I wanted to be in this city. The whole experience was incredibly difficult. It reinforced what I already knew but thought I could override – that I'm better at crisis management, high-risk, in-the-moment work than I am at day-to-day repetitive implementation and execution which the new job was. I like working on things that have a defined start and finish date. I'm not a good day-to-day manager. I'm not organised enough. My brain moves in too many directions at once. I was fortunate in that I was able to take a sideways move in the organisation after six months and I'm now in a role that suits me much better. If this one hadn't turned up I would have had to leave.

Table 8.1 summarises the difficulties he experienced, in relation to the five attributes mentioned, in his first weeks in the new role.

Table 8.1 **Attributes needed to start a new role**

Attribute	Luke Maxwell
An ability to develop links with others in their organisation through setting up networks, coalitions and friendships	I wasn't sure about my relationship with my boss. He'd given me the job on the strength of a recommendation from a friend of mine. Although there's a lot of mutual respect it was a stilted dynamic. He's very quiet, very smart, with a forceful personality. I wanted him to be my mentor as I thought I could learn a lot from him, but that didn't really work out. I couldn't really read him.
Strong motivation and the appropriate skills to learn what is needed	Looking back it was clear that I had no interest and no excitement in taking this role. It was a move prompted by a desire to be in a particular geographic location and didn't capitalise on any of my technical expertise. I wasn't proud of getting the job, and I did no homework to prepare myself to do it. I went in totally cold.
Astute situational awareness and responsiveness requiring insight, subtlety, intuition and an informed perspective	I got some resistance from a couple of my staff and the relationships were pretty contentious; in particular, one person who had thought that she was going to get the job that I got. Her approach was to carve out two things that were "hers" and to stay out of my way. I decided at that point not to pick a fight with her. The people took the tack of going over my head on things (to my superiors), and they in turn went directly to my subordinates; for example, my boss would invite my subordinate to meetings and not me, so I wasn't sure what my role and position was. For a long while I thought I was ineffective and that I was going to lose my job. I felt I had no power to bring people to heel. All I wanted was to be in the loop. I found the first six months very isolating.
The possession of values that match those of the organisation or are adaptable to them	I wanted to promote a strong service delivery environment, thinking about what we did from a customer's perspective, which is not the norm in this organisation.

Attribute	Luke Maxwell
An ability to align personal knowledge, experience, values and sense of importance with the organisation's values, goals and plans	I've been accused of creating a hostile work environment, but a colleague pointed out that I am simply trying to create a work environment. People need to know what is expected from them up front. Here I'm working with a team I inherited, more or less picked at random. I haven't had the luxury of picking winners and there's no time to lose before performance is required. There's no time to sit back and do the homework: "the ticking clock is keeping me from settling in".

For a newcomer to an organisation, learning the culture is almost equivalent to gaining "the seat perilous" (in Arthurian legend the seat across the Round Table from King Arthur reserved for the knight who completed the quest for the Holy Grail) – it is not for the faint-hearted. In a survey conducted at IMD:[3]

> Fully 87% of the 143 survey respondents either agreed or strongly agreed with the statement, "Transitions into significant new roles are the most challenging times in the professional lives of managers". And more than 70% agreed or strongly agreed that "success or failure during the transition period is a strong predictor of overall success or failure in the job".

What makes for success is the ability to simultaneously fit in socially and get on in performance terms. This has little to do with the technical or professional expertise of the newcomer and a lot to do with their personality and their ability to learn the culture. As one headhunter says:[4] "People are hired for their ability and fired for their personality." The head of a coaching firm reinforced this point, observing:[5]

> The combination of your performance and your personality determines how you're viewed. Probably 95% of firings are the result of failing to fit into a company's culture. If people don't know you, they can't trust you.

Julie Roehm, senior vice-president of marketing communications at Walmart, was loudly and publicly fired in December 2006, just ten months after starting the job. Talking about this she acknowledged mistakes, among them moving too quickly and not adapting to her new workplace. Her perceptions painted a picture of warring fiefdoms and a passive-aggressive culture that was hostile to outsiders. Although she was justifiably criticised for being tone-deaf to Walmart's culture, "Walmart", she says, "would rather have had a painkiller [than] taken the vitamin of change." What has she learned? "The importance of culture. It can't be overestimated."[6] She now ranks cultural fit – geographic and corporate – at the top of her list, when looking for a job, adding that her "aggressive-aggressive" personality, as she describes it, does not fit with the "passive-aggressive" politeness of the South (the southern United States where Walmart has its headquarters).[7]

Before joining Walmart, Roehm earned an edgy (that is, a boundary pushing) reputation as director of marketing communications at Chrysler Group. Her hiring by one of America's most colourless companies always struck friends and industry insiders as odd. Few were surprised when Roehm and Walmart parted ways.

This example illustrates the reality that people joining an organisation or moving to a new role within their organisation have to learn the culture and subculture(s) in order to operate successfully within them. Although most of the ways that newcomers approach learning the culture are the same as the ways established organisation members continue to learn it, for new joiners the stakes are higher.

This chapter examines organisational culture from the perspective of employees who are new to an organisation or have a new role, and to whom the following are crucial:

▶ how they recognise and learn what the culture is;

▶ what they should do to fit in and make progress;

▶ the help they are given by their managers to assimilate.

Beginning a new job usually involves both excitement and a degree of fear because of the tightrope that has to be walked in order, as has been said earlier, to "fit it" and "get on"; in other words, be socially acceptable and do the job effectively. Rigorous selection and recruitment processes – designed to weed out internal or external people who might not fit in or get on – are not consistent predictors of whether someone will succeed or fail in the job.

To help mitigate the risks associated with integrating new employees (what academics call "organisational socialisation"), most large organisations have an induction or orientation process that usually provides such information as organisation charts, statements of values and explanations of particular processes. But many organisations fall short in providing information on less tangible aspects, such as assumptions about the role, the way of operating in it, the style to use for getting quick results, and the organisational norms and expectations – in a word, the culture.

For most newcomers to an organisation it is getting to grips with the tacit and inexplicable "way we do things around here" that is much more important in determining their success than the explicit information they are given. But this tacit knowledge is difficult for newcomers to grasp without the help of "insiders" who point them in the right direction and explain what is expected. People experience similar situations trying to enter any culture different from the one they already know. The example of Joanna Bentley joining Eton College, a famous formerly all-male British school, from a girls' state school in the north of England illustrates this:

> The very first day ... I sat in the Chapel on the first assembly and I couldn't believe it – there was just me and lots of boys. They all regarded me with awe, but nobody really wanted to get to know me properly the first few weeks ... It would be impossible for a girl or even a boy to come to Eton in the sixth year (aged 17), as I did, and absorb themselves and know what was going on straightaway. I needed lots of help – the main thing was the language, which is so completely different from anything I've ever known ... When somebody said to me "Which beak are you up to this half?" I just nodded and smiled; in fact it means which teacher is going to teach you this coming ... half term (semester) ... It's a school with all sorts of rules and traditions that don't exist in any other academic environment, certainly not in newer schools.

A visitor, an immigrant, or a new employee integrating into an unknown culture needs to be able to navigate and network effectively. To do this means being skilled at asking questions, making connections, analysing and interpreting a wide range of new information, establishing rapport and demonstrating credibility – all without coming across in a way that puts people off.

Fortunately, the culture can be learned if four factors are in place:

▶ The joiner has the attributes noted in Table 8.1 and the ability to learn the way things are done, including ways of behaving, operating and thinking as well as norms and values (the fitting-in aspects).

▶ The joiner has the capacity to learn this within an acceptable time frame.

▶ Established employees are willing to support and help the newcomer.

▶ The new joiner can and will pay the "price of membership", that is, what has to be paid to become accepted as an insider (the getting-on aspects).[8]

Confirming the headhunter's observation made earlier, none of these factors relate to any apparent technical expertise, formal qualification, or ability to do the job successfully. They all relate to the way the newcomer is able to integrate (or not) into the organisation's culture, which is much more related to his or her personality.

Figure 8.1 models the factors and the individual's ability to perform successfully. The bottom horizontal axis is what and how the recruit is learning; the left vertical axis is the people the recruit is learning from; the right vertical axis is the price the recruit has to pay for joining; and the top horizontal axis is the time that the organisation "allows" for learning. The factors interact in unique ways related to the individual's context and role, but, as stated, to be successful the recruit has to be able to both fit in socially and get on in performance terms. Optimum performance is the outcome of meeting both these conditions well. How this is done is discussed in the following sections.

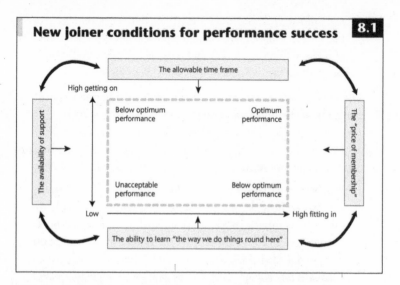

New Joiner conditions for performance success `8.1`

The ability to learn "the way we do things round here"

Whether moving roles within an organisation or joining a new company, people have to immediately (usually within a period of a few weeks) learn a certain amount. How much they need to learn depends, among other things, on the role, their experience, the context and the performance objectives. But generally they must be able and willing to learn – suspending preconceptions, assumptions and (if possible) judgments – from four categories:

▶ **The industry.** Although there is a lot of talk about "transferable skills" – so, for example, a marketing expert in one industry should be able to transfer to a marketing role in another industry – this is more difficult than it appears, as the Roehm example on pages 191–2 shows. The skills may be transferable to the new context but they may need adaptation or development. Without knowing about the industry it is hard to judge how transferable they are, so it is essential that new recruits learn the background, history and current context of the industry they are working in. As one person says:

> I will do much better when I know the business. I'm on a very steep learning curve. This company is one with lots of rules,

regulations, processes and bureaucracy that are in the legacy of the place. It's hard to understand what's to be enforced because of legislation or regulation and what is not allowed. I need to learn about the industry as quickly as possible.

▶ **The organisation.** This covers "the politics, power and value premises of the organisational system, leadership style, special languages and so forth".[9] These implicit aspects of the organisation are difficult for a newcomer to get to grips with early on, as this person joining a large multinational comments:[10]

People here "know how it is". You can't pick up things by osmosis so how do you pick it up? You don't get a book. An awful lot is unwritten and unstructured. Decisions are made in corridors. The organisation is very cloudy. When you come in from outside it's extraordinary. The culture here is based on networks and gossip – who knows who – and my network isn't up enough yet. A large part of what we do is about relationships – I'm conscious that my work is being kept back as I learn the ropes.

▶ **The role.** Learning "focuses on the boundaries of authority and responsibility, expectations and the appropriate behaviours for the position". Learning about the role involves learning what is acceptable and unacceptable for that position as well as the specific expertise required. Lack of job-specific knowledge not only makes it more difficult for people to do their job effectively, but also affects their credibility with members of their workgroups and beyond that their acceptance as a group member. For people moving to a new role internally, the issues can be just as pressing as for someone coming from outside. One manager moving from a corporate position to an operational one comments:

A lot of judgments about how well I can do the job are made on the technical knowledge I have of the "train set". I've sometimes felt I'm less of a human being because I don't know anything about door seals.

▶ **The group processes.** These are "concerned with co-worker interaction, group norms and values and the workgroup's

Table 8.2 Ways of learning a new culture

Learning method	Example	Skills needed
Feedback and guidance given by boss and colleagues	"You can learn from each other around the coffee machines." "My boss is very good at giving me feedback on how I'm doing."	Rapport building Listening Openness to feedback
Comparison with previous experiences	"I hadn't been in a head office environment before. The differences between head office and field are very marked. I have had to adjust my working style."	Assessment Judgment Adaptability
Observation of what is going on in the context	"It was odd seeing people sitting in meetings openly checking their e-mails on their BlackBerrys. In my last job the protocol was to turn off devices in a meeting, but have lots of catch-up breaks".	Patience Objectivity Curiosity
Trial and error	"It's the dead-rat syndrome. I offer things up and judge by the looks on people's faces whether they want them or not."	Risk taking Persistence Resilience
Investigating and asking questions	"If I want to find out something, I have to go out and find it. My attitude has been to question."	Healthy sense of scepticism Research Questioning

normative structure", and underscore the fact that joiners have to learn the norms and values not only at an organisational level but also at a subculture level. For those moving internally, the local culture may be substantially different from that in other parts of the organisation, which can be both surprising and difficult to handle. The boss of one manager who had moved internally makes the point:

> This department is different – he inherited a tough team with

strong personalities and he's had a hard time adjusting his style. His people skills here are a big issue – people don't think he's on their side even if he is. Yet he was known as a great "people person" in his last role.

Identifying the content of what people new to a role are learning is easier than assessing how they are learning it. But five learning methods used in various combinations, both consciously and unconsciously, are cited. Each of these requires deployment of a range of skills, as Table 8.2 illustrates.

People coming new to an organisation from outside are at a disadvantage when it comes to quick and effective performance; they have more to learn and less to draw on in terms of networks and knowing who to go to than insiders changing roles. This organisational know-how is particularly necessary at senior levels – a point discussed in some research on the best-performing CEOs in the world:[11]

> *In our analysis of the 1,999 CEOs, we determined that insiders tend to do better. On average, they ranked 57 places higher than outsiders in the full list.*
>
> *Industry and firm-specific knowledge is critical when it comes to generating long-term growth. Among the up-through-the-ranks leaders on our list are Yun Jong-Yong, who joined Samsung straight out of college and worked there 30 years before becoming CEO, and Mukesh Ambani, who joined Reliance Industries in 1981, when it was still a textile company run by his father.*

This finding is endorsed by Joseph Bower, author of *The CEO Within: Why Inside Outsiders Are the Key to Succession Planning*. In an interview he makes the point:[12]

> *The great advantage of an internal candidate is that he or she knows the people, systems, and culture of the company. That means the candidate knows the company's strengths and weaknesses, who can be relied upon to help change things, where world-class competence does or does not reside, and how things can best be transformed.*

But the statement is qualified by his observation:

> [With this] you need an outside perspective to have a true, even brutal, understanding of what needs to change if the company is to succeed in the competitive environment that lies ahead. The inside-outsider knows that if his or her vision of the way the world is headed is remotely right, then real change is needed and he or she has the understanding of the company and confidence of its people to drive that transformation.

However, having an inside-outsider perspective is not a guarantee of performance success. Even someone with the attributes, skills and technical expertise to get on and fit in may be thwarted by one or more of the other three factors required for cultural integration and performance success.

The acceptable time frame for learning

Like it or not, the early days shape people's perceptions of the newcomer and this, in turn, has an influence on the likelihood of success in role. As one manager put it: "You've got three months while people circle round you and then they make up their minds."

Typically, within the allowable time period (different depending on the organisation but often quoted as "the first 100 days") the individual is going through four stages. These are not tied to any particular time frame, so it is not possible to say that stage 1, for example, takes two weeks. Rather passage through the stages depends on the context and attributes of the new recruit.

There is a tendency to think that these first 100 days in a new role are the most important, and theorists talk of "stage models" of organisational socialisation during this period (see Table 8.3),[13] but it is useful to remember that organisational socialisation is a continuous process for everyone in the organisation all the time. People are making constant adjustments to their standing in their role and the organisation; it is just that once someone is established in an organisation the adjustments become more second nature and less something to be consciously worked at.

Table 8.3 A model of cultural learning within the allowable time frame

Stages in learning the culture	Task	How to do this
Stage 1	Confront and accept organisational reality. **Comment:** What is learned through the interview and due-diligence process rarely squares with what the reality is on joining.	"Spend time with people who can tell you about the hidden rules of success in your new workplace. Seek out the regulars (your team mates, the guy in purchasing whom you'll be calling often), the dealmakers (project leaders, people in-the-know) and the potential mentors. Establish an initial connection so that you can build a relationship. Trust and information will follow naturally."
Stage 2	Achieve role clarity. **Comment:** The job someone is expecting to get and do is not necessarily the one that needs to be done once he or she arrives in the organisation.	"Once you've spent about a month and a half on the job, you should have a solid sense of your responsibilities. How do they differ from what you were led to expect? Are there new opportunities that you might pursue? Get your questions down on paper, along with a list of your top projects and your most pressing deadlines. Then review them with your boss. The goal: to create a real-world job description that you both agree on."[a]
Stage 3	Locate yourself in the organisational context. **Comment:** Knowing how to position yourself in relation to others is crucial to building the necessary trust that must be developed in order to be fully effective.	"I'm new and my colleague doesn't know me, so if I start stomping around in his vineyard he's never going to trust me. I give him input on the things he's asked about ... if he can see that I'm competent ... I think he'll eventually open up to some feedback about the service standards."[b]

Stages in learning the culture	Task	How to do this
Stage 4	Detect signs of successful cultural integration (or lack of it). **Comment:** Organisations have different and subtle ways of "telling" people they have joined. In some places there is a formal rite of passage, for example in the military. In others it is social recognition of some form, and assumes that performance objectives have been met.	"My business results combined with my manager hearing good things about me from the organisation will prove I've 'joined'. The icing on the cake would be getting a place on the innovation tiger team."

a Dahle, C., "Fast Start – Your First 60 Days", *Fast Company*, December 18th 2007.
b Downey, D., *Assimilating New Leaders: The Key to Executive Retention*, AMACOM, 2001.

Judgments on performance come in various forms, often as direct or indirect feedback from the boss or colleagues. Within six weeks of one external recruit joining the company his manager commented:

> The main angst is his speed to getting to work with peers and colleagues. He's already taken some levels of feedback. Some subordinates have suggested he's not getting up to speed as quickly as they would like.

Three months later the same manager noted:

> He hasn't picked things up and isn't able to contribute effectively. I'm getting warning bells from the people he's managing.

The following month the executive left the company.

Conversely, the manager of another external recruit said after six weeks:

> We chucked her in and helped her when requested. She's swimming very well.

Three months later the manager was delighted to say:

> She's been an outstanding success. She's comfortably achieved far more than I expected of her. She's recognised as the best of my managers although she's the newest.

Why some people are able to make an impact within the allowable time frame and others are not is, again, not easy to identify because each individual plays out the interactions between the four factors and his or her attributes differently. But those that have a carefully planned and supportive integration process are less likely to stumble than those who are just left to get on with it.

Helping new people to learn the culture

People coming to a new role cannot learn the culture in isolation. They are dependent on the involvement of others, including their manager, their peer group, co-workers, other staff in the organisation and often others outside the organisation – for example, mentors, ex-employees and customers. Sometimes these others give friendly help and sometimes they are hostile. Here is one person's experience:[14]

> I once spent three weeks trying to get a copy of our client's year-end sales analysis from a co-worker two doors down. We worked for the same advertising agency, on the same account, and for the same client, so I figured we were on the same team, right?

> At first he "couldn't find it". Then it was "probably in Angela's office" ... Then he was late for a meeting and would "be sure to have it by tomorrow". He didn't. Finally it escalated into a scene ... in front of the elevator. Surrounded by cronies, he started to shine his key chain flashlight up my nose and into my pockets, repeating, "Well, maybe it's in here. Is it in there? Nope. I just can't find those statistics anywhere. Sorry."

As the elevator door closed I could hear the laughter echo up through the elevator shaft.

The realisation dawned that although both workers were on the same team they were not "playing the same game". The person's intent was to serve the customer (in a culture that valued customer service), so her co-worker's response "stunned" her. She asks:

If one game was the "Serving the Customer Game", what was the other game? Who made up the teams? What were the rules?

This vividly told incident illustrates the culture game being played in that organisation. This person's response was to learn to play the game. She says:

I learned the rules. I learned to make friends in high places, to withhold information, to say I was going to do things I had no intention of doing.

What this incident says about the culture of this organisation is open to debate, but it illustrates the fact that people learn it from others in all kinds of situations, both caring and hurtful. For new joiners, one of the best ways they can learn the culture is through a thoughtful and perceptive manager who provides constructive feedback and a shoulder to lean on. As an example, this new joiner says:

My line manager is good at feedback and has taken the time to say I'm bringing a fresh outlook to the role, which is what they were looking for. He's been extremely supportive, doing what he can when everyone else has had too much else to concentrate on.

A supportive manager paves the way for the new joiner. One such manager talking of his role in helping his new joiner says:

I pre-sold him in. I've got to help package and present him, and when he joined it was important for him to have me available and for me to be seen to be standing beside him. I took him round with me and we built up trust and rapport.

Without this type of manager support many new joiners flounder and lose their way.

Almost equally important is peer support, less from a feedback role and more from a social inclusion role. When this is withheld people feel uneasy. As one person says:

> With my peer group some testing of me is taking place. I get the feeling that it's a kind of "Let's see what you can bring here. Let's see if you can come up to scratch". There's a need for the network to show approval before someone is accepted and trusted. But they aren't going to tell you if they've decided that they don't like you. You just keep bumping into walls.

This person refers to "some testing", which is commonly talked about in various ways by both new joiners and their managers. As one manager says:

> He has to learn the technicalities of the role – metrics, suppliers – and do it quickly. He's managing a lot of specialists and seasoned practitioners. He'll have to earn his stripes on this. This organisation is generally tough to penetrate across disciplines.

Paying the price of membership

The "price of membership" refers to the cost to the new joiner of being culturally assimilated – of earning their stripes. It marks the point of crossing the boundary from being an outsider to being an insider.

Sometimes the price paid is obvious and perhaps costly, and sometimes it is barely noticeable. It is paid in various ways. It can be a single payment, or the equivalent of an instalment plan with an end point, or a regular "tax" that everyone pays – the type of payment that is extracted from all employees regardless of whether they are new or not. The most common types of price of membership for new joiners are:

▶ an initiation test;

▶ an endurance and/or proving process;

▶ gradual personal change and/or adaptation.

Initiation test

This is not usually the orchestrated "head in lavatory pan" type of trial, but it can feel like it, as it is usually a high-profile, make-or-break event, often related to the completion and presentation of a first task or project that has to be quickly and successfully achieved. Consider this example of the type of thing people describe as an initiation test:[15]

> It's barely two weeks into her new job at the advertising giant Foote Cone & Belding, and Molly Buchholz's nerves are fried. Buchholz, a 29-year-old account executive, has just had a dispute with the company's media director, her first with a Foote Cone colleague. Despite the media director's objections, she has advised her client, Lucent Technologies Inc., to turn down a flashy sponsorship deal with a National Hockey League team. She tried to disagree without being disagreeable, but she fears that the colleague is less than amused.
>
> "There's been some grumbling," she says. "But if I don't express my opinion around here, I'll just be a puppet."
>
> Though she believes she made the right decision, Buchholz frets over the fallout: did she come off as pushy? Did she break an unwritten rule? Did she insult someone whose support she'll need down the road? Buchholz was a star performer at her previous gig, with Saatchi & Saatchi Worldwide, but she feels tentative at her new one. She doesn't yet speak Foote Cone's language. Learning it has been exhausting.
>
> "I spend a lot of time worrying about how I act and react in different situations," she says. "I feel like I'm under a microscope."

In this case Buchholz "passed the test". The senior vice-president in her division endorsed her decision and she was able to proceed with confidence into the role.

An endurance and/or proving process

Often this is about showing that the joiner can play the game in the approved way (even although the rules are usually not that clear), or proving that they are a safe pair of hands, capable of handling certain projects. It is a difficult time for newcomers, as this manager explains:

> At the peer group level people were testing me to see if I was an honest player or whether I was political, self-promoting, or overambitious, so in terms of fitting in socially it wasn't an initiation test - it was a much longer drawn-out process - more like a slow torture rather than a brief period of abuse. It was a proving period to see how I performed. I survived - after three months I was through the worst and now I'm doing fine.

Another commented:

> There are a number of technical aspects associated with the role that I don't understand yet. Some more graunchy, nitty-gritty things I don't know so much about and need to learn. Being able to demonstrate technical knowledge is my rite of entry to the group. I haven't got there.

Gradual personal change and/or adaptation

This starts to happen within the first weeks of starting the new role as people learn that what worked in their previous role is not always appropriate for the current role. In the example below the new employee describes how in her previous company the norm was to give feedback, input and constructive critical comment during a meeting. In her new company the norm was to give feedback in private after the meeting:[16]

> Here [the new company] people will analyse every piece of detail of everything, but only in private. Say if someone presents something in the meeting then literally ten minutes after the meeting ends people will call and say: "How did I do? Should I have done this? How was it received? etc." I think that having that critical dialogue [in a meeting] is exciting, energising, and expected. Here, however, it is seen as being confrontational ... or you are viewed as difficult. Which is interesting when you think that what makes you successful at one organisation actually makes you unsuccessful at another.

In this instance, the new joiner made efforts to adapt her style and approach but finally chose not to continue working in an environment where she did not feel she could be herself. She left after one year.

Signs of unsuccessful integration

Some people make the conscious choice not to pay the price of membership while others cannot do so for various reasons. Here some managers comment on their new joiner's inability to integrate (all four of the joiners these managers were referring to left the organisation within six months):

Manager 1: She's not a good delegator and hasn't learned this yet, so she hasn't been able to deliver what we wanted from her.

Manager 2: With his work team he's learned how to be effective. He's having issues with his superiors – he needs to learn better upward management if he's going to get on.

Manager 3: He doesn't fit into the role – he's a backroom guy rather than front of house.

Manager 4: He learned the business quickly but hasn't learned to change his style.

Again it is noticeable that all the comments relate to style and personality rather than technical expertise. However, remember that no new joiner will be successfully integrated unless they meet performance objectives and are able to fit in.

Signs of successful integration relate to the four domains that new joiners have to learn (see Table 8.4).

Table 8.4 Integration and the price paid

Domain	Example sign of integration	Related price of membership
Industry	Being called on for industry-related expertise: "We needed someone to give an industry perspective and speak for us. He's new to our industry but he's done a quick and effective learning job."	Spending time on developing the industry knowledge and learning the language: "I've put a lot of time into learning the nuts and bolts of the operation, talking to people at all levels and in different roles. It's been a good investment of time."
Organisation	Having ideas accepted: "She's brought in various process aspects that she believes in and has made them effective across the organisation."	Using a different power base: "Where I worked before I could use positional power to get things done. Here I can only achieve the goals using personal power and influence. This took me a while to grasp and apply."
Role	Being noticed as a role model: "She's presenting as a great model for professionalism, cross-functional thinking, communicating and commitment. All in all she's a great ambassador."	Modifying expectations: "I realised that the way to get the department running effectively, meeting its targets, and delivering to plan was to lower my expectations – start from where my team is rather than where I wanted them to be."
Group	Being able to influence the group: "He's come up with several ways round problems. He's got some fresh approaches he's been able to implement."	Changing style: "I've had to be more assertive and more directive than in my previous role, and I've had to adapt my attitudes a lot – all despite my intentions of remaining my own man."

Recap points

▶ Staying in tune with the organisational culture is a continuous process of learning and adaptation for all of an organisation's members. It is essential for newcomers to be adept at reading and adjusting to the culture. If they cannot do this, they will be shunned or expelled from it.

▶ There are five attributes a newcomer needs to have and demonstrate on entering a new culture. These relate to aspects of fitting in socially, and getting on in terms of achieving performance objectives. They are related more to personality than to technical expertise.

▶ People new to a role have to learn it from four different angles: industry, organisation, job content and group processes. Each is equally important in achieving successful performance.

▶ Having the right attributes to learn the culture is not enough. People cannot learn the culture by themselves; they are reliant on the help of others both in and outside the organisation. They have to show they have learned it within an acceptable time frame (often quoted as 100 days), and they have to pay the price of membership.

▶ People will not be accepted into the organisation unless they can both meet performance objectives and fit in socially.

▶ Recognising the signs of successful acceptance means reading social and cultural signals accurately. The clues are often subtle, although in some organisations there is a formal rite of passage, such as admission to a partnership in an accounting company.

▶ People can make conscious choices about whether to aim for cultural admission, but often the existing members of the organisation make the choices for them.

One person's way of learning the culture: Nik

Nik opened the discussion on how he learns the culture of a country and an organisation by giving some biographical information:

> I was born in Iran, and when I was 14 went to live in the UK. Three years later I moved to the United States and I've been here since

*then. It's 34 years now and although I've been primarily based in
the United States my whole working life has been one of working
in the retail business in other markets – the Middle East, North
and South America, eastern Europe, Europe, Japan, South Korea,
Australia and South-East Asia, and now I've just taken a job in
China. I travel a lot; for example, I've been to China four times in
the last four months as well as to other countries. I speak English,
Persian and passable French. I consider myself a global person but I
know that I'll have to fine-tune my globality for this new role.*

The job in China was a lateral move in his current organisation,
where he has worked for seven years. It is an organisation in which
he feels comfortable and recognises a values match (one of the
necessary new-joiner attributes). He decided to take the job mainly,
he says:

*[Because] I thought it would expand my horizons – China is the
final, major territory for our time in our business – and it's a very
significant move for the company to take this leap. It's a very large
market with a lot of potential.*

*I've noticed people fall into one of two camps – one group enjoys
homogeneity, and the other difference. I'm very much in the latter.
I've always been intrigued by difference, I find it stimulating. When
I come across something different I dissect it and learn as much as
I can about it. I accept what I like and drop what I don't. I couldn't
turn down an opportunity like this.*

It is evident that Nik has the strong motivation and the appropriate
skills to learn what is needed (another of the five attributes a new
joiner requires). His motivation comes from his curiosity and his
learning approach comes from his interest in "dissecting" difference.
He explained how he does this:

*What I've found is that the national culture of a country has a
strong influence on the culture of the organisation – even if it
is a multinational the local operation reflects the society which
it's based in. This means I have to be very aware of the national
culture – that's where my curiosity and interest in difference comes
into play. For example, as soon as I arrived, for the first time, in
Shanghai Pudong International Airport I started to pay attention
to the details. I noticed the way the people at the immigration
check approached what they were doing and asked myself things
like: Are they making eye-contact with me? Are they smiling? Are
they approachable? Do I feel welcomed? When I went out into the*

airport concourse I was looking at what people were wearing, the styles, the colours, the haircuts, the approach to foreigners who look different and comparing how people here seemed to respond to them and how I observed similar situations in other airports.

Then travelling into the city I was watching the traffic, noticing if the cars were clean, how organised the traffic flow was – in some cities there can be a huge volume of traffic but it is well organised with lanes, lights, and so on, while in others the same volume is totally chaotic. Noticing these types of things gives me insights into how the people I'll be working with will behave because, as I said, the national culture spills over into the business culture. It's the details that get me to the bigger picture because they help me see what's important to people. Once I have the detail I can make sense of the whole thing.

Thus Nik reveals his personal competence in reading situations and getting them right. As stated earlier, this attribute requires commitment, insight, subtlety, intuition and an informed perspective. He made the point that before he goes to a new place he does a lot of research: he reads about the place he is going to; he talks to people who are from there, have been there and/or lived there; he gathers information and prepares to adapt as necessary. He says:

What I'm doing is continuously comparing the new information and experience with what I already know, analysing the new situation and absorbing, as much as I can, its essence.

At several points during the discussion Nik mentioned the need to be polite and respectful of other people's cultures, saying that being "polite gets you to a lot of places". Developing this theme he says:

Business is first and foremost about building personal relationships – not business relationships. To build personal relationships means I have to be respectful, charming and patient. In a way, in this situation, you're courting the other person or people and it takes time, understanding and trust. When I meet people from other cultures I think of them as my dance partner. I follow their lead. I learn the norms and procedures from them. Over the years, and maybe as a result of my personal heritage, I've learned how I can live and work harmoniously in different cultures. I'm not a "one note" person – harmony is critical and in my experience comes from trying to see things through the other person's lens and being fair. Once you have the personal relationship the business relationship follows.

211

The notable thing about Nik's approach is that his own values of respecting others, playing fair, living harmoniously and reaching out all work towards his being adaptable to any culture; they are firmly held values, but they are inclusive, not exclusive ones. He sees nothing but failure coming from pushing people to do things his way, or working from positional or other power, making the point that "in the long term trying to take the upper hand will fail".

The ability to gain the trust and respect of the people he works with illustrates another attribute that is required to fit in and get on: the ability to develop ties with co-workers through setting up networks, coalitions and friendships. When he left his most recent job (to take on the China role), Nik says he was touched to receive:

> ... so many kind notes from people saying how much they had enjoyed working with me. One of them said that I'd been their rock to lean on. I loved that because it was a complex and difficult job I was doing then and I was working remotely from them. They were my partners on the ground and we couldn't have achieved the success that we did without being able to trust each other from a position of mutual respect.

Clearly, for Nik, the focus on building relationships as a precursor to getting results is strong, but he does not lose sight of the fact that his success in his role will be judged by his ability to achieve the business results. It is evident that he has the ability to align his personal knowledge, experience, values and sense of importance to his organisation's values, goals and plans. He knows what he is in China to do and he is going to do it. He makes the point:

> I'm not being specifically tested – but people are definitely observing what I'm doing. The final verdict will come when we're fully up and running here. I feel pretty confident but it is a probationary period both for me and for the company in this new territory.

Learning from Nik's way of learning the culture

▶ **Be aware of the part that individual heritage and experience play in learning the culture.** Nik was able to take past learning and experiences, transfer them to new situations and keep building his skill at attuning himself to new cultures. Some people find this difficult, particularly if they are not able to adapt and then sensitively apply past learning to a new situation. (In this situation new joiners often say things like "in my last company we did it like this", which irritates people in the new company.) Skilful learners are open to new ways of doing things and, as they meet new situations, continue to hone their cultural fluency (see Chapter 6). For Nik this involves staying curious and being excited and energised by new situations.

▶ **"Do unto others as you would have them do unto you".** No one likes being forced, cajoled or coerced into doing things. Newcomers who exert power rather than seek involvement reduce their chances of fitting in and getting on in the long term. Remember (see Chapter 6) that the right culture includes an environment where people feel they are making a meaningful contribution that adds value. Establishing rapport, building supportive relationships and showing respect for each other lays the groundwork for successful performance in the long term.

▶ **Pay attention to the protocols of the culture.** It is easy to ride roughshod over the artefacts, symbols, rituals, norms and procedures that those in other cultures value. Finding out and paying close attention to what matters to people in different cultures is an essential step in getting along with them – which itself is a necessary condition of successful performance.

Summary

▶ Learning how to fit in and get on in an organisational culture is not easy. However, it can be done with a carefully planned approach, a respect for the norms and protocols of the new organisation, and the skills and attributes required to establish and build trust with the existing members of the organisation.

▶ Often cultural assimilation has to take place within a given (though maybe unstated time frame) and is marked by the payment of a price of membership.

Exercise 8: Reading cultural clues in Appendix 3 is an individual exercise to help people consider how they read cultural clues and what type of organisation they would feel more comfortable joining.

Appendices

Appendices

Glossary

Accountability versus responsibility Accountability means an employee's obligation to report progress, at the request of a third party, of agreements and expectations. Responsibility means owning, or feeling a sense of ownership, of tasks and situations for which a person is accountable. Thus defined, someone takes responsibility and is held accountable.

Biome A regional ecosystem characterised by distinct types of vegetation, animals and microbes that have developed under specific soil and climatic conditions.

Bounded chaos Apparently random and unpredictable behaviour (see chaos theory) but within a defined structure or parameters.

Chaos theory In mathematics, chaos theory describes the behaviour of certain dynamic systems – that is, systems whose state evolves with time – that may exhibit dynamics that are highly sensitive to initial conditions (popularly referred to as the butterfly effect). As a result of this sensitivity small differences in initial conditions (such as those due to rounding errors in numerical computation) yield widely diverging outcomes for chaotic systems, rendering long-term prediction impossible in general. This behaviour is known as deterministic chaos, or simply chaos. Everyday examples of chaotic systems include weather and climate.

Collateral Printed materials to present business information, such as leaflets, folders, brochures, fliers, fact sheets, direct mail items.

Consumerisation of IT IT equipment has reached the point where at no or relatively low cost, consumers can access online services including e-mail, instant messaging, desktop applications, document management and file storage that equal or exceed most corporate equivalents. To take advantage of this phenomenon, IT departments are beginning to give corporate users access to the scale and innovation of the consumer market. This means repairs can be made by Geek Squad or similar shops, device connections are made through the internet, the use of web-based software is encouraged, and employees connect to a corporate network only to access data and applications that must remain inside a firm's firewall.[1]

Cultural fluency   Familiarity with cultures: their natures, how they work and the ways they intertwine with our relationships in times of conflict and harmony. Cultural fluency means awareness of several dimensions of culture, including communication, ways of naming, framing and taming conflict, approaches to meaning making, identities and roles, diversity. When people of two different cultures interact, cultural fluency is the appropriate application of respect, empathy, flexibility, patience, interest, curiosity, openness, the willingness to suspend judgment, tolerance for ambiguity and sense of humour.

Edgy   Boundary-pushing; taking things further than they have been before.

Engagement   Employees' drive and commitment to use their ingenuity and resources for the benefit of the company.

Face value   Accepting someone or something just as it appears; believing that the way things appear is the way they really are.

Gen-Y   The population group in the United States born between around 1976 and around 2000. They are sometimes called echo boomers because some of them are the children of baby boomers. Others, especially those born in the late 1980s and after, may be the grandchildren of baby boomers. Other names for this group are the Millennials and the Internet Generation.

Global reach   Having the ability to attract, supply and keep customers in many different parts of the world.

Greenfield site   Agricultural or forest land, or an undeveloped site earmarked for commercial development or industrial projects. Also used as a metaphor for an undeveloped aspect of something.

Healthy culture   A culture where employees are engaged and committed, customers are satisfied and other stakeholders are included in organisational discussions. Employees feel a sense of ownership in the culture and are encouraged to take responsibility for the part they play in nurturing and developing it.

Horizon scanning   The systematic examination of potential threats, opportunities and likely future developments that are at the margins of current thinking and planning. Horizon scanning may explore novel and unexpected issues, as well as persistent problems or trends.[2]

It seeks to forewarn, while helping decision-makers develop appropriate strategies to protect against, and/or take advantage of these futures. It also attempts to:

- present a "picture" of possible futures, their challenges and opportunities;
- identify the implications of such futures on organisations, markets, governments, technologies and economies; and
- provide information, thoughts and ideas to help shape strategies that meet these futures.

In its broadest sense, horizon scanning helps plan for preferred and alternative futures, increasing an organisation's resilience to, and ability to profit from, potential futures.[3]

Hotelling   A method of using workspace efficiently. Where workers are only occasionally in the office, because they are travelling, teleworking or at client sites, workstations are made available on a bookable basis by the day (similar to hotel rooms).

Intangible asset   An identifiable non-monetary asset without physical substance. A resource that is controlled by the enterprise as a result of past events (for example, purchase or self-creation) and from which future economic benefits (inflows of cash or other assets) are expected.

Mission A brief description of a company's fundamental purpose. A mission statement answers the question: Why do we exist? The mission statement articulates the company's purpose for those in the organisation and for the public.

Move the needle Make something progress in the right direction as the needle on a car's speedometer moves around the dial as the car's speed increases.

Organisation In this book used as shorthand for the leaders in the organisation or members of the organisation.

Organisation culture Described in this book as analogous to a climate zone where biome distribution, latitude, humidity, elevation, distance from the sea and direction of the prevailing winds interact as a dynamic and chaotic (that is, unpredictable within certain boundaries) system to form subclimate zones and day-to-day weather patterns. The climate and the weather patterns are mediated by factors including human activity.

Organisational socialisation An interactive, complex, contingent and continuous process during which an individual in job change demonstrates success and capability in both fitting in and getting on in the new organisation.

Partner network Organisations that work together to achieve similar goals.

Power brands The top few brands that deliver the highest value to an organisation.

Presenteeism Being physically at work but mentally elsewhere, doing the minimum needed to avoid any penalties

Price of membership The price that has to be paid to join the organisation, such as membership fees for an association or club. In joining an organisation the price is not monetary but emotional or behavioural or otherwise related to being accepted as an insider by community members.

Pulse survey A powerful type of survey used to monitor the internal operating health, or climate, of an organisation. "Pulse" is used in the medical sense of measuring the heartbeat. When a person's pulse is measured graphically it shows a line with a "blip" every time the heart beats. In a similar way an organisational pulse survey shows the heartbeat of the organisation. It usually comprises no more than five questions and the single aggregated score indicates the organisation's current health. Users can then "drill down" to reveal the components of the overall score.

Purpose   An organisation's fundamental reasons for existence beyond just making money – a perpetual guiding star on the horizon – not to be confused with specific goals or business strategies. Vision, mission and purpose are used synonymously in this book.

Role modelling   Leading by example.

Same-store sales   Sales revenues of retail stores that have been open for a year or more. Most retail companies report this metric monthly. Same-store sales are also called "comps". New sales come from two sources: sales growth and opening new stores. Analysts and investors prefer monthly same-store sales growth because this indicates that compared with the previous month store traffic is increasing and/or shoppers are willing to pay more for products. These two factors increase sales revenues without the opening of new stores, which is often a more capital-intensive way of growing.

The seat perilous   In Arthurian legend, the seat across the Round Table from King Arthur reserved for the knight who completed the quest for the Holy Grail.

Social capital   The value created from investing in good community and human relationships.

Strapline   A catchy phrase typically connected to a brand or logo and found in marketing materials and advertising.

Strong culture   There is consistency in what people (inside and outside the organisation) see, hear and feel about it. Employees are clear how things are done, and are willing and able to help the organisation achieve its goals.

Systems of meaning   Sets of relationships between a group of variables (like words, behaviours, physical symbols) and the meanings that are attached to them. Relationships in meaning systems are arbitrary: there is no particular reason why the word "cat" should refer to a furry four-legged animal, for example. However, when a society agrees upon certain relationships between a certain class of variables (like words or behaviours) and their meanings, a system of meaning is established. Language is perhaps the most formal of human meaning systems. At the same time, we all know what it means to wink at someone or to give someone "the finger"; this suggests that human behaviour, like language, can be a part of complex and established systems of meaning.

Systems theory The relationship and functioning of the inter-related elements comprising a unified whole. A system typically consists of components, elements and/or subsystems that each affect the other and depend upon the whole. For example, consider a car. It has a number of parts and subsystems (electrical, fuel, and so on). Knowing the details of one or more parts or subsystems will not help to produce a moving vehicle. The interrelationship between all the parts and subsystems (including the driver) that form the moving car – the system – has to be grasped.

Toyota Way words *Andon* (signal for help), *genchi genbutsu* (go to the source and see for yourself), *hansei* (relentless reflection), *jidoka* (standardise tasks), *kaisen* (continuous improvement), *muda* (waste), *mura* (unevenness), *muri* (overburden).

Values Core values are an organisation's essential and enduring tenets, a small set of general guiding principles. Values are not to be confused with specific cultural or operating practices, nor are they to be compromised for financial gain or short-term expediency.[4]

Vision statement A picture of an organisation in the future but also an aspiration and an inspiration: the framework for strategic planning.

Walk the talk Demonstrating in actions what is said in speech.

Wal-Mart, Walmart Wal-Mart Stores Inc (NYSE: WMT) is the legal name of the corporation. Walmart (one word and without punctuation) is a trademark of the company and is used analogously to describe the company and its stores. Use the legal name when it is necessary to identify the legal entity, such as in financial results reports, Securities and Exchange Commission filings, litigation and governance matters.[5]

Cultural assessment tools

Quantitative tools to assess an organisation's culture should be used in conjunction with qualitative methods. Any culture assessment is only an indicator and outcomes of assessments should be used with care. Here is a selection of tools, none of which is recommended over another. Descriptors are abbreviated from the relevant websites and do not necessarily coincide with the author's views of the validity of the tool.

Campbell Organisation Survey

Assesses an organisation's climate, offering insights on areas that need improvement and those that should be celebrated. The COS can be used with all employees or members of a targeted work group. It allows organisations to survey employees on their satisfaction in such areas as feedback, top leadership and organisational planning.

www.ccl.org/leadership/assessments/COSOverview.aspx

Competing Values Framework and Assessment

Provides a measurement of the values and beliefs driving an organisation's leadership, project teams and enterprise-wide employees that shape innovation and growth.

http://competingvalues.com

Corporate Culture Questionnaire

Measures the prevailing culture of an organisation (its dominant system of beliefs and practices) and helps to guide the development of strategy and to evaluate change programmes. An SHL tool.

www.shl.com/WhatWeDo/CultureAndMotivation/Pages/
CorporateCultureQuestionnaire.aspx

Corporate Culture Survey

Measures and evaluates seven dimensions of an organisation's culture: teamwork, morale, information flow, employee involvement, supervision, meetings and customer service. A Glaser survey.

www.theglasers.com/Service-survey.html

Culture Assessment

Provides an assessment of an organisation's cultural strengths and critical barriers to success. Published by Hagberg Consulting Group.

www.hcgnet.com/Tools.asp?tool_id=4

Denison Organisational Culture Survey

Provides a measure of an organisation's progress towards achieving a high-performance culture and optimum results.

www.denisonconsulting.com/products/cultureProducts/
surveyOrgCulture.aspx

Diagnosing Organisational Culture Instrument

Evaluates significant cultural patterns within an organisation. For a culture requiring change, the tool suggests how to effect that change.

www.pfeiffer.com/WileyCDA/PfeifferTitle/productCd-0883903164.
html

Great Place to Work Culture Audit

A management questionnaire used to gain a better sense of the overall culture of the organisation. It is available only to applicants accepted in the Great Place to Work process.

www.greatplacetowork.in/best/culture-audit.php

Organisational Beliefs Questionnaire

A 50-item questionnaire designed to assess an organisation's culture by examining the values and beliefs shared by most people in that organisation. This is done by looking for behaviours and actions that reflect – or contradict – certain values and beliefs.

http://pace.leadingandfollowing.com/OBQ.htm

Organisational Culture Assessment Questionnaire

A 30-item questionnaire designed to help understand an organisation's culture and identify ways to deal with cultural-based problems. The OCAQ assesses the values and beliefs that help or hinder organisational performance in five crucial dimensions.

http://pace.leadingandfollowing.com/OCAQ.htm

Organisational Culture Inventory

Provides a picture of an organisation's operating culture in terms of the behaviours that members believe are expected or implicitly required. By guiding the way in which members approach their work and interact with one another, these "behavioural norms" determine the organisation's capacity to solve problems, adapt to change and perform effectively.

www.humansynergistics.com/products/oci.aspx

The Organisation Shadow-Side Audit

Shows how to diagnose what is happening inside your organisation, often beneath a veneer of rationality and "spin". The shadow-side model can be thought of as a lens through which an organisation can be seen and understood in a fresh light. This self-assessment audit explains and reveals that lens.

www.organisational-leadership.com/shadowside_audit.cfm

The Situational Outlook Questionnaire

Measures people's perceptions of the climate for creativity, innovation and change in their immediate working environment. The SOQ is used to help foster and maintain a climate that can support innovation and change.

www.soqonline.net

Strategic Organisational Management Index

A proprietary process that reveals and uncovers employees' perceptions, attitudes, strengths and weaknesses that affect your corporate performance and profit. The STORM Index includes identification of corporate culture.

www.stormindex.com

Target Culture Modelling or "Culture Sort"

Ensures that culture is consistent when two companies merge. It is used by many companies merging and many others implementing new strategies. A Hay Group tool.

www.haygroup.com/

Useful exercises

Exercise 1: Getting to grips with an organisation's culture

Understanding what an organisation's culture is means looking at it from the three perspectives discussed in Chapter 1, and recognising that these cannot be turned into checklists with items that can be manipulated independently.

Exercise 1 involves compiling a short, realistic guide (in any medium) that would help a visitor or newcomer to an organisation understand something about its culture. The aim is to find out how the two higher-level perspectives – integration and differentiation – manifest (or not) in a specific enterprise. Asking insiders (employees) and outsiders (customers, suppliers) helps give a rounded picture.

Instructions

1 Find out if there is a strapline or similar that acts as the organisational integrator encapsulating a strategy that all employees understand and are clear about (for example, McDonald's "Plan to Win", which has the aim of "better not bigger", or Xerox's mid-1990s strategy to "Get Canon").

Use the questions in Table 1 – the integration perspective – as a starter.[1]

2 Look for a consistent "set" of principles, values and/or assumptions that indicate what the company stands for and enable people in the company to manage their diverse and often competing

interests and objectives in delivering the strategy. (This may be implied or explicit and can include stories about the way things happen, or the legacy of the organisation; for example, McDonald's people frequently refer to the way Ray Kroc, the founder, spoke about things.)

Observe how these reflect differently in different parts of the organisation depending on who is asked, their role and level in the organisation, reflecting the differentiation perspective.

Use Table 2 – the differentiation perspective – to help gather the information on the differentiation perspective of the culture of the organisation.

3 Collect examples of both cultural consistency and cultural challenges at the integration and differentiation levels. Note that the challenges are more likely to come from the countercultures (discussed in Chapter 2).

Table 1 What is the strapline that encapsulates the strategy? (Integration perspective)

Strapline/strategy	Is it evident? Where? How? At all levels in the organisation or only at some levels? What do people say about it? (Are they enthusiastic, cynical, committed, etc?)

Table 2 What are the values/principles/ assumptions that indicate what the organisation stands for but are reflected differently across the organisation? (Differentiation perspective)

Values, principles, assumptions	Are they evident/obvious? Are they shared? How is the sharing obvious? Is it at all levels or at some levels?

Organisation's relationship to its environment	Is it "right" to relate to the external world in a dominant, submissive or harmonising way?
	What do people hold as being more important: internal integration (internal focus) or external responsiveness/adaptation (external focus)?
	What is the "right" way to behave in response to incidents and crises (eg, identify and punish those who were to blame, impose constraints to stop it happening again, learn from them and educate the organisation)?
Employee activity	What is the "correct" way to behave: to be dominant, take a harmonising stance, be passive, be fatalistic, etc?
	What constitutes time wasting? Is there a concept of "real work" and, by inference, other work that is less legitimate?
	In the final resort, is achieving the desired ends more important than/equally important to/less important than the means used?
	What relative weightings are given to reflection and action?
	Is there a rational, "one best way" approach to everything, if only it can be found?

Attitude to people   What is the view of people? That they are basically good, neutral or bad, selfish or altruistic, etc?

Left to their own devices are people viewed as inherently self-motivated or do they require some external stimuli (eg, rewards and punishments) to contribute?

Are people's traits considered perfectible? Is talent shared by the few or the many – that is, will there always be a cadre of people who are different – the leaders?

Is it acceptable for people to show weakness and/or to admit that they don't know something?

What key traits are evidentially essential to progress in organisation?

What traits are rewarded or forbidden? Which are discouraged but practised anyway? What lifestyles are encouraged?

Who's been laid off/made redundant? Who's been promoted? Who do people go to for information? Who are the players?

How is career progress made? Who gets promoted and who doesn't?

Do career actions support the stated values (eg, departments keeping their best people to themselves)?

What do successful/unsuccessful career paths say about what is necessary to get on?

Is the view that the best people will inevitably come through (sink or swim) or that people need help and support to succeed?

Who are the role models? What makes them a role model? Are they modelling the desired characteristics or the maverick characteristics?

Interactions	Is life basically competitive or collaborative?
	Is it better to organise based on individualism (eg, self-interest, individual drive and initiative, impersonal) or collectivism (loyalty, sense of duty, community and participation)?
	What is the "correct" way for people to relate to each other (eg, formal or informal, on equal terms or with deference to elders and betters)?
	Is it "right" to show emotion or affection?
	Is the organisation seen as a commodity (to be bought and sold if the price is right) or as a community?
	How is status afforded: by position, contribution, skill, association or what?
	Do people have to "play politics" to get on?
	Is it "right" for relationships and information to be open or for privileged access to be maintained?
	What is the "right" way to distribute power in the organisation?
	Is it acceptable to challenge senior people openly?
Time scales	What is the organisation's basic orientation in terms of past, present and future? What is the "proper" place to focus attention (eg, past experience, today's activities, short-term future, long-term future)?
	What time units are most relevant to the conduct of everyday business (eg, minutes, hours, days, months, years, decades)?
	Is the notion of cause and effect taken for granted?
	What is the "proper" way to behave in relation to time keeping and punctuality? Should this differ from group to group? Is seniority relevant?
Diversity	Is a group/organisation seen as being best if it is highly diverse or highly homogeneous?
	How are challenges to established/group thinking handled? Are they welcomed or suppressed?

Supporting the values, principles and/or assumptions

Rituals and routines	What are they? What value do they add?
	What are their benefits and limitations (eg, rites of passage, routine meetings, awards given, etc)?
Stories and myths	What are the stories told in the organisation (eg, McDonald's tells stories of the founder, Ray Kroc). Where, when and why did they arise?
	What are the (often ill-founded and untested) beliefs that powerfully affect the way in which organisation members behave (eg, "it's no use trying anything new")?
Organisation-specific phrases or language	What jargon, acronyms or technical vocabulary are in common use? What is the "meaning behind the words" (eg, "what gets measured gets done", "movers and shakers", "size of territory is a measure of your value to the organisation", "left-hand column", "guard rails", etc)?
Workspace organisation, design and protocols	What is the workspace design: open-plan, own offices, hotelling, cubicles (and the pecking order these imply)?
	What are the colour schemes, picture/plants decorations, lighting?
	Is there a clean-desk policy (or design your own space)?
	What is the communal space like (kitchens, coffee areas, print rooms, vending machines, restaurants, receptions areas, etc)?
	What is the noise level?

Processes	How is control achieved (eg, command or self-control)?
	How is technology used (security levels, collaborative software, internet access, etc)?
	What are the measurement processes (individual, business unit, organisation)?
	How are decisions made?
	How is information held (close to the chest, transparently, need-to-know basis, etc)?
Structures	How are people organised (eg, self-managing teams, matrix, hierarchy)?
	How many levels are there in the organisation?
Visuals	What impression does the logo, online page set-up, marketing material convey?
Risk-taking and innovation	What is the "correct" attitude to risk-taking and risk-takers?
	Is it right for people to "stick their necks out" from time or should they "stick to the knitting"?
	Is it acceptable to be "off the wall"?
	Which, in general, are more important: rules or ideas?
	Does it pay to try to be right?
	Does it pay to "rock the boat"?
Ambiguity	What is the response to conflicting demands?
	How far do people adopt a "both and" stance, or feel the need to be decisive and decide one way or the other?
	How comfortable are people with ambiguity and "mess"?
	How much do they seek order and certainty?

Exercise 2: Developing a tailored measurement process

Several of the companies mentioned in Chapter 2 have developed a unique set of cultural indicators, generated by employees (sometimes with the help of an external consultant), which they use to measure or assess their culture. This is a pragmatic and cost-effective approach. Its value is that it does not depend on predetermined categories or dimensions but instead asks insiders to identify attributes they feel either do (or should) characterise their organisation's culture. Exercise 2 is useful to organisations that want to develop their own measurement process.

Instructions: Part 1[2]

1 Form groups of 10–15 people (the number will depend on the size and complexity of the organisation) that represent cross-sections of the culture being assessed.

2 Share with them the business issue or opportunity behind what is being done.

3 Give group members a model of how to think about culture (for example, the three perspectives model).

4 Facilitate a group discussion beginning with the key cultural attributes that they share. (Use the information gained from Exercise 1, or start this group session with that exercise.)

5 Assess which of the elements of the culture will aid them in solving the business problem and which elements will hinder solving it.

6 Look across the group discussions for elements that appear to be relevant to and representative of the culture.

Instructions: Part 2

1 About a week later, with 4–6 people drawn from the original group of 10–15, confirm the elements that represent the culture. (Doing this a week later allows time for rethink and reflection.)

2 With the business issue or opportunity in mind, identify which

of the elements will be most useful to track/monitor progress towards the goal.

3 Once these are agreed determine what needs to happen to monitor them effectively. (See the Zappos example on pages 42–8 for some ideas.)

4 Agree the schedule and process for monitoring, reporting back and taking any necessary action on the results.

Here's how Alan Lafley, CEO of Procter & Gamble from 2000 to 2009, conducted a similar exercise and took action on the helping and hindering elements.

When he became CEO in 2000, Lafley realised that P&G, although struggling, was in better shape than press reports suggested. In particular, he recognised that the company's culture, far from being a hindrance, was an asset that could be used in a transformation. So he reversed his predecessor's sharp critique of the culture and affirmed its competitive value in discussions with managers and employees across the company:[3]

> I started with P&G values and said, "Here's what's not going to change. This is our purpose: to improve the everyday lives of people around the world with P&G brands and products that deliver better performance, quality, and value. That's not going to change. The value system – integrity, trust, ownership, leadership, and a passion for service and winning: not going to change. The six guiding principles, respect for the individual, and so on: not going to change. OK, so here's the stuff that will change. Any business that doesn't have a strategy is going to develop one; any business that has a strategy that's not winning in the marketplace is either going to change its strategy or improve its execution." And so on. So I was very clear about what was safe and what wasn't.

Exercise 3: The characteristics that make a culture distinctive

This exercise gives insight and practice in recognising the characteristics that contribute to making an organisation's culture distinctive and of value – that is, those characteristics that make the culture matter in terms of the asset value it can add.

Instructions

Look at Table 3. The left-hand column lists the ten characteristics that contribute to culture (discussed in Chapter 3). The right-hand column suggests related or similar characteristics.

With a specific organisation in mind, using the lists in Table 3:

1 Identify the characteristics that are distinctive to that organisation and add value to the culture (or if not paid attention to diminish cultural value) – note that they may have different labels from those listed but still be similar.

2 Identify other organisation-specific characteristics – for example, Swedishness is one specific to IKEA that is distinctive and adds value – that are not on this list.

3 Determine and agree what action needs to be taken to protect and add value to these cultural assets.

Table 3 Cultural characteristics

Characteristics	Examples of related characteristics
A story or stories	Legacy
	Sacred cow (or a herd of sacred cows)
	A hero/heroine
A purpose and a set of values	Governance principles
	Operating principles
	An ethical code
A business strategy	Organisational reviews
	A rolling plan
	An organisational roadmap

Characteristics	Examples of related characteristics
An attitude to people in the workforce	Statement of inclusion and diversity
	Career development routes
	A set of employee/employer expectations
A global mindset	A corporate social responsibility manifesto
	A sustainability strategy
	Partnership(s) with non-governmental organisations (NGOs)
A relationship network	A structural hierarchy
	A collaboration forum or forums
	A multiple stakeholder perspective
Digital presence	A willingness to try out new technology
	A forward-thinking IT department
	An experimental mindset
Reputation	Brand recognition
	Consumer trust
	Service recovery skills
A customer proposition	Customer relationship management (CRM)
	A unique market niche
	A customer first mindset
A horizon-scanning capability	Forecasting and trend analysis capability
	A spirit of curiosity and inquiry
	R&D skills

Add in others

Exercise 4: Connecting business success and culture

This is a two-step exercise that helps make the connection between business success and culture.

Step 1

Define "business success", beyond financial results, for the organisation in a clear and concise way. To do this:

1 Consider success in the five dimensions listed below.[4]

2 Decide whether success is for the short, medium, or long term (or a combination of these).

3 Agree what success in these dimensions (collectively and independently) would look like.

▷ Social: to address conditions that affect us all, including poverty, violence, injustice, education, public health, and labour and human rights.

▷ Economic: to help people and businesses meet their economic needs
– for people: securing food, water, shelter and creature comforts;
– for businesses: turning a profit.

▷ Environmental: to protect and restore the Earth – for example, by controlling climate change, preserving natural resources and preventing waste.

▷ Cultural: to protect and value the diversity through which communities manifest their identity and cultivate traditions across generations.

▷ Political: to work with governments and legislators in an ethical way, to manage conflicts of interest and to compete fairly.

Step 2

Identify the cultural assets that add value to the organisation and will help drive business success. (See Exercise 3 for instructions on how to do this.) Assess how effectively these assets are being nurtured in the pursuit of success.

Exercise 5: Determining accountability and responsibility

Use the continuum and statements in Table 4 in workshops or interviews to create discussion about the clarity of accountability and responsibility in the organisation. Do this by asking participants where they think the organisation stands in relation to each statement and what examples they can give to support their position.

Focus on where things are going well and find out what the conditions are that enable this and whether/how they can be replicated as appropriate in other parts of the organisation.

Note where and how to take actions to address weak areas and develop the strong ones. (Be aware that this is a discussion tool, not a survey.)

Table 4 Continuum and statements

0 ⟶ 10

Leader (CEO) does not define cultural expectations	Leader (CEO) has clearly defined what his/her cultural expectations are from employees
Leader (CEO) appears to take no accountability for the culture	Leader (CEO) is clearly accountable for the culture and has cultural expectations high on his/her agenda
Leader (CEO) talks about the desired culture but does not "walk the talk"	It is clear to all stakeholders that the leader (CEO) role-models the culture he/she expects

0	→ 10
Managers do not role-model cultural expectations	Managers clearly and consistently role-model cultural expectations
Cultural accountability is fragmented with many people held accountable for it	Accountability for the culture is taken by a small group of people who are charged with steering or nurturing it
Employees are unclear how they are accountable to the culture in specific ways	Employees know how their conformance to cultural norms will be measured and rewarded or sanctioned
Few employees take responsibility for the culture	There is quantitative and qualitative evidence that each individual takes positive cultural responsibility
Formal rewards and sanctions are not aligned to support cultural expectations	Formal rewards and sanctions are closely aligned to support cultural expectations

Exercise 6: The two swords[5]

This is an exercise in cultural fluency. Miyamoto Musashi, a 17th-century Japanese *samurai*, learned to handle two swords at the same time. To be skilful, effective and successful in your own culture by being assertive, quick and to the point is one mode of behaviour. To be skilful, effective and successful in another culture by being unassertive, patient and indirect is another mode entirely – like being able to handle two swords at the same time.

This exercise helps in learning how to respond to two (or more) cultures.

Step 1

Ask individuals to read the following list of adjectives that could describe a manager and circle the ones that apply to them:

assertive	witty	procrastinator	easily
energetic	original	enjoy	distracted
decisive	colourful	responsible	serious
ambitious	calm	resourceful	idealistic
confident	easy-going	individualist	sceptical
quick	good-natured	broad	abrasive
aggressive	tactful	interests	cynical
competitive	forceful	limited	conscientious
impatient	unemotional	interests	flexible
impulsive	good listener	good team	mature
quick-	inhibited	worker	dependable
tempered	shy	enjoy	honest
intelligent	absent-	working	sincere
excitable	minded	alone	reliable
informal	cautious	sociable	adaptable
versatile	methodical	co-operative	curious
persuasive	timid	quiet	
imaginative	lazy		

Using these qualities skilfully is like handling one sword.

Step 2

Now ask individuals to think of a business trip to another country, or a meeting with a different department, and ask them to circle the qualities that they think the other people will be looking for in them (the second sword).

Step 3

Discuss what individuals will have to do and/or learn to be able to wield the second sword successfully as they meet people with different cultural expectations and norms.

Exercise 7: Culture change

This exercise provides a structure for planning for culture change in a non-programmatic way. It should be conducted at various levels and in various places in the organisation to get a rounded view.

Step 1

For each of the six conditions for culture change in Table 5 consider whether the organisation meets them and how they manifest. (Add appropriate examples to those given in column two and ensure there is evidence to support the examples.)

Step 2

Where there are shortfalls, develop subtle (non-programmatic) approaches that can help meet the conditions.

Table 5 Six conditions for culture change

Condition	Example of how this manifests
Stating clear and well-articulated business reasons for wanting to change the culture that are demonstrably tied to the business strategy and/or presenting business issue	We communicate our business plan and goal with absolute clarity. (How do you know?)

Condition	Example of how this manifests
Affirming the principles for delivering the business strategy and/or resolving the business issue through a set of values or similar are espoused, shared and acted on by the workforce (albeit reflecting differently in different parts of the organisation) and are appropriate to the business model	Our business model is appropriate to our culture and vice versa. (How do you know?) We work on the basis that an organisation's culture reflects differently – there are subcultures and countercultures – but within the same broad boundaries, in different parts of the organisation. We have a strong set of corporate values or equivalent that people are committed to. (How do you know?)
Aligning the measures, language, policies, work practices/processes, physical environment and other infrastructures with the principles and focusing on delivering the business strategy	We have created a common language. We reward the right responses more frequently than punishing the wrong responses. (How do you know?) We know why we measure aspects of the culture and measure judiciously using a mixed approach. We have harmonised and aligned the HR policies, practice and processes that mediate the culture.
Committing leaders to evidently, consistently and credibly modelling the desired/required "way we do things round here"	Our leaders role-model the behaviours and cultural norms they want employees to model.

Condition	Example of how this manifests
Recognising the limits and boundaries of any possible culture change (including history, legacy, business model, and resource constraints)	We have a grip on the culture of the organisation and understand why the culture is what it is. (As Frank Nicolai, former CEO of American Management Systems, says: "If you don't know what you have and do not understand why it got that way, you reduce your chances of changing it positively to a culture that supports the visions and mission.") We know what our unique cultural assets are and we nurture them – keeping what works.
Accepting that planned culture change takes a long time (years rather than months), and that culture is changing all the time irrespective of any planned change	We know that culture change is a continuous work in progress.

Exercise 8: Reading cultural clues[6]

This is an individual exercise to help people consider how they read cultural clues and what type of organisation they would feel more comfortable joining. It is a useful exercise to do jointly with a coach or mentor so the responses can be discussed and form a basis for reflection.

Step 1

Read the following accounts of two interviews:

▶ **Interview 1.** This place seemed crazy. Other places I'd been interviewed at were much more organised. There was an interview schedule that was strictly followed: I'd meet with several of my peers, with my proposed boss in the morning, and then later in the afternoon when I'd met everyone else. I felt they were concerned about my feelings and respectful of my time.

▶ **Interview 2.** At the last company I went to they really kept me waiting. Finally I met with the senior guy. Midway through the interview his assistant came in and pulled him out of the room. He explained that this was an emergency and left. One of his other subordinates joined me. The whole day was like this. Nothing went as planned. It was chaotic. I don't think a single one of those interviews lasted as long as they were supposed to, and most of them were cut short by half. While I know this is routine in more dynamic industries, it struck me as unprofessional.

Step 2

Answer the following questions:

▶ Which interview was best?

▶ What cultural clues does each interview present?

▶ What can be learned about each culture from these clues?

▶ What are the cultural values that come across in each organisation?

▶ How would someone learn to fit in and get on in each – would the approach be the same or different?

▶ Would each of the two organisations attract different types of people to work in them? What makes this seem likely/unlikely?

▶ What types of questions should the interviewee ask to judge his/her level of fit with the organisation?

Step 3

Reflect on how the details that can be picked up from situations like this contribute to getting an impression of the bigger picture and the type of learning (content and approach) required to fit in and get on in an organisation.

Notes and references

1 What is organisation culture?

1 Hanessian, B. and Sierra, C., "Leading a Turnaround: an interview with the chairman of D&B", *McKinsey Quarterly*, No. 2, 2005.

2 Detert, J.R., Schroeder, R.G. and Mauriel, J.J., "A Framework for Linking Culture and Improvement Initiatives in Organizations", *Academy of Management Review*, Vol. 25, No. 4, 2000.

3 See, for example, Martin, J., *Organizational Culture: Mapping the Terrain*, Sage Publications, 2002; Martin, J., *Cultures in Organizations: Three Perspectives*, Oxford University Press, 1992.

4 www.nytimes.com/2008/06/02/business/media/02bertelsmann.html?_r=1&scp=4&sq=markus%20dohle&st=cse

5 Kelly, K., "Panic Over Random's Act", *New York Post*, May 21st 2008.

6 http://en.wikipedia.org/wiki/File:MagrittePipe.jpg

7 http://knowledge.wharton.upenn.edu/article.cfm?articleid=1631

8 www.investmentnews.com/apps/pbcs.dll/article?AID=/20081006/REG/810069969/1094/INDaily01

9 US Department of Defense news briefing, February 12th 2002, converted into poetry by Hart Seely, *Slate*.

10 Hofstede, G., "National cultures and corporate cultures" in Samovar, L.A. and Porter, R.E. (eds), *Communication Between Cultures*, Wadsworth, 1984.

11 Armstong, M., *A Handbook of Human Resource Management Practice*, 10th edn, Kogan Page, 2006.

12 Schein, E.H., "Organizational Culture and Leadership" in Shafritz, J. and Ott, J.S. (eds), *Classics of Organization Theory*, Wadsworth, 2001.

13 Morgan. G., *Images of Organization*, Sage Publications, 1997.

14 O'Reilly, C.A. and Chatman, J.A., "Culture as social control: Corporations, cults, and commitment" in Straw, B.M. and Cummings, L.L. (eds), *Research in Organizational Behavior*, Vol. 18, JAI Press, 1996.

15 www.nasa.gov/mission_pages/noaa-n/climate/climate_weather.html

16 Taken from Copenhagen Business School's description of a short course, Organization Culture, June 7th–9th 2011.

17 Reed. S., "Can Shell Put Out This Fire?", *Business Week*, May 3rd 2004.

18 Goldberg, M., "Fallen Arches", 2002 (http://radio-weblogs.com/0107127/stories/2002/12/18/mcdonaldsTargetForAntiamericanFeeling.html).

19 www.marketwire.com/press-release/Chief-Executive-Magazine-987587.html

2 Can culture be measured?

1 The autos task force, created just after the Obama administration took office in January 2009 (led by Steven Rattner, a former investment banker and co-founder of the Quadrangle private equity firm), engineered the bankruptcy reorganisations of GM and Chrysler, forcing both companies to cut debt and achieve concessions from labour and vendors. www.reuters.com/article/politicsNews/idUSTRE56G5Q420090717

2 "A Cliffhanger to See if a G.M. Turnaround Succeeds", *New York Times*, July 26th 2009.

3 Schein, E., *The Corporate Culture Survival Guide*, Jossey-Bass, 1999.

4 Wilkins, A.L. and Ouchi, W.G., "Efficient Cultures: Exploring the Relationship Between Culture and Organizational Performance", *Administrative Science Quarterly*, Vol. 28, No. 3, September 1983, pp. 468–81.

5 *The Capstone Encyclopedia of Business*, Capstone Publishing, 2003.

6 One of the theoretical debates on organisation culture centres on whether an organisation "has" a culture or "is" a culture. Simplifying considerably, the former view holds that culture can be passed on to organisational members whereas the latter argues that organisations "are" cultures. For a manager, the distinction does not matter: in the day-to-day circumstances managers are working in, and speaking about, an organisation both has a culture and is a culture. This book uses the concepts interchangeably.

7 Matar, H., *In the Country of Men*, Penguin, 2006.

8 Cresswell, J.W. and Garrett, A.L., "The 'movement' of mixed methods research and the role of educators", *South African Journal of Education*, Vol. 28, 2008, pp. 321–33.

9 Human Synergistics Organisational Culture Inventory (www.humansynergistics.com).

10 Words from the poem *Pied Beauty* by Gerard Manley Hopkins.

11 Schein, E.H., "Five Traps for Consulting Psychologists", *Consulting Psychology Journal: Practice and Research*, Vol. 55, No. 2, 2003, pp. 75–83.

12 www.fastforwardblog.com/2008/05/22/zappos-how-twitter-can-work-in-a-corporate-environment/

13 *Contagious Magazine*, Issue 18 (www.contagiousmagazine.com/).

14 www.zappos.com/n/showtestimonials.cgi?page=1

15 www.npr.org/templates/story/story.php?storyId=11980729 (NPR story on Zappos).

3 Does culture matter?

1 Kaplan, R. and Norton, D., "Measuring the Strategic Readiness of Intangible Assets", *Harvard Business Review*, Vol. 82, Issue 5, May 14th 2004.

2 Intangible assets are generally categorised as either legal intangible assets or competitive intangible assets. There are internationally agreed accounting rules for valuing certain types of intangible assets such as IAS38. This chapter is concerned with competitive intangible assets and does not discuss whether or not they could/should be accounted for.

3 Smith, P.A., "Systemic Knowledge Management: Managing Organizational Assets For Competitive Advantage", *Journal of Systemic Knowledge Management*, April 1998.

4 www.allbusiness.com/lecture/11758637-1.html

5 "'You've got to find what you love,' Jobs says", *Stanford Report*, June 14th 2005.

6 www.businessweek.com/magazine/content/06_32/b3996057.htm

7 Fog, K. and Budtz, C., *Storytelling: Branding in Practice*, Springer-Verlag, 2005.

8 Collins, J., *How the Mighty Fall*, HarperCollins, 2009.

9 www.themanager.org/Strategy/Trader_Joe_Corporate_Culture_Strategy.htm

10 See McGregor, D., *The Human Side of the Enterprise: Annotated Edition*, McGraw-Hill, 2005.

11 Roman, K., "The House that Ogilvy Built", *Strategy+Business*, Issue 54, 2009.

12 Rocafort, M., "Ogilvy's Magic House", *Strategy+Business*, Issue 56, 2009.

13 Harris, J., "How and why does culture matter?", *Economic and Political Weekly*, January 8th 2005. Quoting from Rao, V. and Walton, M. (eds), *Culture and Public Action*, Stanford University Press, 2004.

14 http://history.nasa.gov/rogersrep/genindex.htm. Report of the Presidential Commission on the Space Shuttle Challenger Accident, Chapter 5. Boisjoly was a Morton Thiokol engineer (a third-party company working with NASA on the project) who in 1988 received the AAAS Award for Scientific Freedom and Responsibility for his efforts to avert the Challenger disaster.

15 www.grameenamerica.com/Microlending/Microfinance/Grameen-Bank-and-Relationships.html

16 http://designerscouch.org/show_article/98/interview-with-vitor-lourenco.html#

17 Cook, J. and Finlayson, M., "The Impact of Cultural Diversity on Website Design", *S.A.M. Advanced Management Journal*, Summer 2005. For the cross-cultural meanings of colour see also the Color Connection Book Series: www.office.xerox.com/business-resources/colorconnection_book4_all.pdf

18 Fombrun, C., *Reputation: Realizing Value from the Corporate Image*, Harvard Business School Press, 1996.

19 Suessmuth-Dyckerhoff, C., Hexter, J. and St-Maurice, I., "Marketing to China's New Traditionalists", *Far Eastern Economic Review*, April 2008.

20 Lafley, A., "The work of a CEO: what only a CEO can do", Speech Transcript: Harvard Business Review McKinsey Prize Awards Dinner, March 24th 2009 (www.pg.com/news/pdf/prizeaward.pdf).

21 Borden, M., "Nokia Rocks the World: the Phone King's Plan to Redefine its Business", *Fast Company*, September 2009.

22 Barwick, S., "Ikea stores appalling at weekends, boss admits", *Daily Telegraph*, February 1st 2001.

23 Ibid.

24 Terdiman, D., "Anatomy of an IKEA product", CNetNews, April 19th 2008.

25 See Ruppel-Shell, E., *Cheap: The High Cost of Discount Culture*, The Penguin Press, 2009, for a critique of "the well polished rags-to-riches story the company (IKEA) wrote for itself".

26 Turner, C., "How IKEA Persuaded Brits to Shop Swedish", www.utalkmarketing.com, May 14th 2008.

27 Rosner, D. and Bean, J., Learning from IKEA Hacking: "I'm Not One to Decoupage a Tabletop and Call It a Day", CHI 2009, April 4–9th, Boston, MA, US.

28 http://dejavu6.ucd.ie/2009/07/29/rip-off-ireland-a-tale-of-12-ikea-stores/

4 Is culture related to business success?

1 Bowe, C., "Man out to shake up Merck", *Financial Times*, March 26th 2006.

2 Leaf, C., "Temptation is all around us", *Fortune*, November 18th 2002.

3 Malcolm, S. and Aillery, M., "Growing Crops for Fuel has Spillover Effect", *Amber Waves*, US Department of Agriculture, March 2009.

4 Ernsting, A., Rughani, D. and Boswell, A., "Agrofuels threaten to accelerate global warming", *Biofuelwatch*, December 2007.

5 http://mgt.ncsu.edu/d/com/weblogs/profiles/jim-owens-interview.html

6 www.southwest.com/about_swa/financials/investor_relations_index.html

7 Sorenson, J., "The strength of corporate culture and the reliability of firm performance", *Administrative Science Quarterly*, No. 47, 2002.

8 Weinzimmer, L., Franczak, J. and Michel, E., "Culture-Performance Research: Challenges and Future Directions", *Journal of Academy of Business and Economics*, Vol. 8, No. 4, 2008, p. 158.

9 De Smet, A., Loch, M. and Schaninger, B., "The Link Between Profits and Organisational Performance", *McKinsey Quarterly*, No. 3, 2007.

10 Osterwalder, A., *How to Describe and Improve your Business Model to Compete Better*, 2007 (http://alexosterwalder.com/speaking.html).

11 "Domino's Pizza Announces Second Quarter 2009 Financial Results", http://phx.corporate-ir.net/External.File?item=UGFyZW5oSUQ9MTEwNz18Q2hpbGRJRDotMXxUeXBlPTM=&t=1

12 *Times Online*, "Lessons Learned, Making Strategy Work – David Brandon, Chairman and CEO, Domino's Pizza", January 15th 2009.

13 Horowitz, B., "Where's your Domino's Pizza? Track it Online", *USA Today*, January 30th 2008.

14 *Times Online*, op. cit.

15 Hornaday, A., "State of Play: a Newspaper Thriller True to its Sources", *Washington Post*, April 17th 2009.

16 Liedtke, M., "Tough Times Turning Newspaper Lenders into Owners", *Huffington Post*, November 29th 2009.

17 www.businessinsider.com/the-death-of-the-american-newspaper-2009-7

18 Wyman, B., "Five Key Reasons Why Newspapers are Failing", *Splice Today*, August 13th 2009.

19 Schulte, B., "The Distribution Revolution", *American Journalism Review*, December/January 2010.

20 Fishman, C., "The Wal-Mart You Don't Know", *Fast Company*, December 19th 2007.

21 Barton, D. and Deutsch, C., "Transforming a South Korean Chaebol: an interview with Doosan's Yongmaan Park", *McKinsey Quarterly*, September 2008.

22 For more on national cultures read work by Geert Hofstede and Fons Trompenaars, both well-known writers in the field, although Hofstede's work has been heavily criticised in some quarters.

23 Boroditsky, L., "How does our language shape the way we think?", *Edge*, June 12th 2009.

24 Tannen, D., in Fasold, R. and Connor-Linton, J. (eds), *An Introduction to Language and Linguistics*, Cambridge University Press, 2006.

25 Kellaway, L., "Are you going forward? Then stop now", *BBC Magazine*, June 16th 2008.

26 Caulkin, S., "Gore-Tex Gets Made Without Managers", *Observer*, November 2nd 2008.

27 "Workplace Democracy at W.L. Gore & Associates", *Workplace Democracy*, July 19th 2009.

28 Kaplan, M., "You have no boss", *Fast Company*, December 18th 2007.

5 Culture: creation, accountability and responsibility

1 Schein, E.H., *Organisational Culture and Leadership*, Jossey-Bass, 1985.

2 Harvard Business School, Global Business Summit, October 13th 2008.

3 Stewart, T. and Raman, A., "Finding a Higher Gear", *Harvard Business Review*, July/August 2008.

4 Lewis, M., "The Man Who Crashed the World", *Vanity Fair*, August 2009.

5 Hatch, M.J., "Dynamics in Organisational Culture", in Scott Poole, M. and Van de Ven, A.H. (eds), *Handbook of Organisational Change and Innovation*, Oxford University Press, 2004.

6 Beckhard. R., *Organization Development: Strategies and Models*, Addison-Wesley, 1979.

7 Mills, E., "Meet Google's Culture Czar", *CNet News*, April 30th 2007.

8 www.reuters.com/article/newsOne/idUSTRE52G3BQ20090317

9 Laurence, J., "Sacked for Telling the Truth About Drugs", *Independent*, October 31st 2009.

10 Norvig, P., "Einstein's '05 Performance Review" (http://norvig.com/).

11 Address of Senator Robert F. Kennedy, "Day of Affirmation", University of Capetown, June 6th 1966 (www.disa.ukzn.ac.za/index.php?option=com_displaydc&recordID=spe19660606.026.022.000)

12 Newcomb, D., "A conversation with Debra Meyerson", *Information Outlook*, October 2001.

13 Meyerson, D., "The Tempered Radicals: How employees push their companies – little by little – to be more socially responsible", *Stanford Social Innovation Review*, Fall 2004.

14 Ibid.

15 Crawford, M., *Shopcraft as Soulcraft*, Penguin Press, 2009.

16 www.guy-sports.com/months/jokes_jobsworth.htm

17 Zurawik, D., "'Undercover Boss' – Reality TV bites into economy", *Baltimore Sun*, February 7th 2010.

18 Henriques, D., "Lapses Kept Scheme Alive, Madoff Told Investigators", *New York Times*, October 31st 2009.

19 Goldfarb, Z., "Tougher financial regulations not coming fast or easy for SEC's Mary Schapiro", *Washington Post*, February 16th 2010.

20 De Botton, A., *The Pleasures and Sorrows of Work*, Hamish Hamilton, 2009.

21 Johnson, P. and Indvik, J., "Organizational benefits of having emotionally intelligent managers and employees", *Journal of Workplace Learning*, Vol. 11, Issue 3, 1999.

22 http://webweaversworld.blogspot.com/2009/03/thoughts-on-being-contractor-freelancer.html

23 "McKinsey Conversations with global leaders: Paul Polman of Unilever", *McKinsey Quarterly*, October 2009.

24 Liker, J., "Toyota Recall and the Lean Movement", The Lean Edge, January 30th 2010 (http//theleanedge.org).

25 The W. Edwards Deming Institute.

26 Liker, J., *The Toyota Way*, McGraw-Hill, 2003, Chapter 4.

27 www.nytimes.com/2009/10/03/business/global/03toyota.html

6 What is the right organisation culture?

1 Lewis, M., *Liar's Poker*, Penguin Books, 1989. Reproduced by kind permission of W.W. Norton (2010 reprint edition).

2 Morgan, G., op. cit.

3 Ibid.

4 Gardner, H., Csikszentmihalyi, M. and Damon, W., *Good Work: When excellence and ethics meet*, Basic Books, 2001.

5 De Botton, op. cit.

6 www.goodworkproject.org/

7 www.blogs.marriott.com/diversity/default.asp?item=2393758

8 http://business.timesonline.co.uk/tol/business/career_and_jobs/best_100_companies/article5746038.ece

9 www.blogs.marriott.com/marriott-on-the-move/2009/06/embracing-marriotts-extended-family.html

10 www.computerworld.com/spring/bp/detail/541

11 Weeks, J., *An Unpopular Corporate Culture*, IMD, September 2008.

12 Catmull, E., "How Pixar Fosters Collective Creativity", *Harvard Business Review*, September 2008.

13 Smircich, L., "Concepts of Culture and Organizational Analysis", *Administrative Science Quarterly*, No. 28, 1983.

14 King, A., *The Ethos of the Royal Marines*, University of Exeter, 2004.

15 http://technology.timesonline.co.uk/tol/news/tech_and_web/article6797859.ece

16 www.businessweek.com/the_thread/techbeat/archives/2008/03/apples_design_p.html

17 Krishnamurthy, S., "CASE: Mozilla vs. Godzilla – The Launch of the Mozilla Firefox Browser", *Journal of Interactive Marketing*, Vol. 23, No. 3, 2009, pp. 259–71.

18 http://blog.lizardwrangler.com/2007/02/06/looking-for-a-general-counsel/

19 Lih, A., *The Wikipedia Revolution: How a Bunch of Nobodies Created the World's Greatest Encyclopedia*, Hyperion, 2009.

20 Schein, E.H., "From Brainwashing to Organizational Therapy: A Conceptual and Empirical Journey in Search of 'Systemic' Health and a General Model of Change Dynamics. A Drama in Five Acts", *Organization Studies*, Vol. 27, No. 2, 2006.

21 Barnes, B., "Disney and Pixar: The Power of the Prenup", *New York Times*, June 1st 2008.

22 Sacks, D., "Scenes from the culture clash", *Fast Company*, January 2006.

23 Lih, op. cit.

24 BBC news, July 24th 2009 (http://news.bbc.co.uk/2/hi/uk_news/8149463.stm).

25 www.immi.se/intercultural/nr15/inoue.htm

26 http://business.timesonline.co.uk/tol/business/
movers_and_shakers/article2852507.ece

27 www.economistconferences.co.uk/press-release/economists-
innovation-awards-corporate-use-innovation-award-winner-
announcement/240

28 www.lz-blog.de/spotlight/2009/07/05/
interview-with-bart-becht-ceo-reckitt-benckiser/

29 http://business.timesonline.co.uk/tol/business/
movers_and_shakers/article2852507.ece

30 www.newswiretoday.com/news/51970/

31 www.secinfo.com/dsvRq.t11.d.htm

32 Moulds, J., "Consumer Champion", CNBC *European Business*,
April 2009.

33 Ibid.

7 Can culture be created, changed, or protected?

1 Smircich, L., "Concepts of Culture and Organizational Analysis",
Administrative Science Quarterly, No. 28, 1983.

2 Morgan, G., op. cit.

3 Marcus, G., ed., *Global Futures*, University of Chicago Press,
1998. Quoted in McDowell, L., "Acts of memory and millennial
hopes and anxieties: the awkward relationship between the
economic and the cultural", *Social and Cultural Geography*, Vol. 1,
Issue 1, September 2000.

4 Chatman, J. and Cha, S., "Leading by Leveraging Culture",
California Management Review, Vol. 45, No, 4, Summer 2003.

5 In March 2010 Zain announced the sale of 100% of Zain Africa
BV (excluding its operations in Morocco and Sudan) to Bharti
Airtel Limited.

6 "McKinsey Conversations with Global Leaders: John Chambers
of Cisco", *McKinsey Quarterly*, July 2009.

7 McGirt, E., "How Cisco's CEO John Chambers Is Turning the Tech Giant Socialist", *Fast Company*, December 1st 2008.

8 Malone, T., "The World According to Chambers", *The Economist*, August 29th 2009.

9 Rao, V. and Walton, M., *Culture and Public Action*, Stanford University Press, 2004.

10 Schulz, M. and Hatch, M.-J., "The Cycles of Corporate Branding: the case of the Lego Company", *California Management Review*, Vol. 46, No. 1, Fall 2003.

11 "After Nine Years, Time Warner to Split From AOL", from a transcript of a PBS interview, May 28th 2009 (www.pbs.org/newshour/bb/media/jan-june09/aol_05-28.html).

12 Schraeder, M. and Self. D., "Enhancing the success of mergers and acquisitions: an organizational culture perspective", *Management Decision*, Vol. 41, No. 5, 2003.

13 Schulz and Hatch, op. cit.

14 Morgan, G., *Images of Organization*, updated edn, Sage Publications, 2006.

15 Schein, E.H., "Five Traps for Consulting Psychologists or How I Learned to Take Culture Seriously", *Consulting Psychology Journal*, Vol. 55, No. 2, 2003.

16 Ibid.

17 http://blogs.zappos.com/ceoletter

18 www.lockheedmartin.com/aboutus/culture/stevens-culture. html

19 De Botton, op. cit.

20 Taylor, A., "Fixing Up Ford", *Fortune*, May 11th 2009.

8 Can culture be learned?

1 Schein, E.H., "Organizational Socialisation and the Profession of Management", *Industrial Management Review*, No. 9, 1968, pp. 1–16.

2 Stanford, N., *Fitting In and Getting On: A Study of Top Level Senior Managers Joining an Organization*, VDM Verlag, 2002.

3 Watkins, M., "Why the first 100 days matters", *Harvard Business Review* blog, March 27th 2009.

4 Brotherston, K., "Soundbites", *People Management*, November 6th 1997.

5 Dahle, C., "Fast Start – Your First 60 Days", *Fast Company*, December 18th 2007.

6 "My Year at Wal-Mart", *Business Week*, February 12th 2007.

7 Sacks, D., "Behind the rebranding campaign of Walmart's scarlet woman", *Fast Company*, July 1st 2009.

8 Schein, op. cit.

9 Ostroff, C. and Kozlowski, S.W.J., "Organisational Socialisation as a Learning Process: The Role of Information Acquisition", *Personnel Psychology*, Vol. 45, 1992, pp. 849–74.

10 All unattributed quotes are taken from Stanford, op. cit.

11 Hansen. M., Ibarra, H. and Peyer, U., "The Best-Performing CEOs in the World", *Harvard Business Review*, January–February, 2010.

12 Silverthorne, S., "Growing CEOs from the Inside", *Harvard Business School Working Knowledge*, November 7th 2007.

13 Wanous, J.P., *Organizational Entry Recruitment, Selection and Socialization of Newcomers*, Addison Wesley Publishing Co, 1980.

14 Simmons, A., *Territorial Games : Understanding and Ending Turf Wars at Work*, AMACOM, 1998.

15 Dahle, op. cit.

16 Downey, D., *Assimilating New Leaders: The Key to Executive Retention*, AMACOM, 2001.

Appendices
1 Glossary

1 Adapted from Ginsburgh J. and Alvarez, E., "The Consumerization of Corporate IT", *Strategy+Business*, Issue 56, Autumn 2009.

2 http://horizonscanning.defra.gov.uk/

3 www.rmprofessional.com/rm/elusive-benefits.php

4 Collins, J. and Porras J., *Built to Last*, HarperCollins, 1997.

5 http://walmartstores.com/AboutUs/

3 Useful exercises

1 Tables have been adapted from an exercise used by Chris Rodgers (www.chrisrodgers.com/).

2 Adapted from an exercise described in Schein, E.H., "Five Traps for Consulting Psychologists", *Consulting Psychology Journal: Practice and Research*, Vol. 55, No. 2, 2003, pp. 75–83.

3 Gupta, R. and Wendler, J., "Leading change: An interview with the CEO of P&G", *McKinsey Quarterly*, July 2005.

4 Adapted from Webach, A., *Strategy for Sustainability*, Harvard Business Press, 2009.

5 Adapted from Moran, R., Harris, P. and Moran, S., *Managing Cultural Differences: Global Leadership Strategies for the 21st Century*, 7th edition, Elsevier, 2007.

6 Adapted from Downey, op. cit.

Index